High-Skilled Migration
to the United States and
Its Economic Consequences

**A National Bureau
of Economic Research
Conference Report**

High-Skilled Migration to the United States and Its Economic Consequences

Edited by **Gordon H. Hanson, William R. Kerr, and Sarah Turner**

The University of Chicago Press

Chicago and London

The University of Chicago Press, Ltd., London
Published 2018
Printed in the United States of America

27 26 25 24 23 22 21 20 19 18   1 2 3 4 5

ISBN-13: 978-0-226-52552-5 (cloth)
ISBN-13: 978-0-226-52566-2 (e-book)
DOI: https://doi.org/10.7208/chicago/9780226525662.001.0001

Library of Congress Cataloging-in-Publication Data

Names: Hanson, Gordon H. (Gordon Howard), editor. | Kerr,
    William R. (William Robert), editor. | Turner, Sarah E., 1966– editor.
Title: High-skilled migration to the United States and its economic
    consequences / edited by Gordon H. Hanson, William R. Kerr, and
    Sarah Turner.
Other titles: National Bureau of Economic Research conference report.
Description: Chicago : The University of Chicago Press, 2018. | Series:
    National Bureau of Economic Research conference report
Identifiers: LCCN 2017035755 | ISBN 9780226525525 (cloth : alk.
    paper) | ISBN 9780226525662 (e-book)
Subjects: LCSH: Foreign workers—United States. | Skilled labor—
    Economic aspects—United States. | United States—Emigration and
    immigration—Economic aspects.
Classification: LCC HD8081.A5 H54 2018 | DDC 331.6/20973—dc23
LC record available at https://lccn.loc.gov/2017035755

♾ This paper meets the requirements of ANSI/NISO Z39.48-1992
(Permanence of Paper).

Contents

Introduction

Gordon H. Hanson, William R. Kerr,
and Sarah Turner

High-skilled immigrants represent an increasing share of the US work-force, particularly in science and engineering fields, while the global pool of workers with collegiate and advanced degrees has also increased markedly. The share of foreign-born workers in science, technology, engineering, and mathematics (STEM) occupations in the United States has expanded from 6.6 percent in 1960 to 28.1 percent in 2012 (Hanson and Liu, chapter 1, this volume). These workers play an ever more prominent role in the US innovation ecosystem by raising the quality and quantity of basic science performed in US universities and contributing to the creation of new ideas, designs, and patents that are commercialized by US industries.

The potential economic impact of high-skilled immigration depends on market conditions and policy choices, particularly visa policies affecting the temporary and permanent flow of workers to the United States. Questions that permeate US policy debates include: Would expansion (or contraction) of the number of visas for skilled workers from abroad reduce the wages of US citizens? Do high-skilled immigrants contribute to economic growth through enhancing prospects for innovation? Will technological progress,

Gordon H. Hanson holds the Pacific Economic Cooperation Chair in International Economic Relations at the University of California, San Diego, and has faculty positions in the Department of Economics and the School of Global Policy and Strategy, where he also is director of the Center on Global Transformation. He is the acting dean of the school and is a research associate of the National Bureau of Economic Research. William R. Kerr is the Dimitri V. D'Arbeloff–MBA Class of 1955 Professor of Business Administration at Harvard Business School and a research associate of the National Bureau of Economic Research. Sarah Turner holds the Souder Family Endowed Chair and is chair of the Economics Department as well as the University Professor of Economics and Education at the University of Virginia. She is a research associate of the National Bureau of Economic Research.

For acknowledgments, sources of research support, and disclosure of the authors' material financial relationships, if any, please see http://www.nber.org/chapters/c13839.ack.

including increased capacity to utilize high-skilled workers abroad, substitute for immigration?

Answering these questions requires a complete economics tool kit. Indeed, these questions demand integration of multiple subfields in economics, drawing on the insights of international trade, industrial organization, labor economics, and macroeconomics. To understand the complete process of market adjustment to inflows of high-skilled workers from abroad requires thinking beyond a static, partial-equilibrium context, which tends to dominate current empirical research on immigration. In order to measure who benefits—and who does not—from high-skilled immigration, it is important to account for multiple margins of adjustment including worker educational choices, firm market-entry decisions, and business selections over product mix, which together combine to determine the level and growth of aggregate productivity.

This volume takes an important step to integrate research advances connecting high-skilled immigration, scientific innovation, and market adjustment. While the study of immigration and immigration policy has a long history, a disproportionate share of the research has focused on low-skilled immigrants and their impact on labor market outcomes for low-skilled US workers. To be sure, low-skilled immigration is an important area of inquiry and there remain unresolved questions regarding its causes and consequences. Yet, the economic dynamics that follow from high-skilled immigration—and the more general expansion of the global scientific workforce—are likely to be distinct from those of low-skilled immigration and arguably more consequential. Given the potential link of immigrants to productivity-enhancing innovation, the flow of high-skilled workers between countries is a first-order determinant of the pace of global economic growth. Although there is an established line of economics research on the importance of scientific innovation for productivity growth, there have been only limited connections between this work and studies of high-skilled immigration.

The full impact of high-skilled immigration and a globalized market for talent depends on the state of technology, the structure of markets, and policies that impact the flows of goods, capital, and labor across borders. What is clear from the work presented in this volume is that the heterogeneity of talent flows across countries, sectoral distinctions in the utilization of high-skilled labor, and the dynamics of adjustment affect our capacity to predict how changes in policy can affect economic growth and the distribution of earnings. An aim of this volume is to clarify the links among talent flows, migration policies, and economic outcomes by identifying the mechanisms of adjustment that are operative.

Markets for skills in the global economy operate at a microeconomic level that depends on country of origin, visa policies, and the state of technology. The opening three chapters take on particular empirical puzzles and observations including country-specific variation in specialization, the distinct use of alternative visa mechanisms among multinational enterprises, and the alternative of "offshore" employment in the hiring of skilled labor.

To provide context for the detailed analyses to come, Gordon H. Hanson and Chen Liu, in "High-Skilled Immigration and the Comparative Advantage of Foreign-Born Workers across US Occupations," demonstrate the differential sorting between natives and immigrants—as well as among immigrants from different countries—across high-skilled occupations. These patterns are broadly stable across time, within countries of origin, and among both foreign educated and US educated of the same nationality. It thus appears that by opening immigration to particular countries, such as China and India, the United States implicitly chooses the occupational composition of its high-skilled immigrant labor force.

In his chapter, "The Innovation Activities of Multinational Enterprises and the Demand for Skilled-Worker, Nonimmigrant Visas," Stephen Ross Yeaple draws attention to how the structure of firms affects access to the pool of talent from abroad. Multinational firms have the capacity to use the relatively unconstrained L visas (which permit companies to bring their foreign employees to the United States for temporary job assignments), while firms without this global reach must draw on foreign-born workers through the oversubscribed H-1B program. Yeaple places these facts in the context of firms making decisions about how to source differentiated intermediate inputs. A theoretical implication of his model is greater access to foreign workers, through whichever existing high-skilled visas, can increase firm-level demand for native-born, high-skilled workers.

Shifting attention to how the digital economy creates alternatives to immigration, John Horton, William R. Kerr, and Christopher Stanton, in "Digital Labor Markets and Global Talent Flows," provide the insight that employers' access to the global talent pool is not limited by the physical migration of workers. Digital markets and contests increasingly provide an alternative platform for the identification and utilization of skills from abroad. Intriguingly, these online employment exchanges appear to complement, not substitute for, immigration. The authors also provide some novel evidence on the elasticity of cross-border demand for labor with wage adjustments.

An explicit objective of the last three chapters is to address questions about how high-skilled immigration affects economic growth and the distribution of earnings. Models that account for aggregate dynamics explicitly provide an opportunity to assess different channels of adjustment, while also permitting counterfactual policy simulations. While these three chapters emphasize somewhat different facets of the labor market and impacts of immigration, each generates a significant insight about the nature of adjustment and potential trade-offs.

In their chapter, "Understanding the Economic Impact of the H-1B Program on the United States," John Bound, Gaurav Khanna, and Nicolas Morales consider a model with endogenous technical change in the information technology (IT) sector in the context of a general-equilibrium model of the US economy. They quantify the effect of high-skilled foreign workers on the earnings of high- and low-skilled workers, total consumption, and economic growth. Assessed over the period from 1994 to 2001, the authors find that immigration increased the overall income of US native-born workers, while also lowering prices and raising output in the IT sector. At the same time, there are substantial distributional consequences to high-skilled immigration. US-born workers shift out of computer science, as wages in this occupation also fell relative to the expected outcome in the absence of immigration. Owners of factors of production that complement computer scientists see increased wages.

Moving to an explicitly dynamic context, Nir Jaimovich and Henry E. Siu, in "High-Skilled Immigration, STEM Employment, and Nonroutine-Biased Technical Change," consider high-skilled immigration in the framework of endogenous nonroutine-biased technical change. Their calibrated model captures the tendency of the foreign born to work in innovation-related activities, the polarization of employment opportunities across occupations for native- and foreign-born labor, and the evolution of wage inequality. A striking result of their analysis, which covers the US economy since 1980, is that the inflow of high-skilled immigrants attenuates increases in skill-based inequality in the distribution of earnings.

Michael E. Waugh continues the emphasis on macroeconomic dynamics in his chapter, "Firm Dynamics and Immigration: The Case of High-Skilled Immigration." He takes the study of the impact of immigration to a dynamic model of heterogeneous firms in a monopolistic-competition framework. The innovation of Waugh's model is to allow the skill intensity of production to vary with a firm's productivity, which impacts the path of relative wages. The short-run impact of immigration is to reduce the wage premium of high- to low-skilled workers more than in conventional models, while output increases over the longer run. In the short run, it is also the case that immigration begets firm entry, which generates increased capital investment, thereby producing a near-term drop in consumption until the economy converges to its new stationary equilibrium at higher income and consumption levels.

While these models differ in what they assume about the competitive nature of markets and the mechanisms behind market adjustment, they embody a common set of themes. First, in all three cases, there is a positive role for immigration in generating aggregate economic growth. At the same time, high-skilled immigration—particularly in the presence of endogenous growth and skill-biased technical change—actually places downward pressure on the wage gap between high- and low-skilled workers.

In bringing these authors together, our aim is to seed a fertile area of research with methods and models from different fields, along with the empirical insights and outstanding puzzles that will stimulate additional innovation in this domain. There is no question that the global pool of high-skilled workers is increasing; yet, the extent to which visa policies and market structure encourage integration across borders is less clear. Even as there is abundant evidence of overall gains from high-skilled immigration and associated innovation, many questions remain to be answered about market adjustments, distributional consequences, and the impact of immigration policies.

This volume is certainly not the last word on high-skilled immigration. Rather, it is our hope that it is a starting point for a rich path of research inquiry that brings together frontier methods and models of economics with new data sources. The completion of this volume, along with a broader investment in fostering research on high-skilled immigration, owes a debt of gratitude to the Alfred P. Sloan Foundation and Danny Goroff. In addition, we appreciate the encouragement provided by Jim Poterba along with the broad-based infrastructure support provided by the National Bureau of Economic Research.

1

High-Skilled Immigration and the Comparative Advantage of Foreign-Born Workers across US Occupations

Gordon H. Hanson and Chen Liu

1.1 Introduction

The increase in the demand for more skilled labor is among the most important changes in the US economy of the last forty years (Katz and Autor 1999). In the narrative crafted by Goldin and Katz (2008), technological advances and rising educational attainment are in something of a race, with the premium for skilled labor rising during periods, as in the 1980s and 1990s, when growth in the supply of college graduates is insufficient to meet the expanding demand for qualified labor. High-skilled immigration changes the nature of the competition between education and technology. Whereas in 1980 the foreign born accounted for only 7.1 percent of prime-age males with a college education, by 2012 this share had reached 17.1 percent. Today, the United States is able to meet the need for a more technologically sophisticated labor force either by growing its own talent through the education and training of native-born workers or by importing talent from abroad (Freeman 2005).

There is growing interest in how and why high-skilled, foreign-born workers enter the US labor market. One important channel of entry is US higher education. Many workers who ultimately obtain US permanent resident visas first enter the country as students (Rosenzweig 2006, 2007). The draw

Gordon H. Hanson holds the Pacific Economic Cooperation Chair in International Economic Relations at the University of California, San Diego, and has faculty positions in the Department of Economics and the School of Global Policy and Strategy, where he also is director of the Center on Global Transformation. He is the acting dean of the school and is a research associate of the National Bureau of Economic Research. Chen Liu is a graduate student in economics at the University of California, San Diego.

For acknowledgments, sources of research support, and disclosure of the authors' material financial relationships, if any, please see http://www.nber.org/chapters/c13841.ack.

of US universities is due in part to their global standing, especially in science, technology, engineering, and mathematics (STEM). In global rankings of scholarship, US institutions of higher education account for nine of the top ten programs in engineering, for eight of the top ten programs in life and medical sciences, and for seven of the top ten programs in physical sciences.[1] The lure of studying in the United States also derives from the contact that it facilitates with potential US employers (Bound et al. 2015). A job offer from a US place of business is essential to obtain a temporary work visa or an employer-sponsored green card. Whether foreign students choose to stay in the United States after completing their degrees depends on immediate US and foreign job-market conditions and on prospects for long-run growth in the United States relative to their home countries (Grogger and Hanson 2015).

In this chapter, we consider the possibility that the incorporation of foreign-born workers into the US economy depends on occupational comparative advantage that is at least in part specific to the country in which an individual is born. There is, of course, a long tradition of using comparative advantage to explain international trade in goods, with modern variants of the theory grounding these advantages in cross-country differences in the productivity distributions from which firms draw their industrial capabilities (Eaton and Kortum 2002). There is also a long tradition in labor economics, dating back to Roy (1951), in which workers are posited to vary in their skills for performing different occupational tasks. Recent work combines Eaton and Kortum (2002) with Roy (1951) to obtain models of comparative advantage in which workers are heterogeneous in their capabilities and in which the parameters of the underlying distribution of labor productivity differ between groups of individuals according to their demographic characteristics (Lagakos and Waugh 2013; Hsieh et al. 2013; Burstein, Morales, and Vogel 2015) or their countries of origin (Burstein et al. 2017).

We begin the analysis by documenting the growing presence of foreign-born workers in the US college-educated labor force. This presence varies markedly by occupation. Whereas the share of US college-educated workers who are foreign born rises modestly from 4.2 percent in 1960 to 11.6 percent in 2010–2012 in education, law, and social-service occupations, it rises more impressively from 6.6 percent to 28.1 percent over this same period in STEM occupations. Also notable is the difference in occupational-employment patterns by immigrants according to their country of origin. In STEM jobs, the share of US workers who are from India rises from near zero in 1960 to 9.3 percent, or one-third of all foreign workers, in 2010–2012. In health-related occupations, it is workers from Southeast Asia whose employment shares have risen most dramatically, reaching 5.4 percent, or one-fifth of all foreign workers, in 2010–2012 from negligible levels five decades previously.

---

1. See world university rankings by field at www.arwu.org.

Specialization patterns are similar for male and female immigrants from the same origin countries.

Next, we use an Eaton-Kortum-Roy definition of comparative advantage to characterize occupational specialization by nationality and over time for college-educated workers. The measure of comparative advantage we use gives the log odds of, say, an Indian immigrant working in STEM over a manual occupation relative to the log odds of a US native-born individual working in STEM over a manual job. We document three features of occupational specialization in the US labor market. First, patterns of specialization by nationality are most extreme in STEM occupations. Among prime-age male college graduates, an immigrant from India is 10.7 times more likely than a US native-born individual to work in STEM over a manual job and 54.6 times more likely to do so than an immigrant from Mexico, Central America, and the Caribbean. Second, occupational specialization for male and female immigrant college graduates is strongly positively correlated across origin countries, with a partial correlation of male-female comparative advantage in 2010–2012 of 0.92 in STEM jobs, 0.86 in management and finance, and 0.71 in health-related occupations. Third, immigrant occupational specialization patterns persist firmly over time. For college-educated men, a regression of log comparative advantage in 2010 against the value in 1990 across birth countries yields very precisely estimated slope coefficients of 0.99 in STEM occupations, 1.02 in management and finance, and 1.01 in education, law, and social-service occupations. We take these results to mean that the factors that drive occupational specialization among immigrants are stable across decades and common to workers in different demographic groups from the same origin countries.

High-skilled immigration has important consequences for US economic development. In modern growth theory, the share of workers specialized in R&D plays a role in setting the pace of long-run growth (Jones 2002). Because high-skilled immigrants are drawn to STEM fields, they are likely to be inputs into US innovation. Recent work finds evidence consistent with high-skilled immigration having contributed to advances in US innovation. US states and localities that attract more high-skilled foreign labor see faster rates of growth in labor productivity (Hunt and Gauthier-Loiselle 2010; Peri 2012). Kerr and Lincoln (2010) find that individuals with ethnic Chinese and Indian names, a large fraction of whom appear to be foreign born, account for rising shares of US patents in computers, electronics, medical devices, and pharmaceuticals. US metropolitan areas that historically employed more H-1B workers enjoyed larger bumps in patenting when Congress temporarily expanded the program between 1999 and 2003. Further, the patent bump was concentrated among Chinese and Indian inventors, consistent with the added H-1B visas having expanded the US innovation frontier. Yet, the precise magnitude of the foreign-born contribution to US innovation and productivity growth is hard to pin down. Because the allocation of labor across regional markets responds to myriad economic shocks, establishing a causal relationship between inflows of foreign workers and the local pace of innovation is a challenge. High-skilled immigration may displace some US workers in STEM jobs (Borjas and Doran 2012), possibly attenuating the net impact on US innovation capabilities. How much of aggregate US productivity growth can be attributed to high-skilled labor inflows remains unknown.

When it comes to innovation, there appears to be nothing "special" about foreign-born workers, other than their proclivity for studying STEM disciplines in a university. The National Survey of College Graduates shows that foreign-born individuals are far more likely than the native born to obtain a patent, and more likely still to obtain a patent that is commercialized (Hunt 2011). It is also the case that foreign-born students are substantially more likely to major in engineering, math, and the physical sciences, all fields strongly associated with later patenting. Once one controls for the major field of study, the foreign-native-born differential in patenting disappears. Consistent with Hunt's (2011) findings, the descriptive results we present suggest that highly educated immigrant workers in the United States have a strong revealed comparative advantage in STEM. The literature has yet to explain the origin of these specialization patterns. It could be that the immigrants the United States attracts are better suited for careers in innovation—due to the relative quality of foreign secondary education in STEM, selection mechanisms implicit in US immigration policy, or the relative magnitude of the US earnings premium for successful inventors—and therefore choose to study the subjects that prepare them for later innovative activities. Alternatively, cultural or language barriers may complicate the path of the foreign born to obtaining good US jobs in non-STEM fields, such as advertising, insurance, or law, pushing them into STEM careers.

To understand possible sources of occupational comparative advantage by immigrants from different origin countries, we compare our measures of occupational specialization across three groups of individuals according to their nativity. Immigrants born and raised in an origin country (who arrived in the United States at age eighteen or older) would have been exposed to foreign educational institutions, at least through secondary school. Immigrants born in the origin country but raised in the United States (who arrived in the United States before age eighteen) would have been exposed to US education, at least at the university level. And individuals whose parents or grandparents were born in the origin country would have been exposed to US education throughout their lives. Occupational specialization patterns are similar across these three groups, suggesting that the country in which one is educated is not the overriding factor that explains employment regularities among highly educated immigrants.

In section 1.2, we present the data used in the analysis. In section 1.3, we describe the presence of foreign-born, college-educated workers in US occupations. In section 1.4, we define and measure occupational comparative advantage among US immigrants according to their country of origin. And in section 1.5, we provide a concluding discussion.

1.2 Data

We use data from the Census Integrated Public Use Micro Samples (Ruggles et al. 2010) for the years 1960 (5 percent sample), 1970 (1 percent sample), 1980 (5 percent sample), 1990 (5 percent sample), and 2000 (5 percent sample), and the American Community Survey (ACS) for 2010 to 2012. We pool ACS files for 2010 through 2012 to increase sample size and, hence, measurement precision.

Throughout our analysis, we restrict the sample to individuals with positive earnings, who are between twenty-one and fifty-four years old at the time of the survey, and who have at least a bachelor's degree. Our focus on college graduates follows from our interest in the high-skilled labor force. The age restrictions we impose allow us to center on prime-wage workers who are likely to have completed their undergraduate studies. To measure employment, we calculate the number of full-time equivalent workers in given national origin, gender, and occupation categories by using weights equal to the sampling weight for an individual times her hours of work last year, which we take to be the product of weeks worked last year and usual hours worked per week. The US native-born population comprises individuals who were born either in the United States or abroad to parents who are US citizens. The foreign-born population comprises all other individuals.

To accommodate a perspective that spans six decades and dozens of source countries for immigrants, we aggregate occupations into six broad categories. Aggregation helps avoid having large numbers of cells with zero entries, which is of particular concern for smaller source countries and in earlier years. The occupation categories are

- STEM (architects, computer programmers and software developers, engineers, life and medical scientists, and physical scientists);
- management, finance, and accounting (accountants, chief executives, financial managers, general managers, market surveyors, and economists);
- health (dentists, pharmacists, physicians, registered nurses, therapists, and veterinarians);
- education, law, social work, and the arts (instructors and teachers, lawyers, social and religious workers, writers, and artists);
- technical, sales, and administrative support (administrative support staff, clerks and record keepers, sales representatives, sales supervisors, and technicians); and

- less-skilled manual work (agricultural workers, construction workers, hospitality workers, household-service workers, machine operators and production workers, mechanics and repairers, and personal-service workers).

These categories divide occupations according to the level of education, the type of training, and the range of skills that are demanded on the job. Most STEM occupations require at least a bachelor's degree, as well as aptitude in quantitative reasoning. Because quantitative skills are grounded in mathematical logic, they may transfer from one country to another with relative ease, making human capital acquired in STEM jobs relatively portable across borders. Although management positions also require some familiarity with quantitative reasoning, they are intensive in the use of communication and other social skills to a degree that STEM positions are not. Health, education, law, and social work are distinguished by requiring a bachelor's degree or higher to enter these professions and by being subject to occupational accreditation processes that are specific to the United States or to individual states within the country. Accreditation may limit the portability of skills for immigrants in these professions. The final two occupational categories—manual work and technical, sales, and administrative support—typically do not require a college degree. The first category includes jobs from which advancement to higher-level positions is usually limited. The second encompasses jobs through which more-educated immigrants may first enter the labor force as they seek to establish their position in a new labor market.

1.3 Foreign-Born Presence in US Occupations

We begin the analysis by describing the presence of immigrants in US occupations, first for college-educated males and then for college-educated females. We then consider the specialization of immigrants from different origin countries in particular types of jobs. For ease of presentation, we present trends for immigrants grouped according to six sending regions: China, Hong Kong, and Taiwan; Eastern and Western Europe; East and Southeast Asia; India; Mexico, Central America, and the Caribbean; and South America. China and India merit attention because they account for a disproportionate share of the recent growth in US high-skilled immigration.[2] Europe, a historic but now less important source of US high-skilled immigrants, offers an instructive contrast. East and Southeast Asia include Korea, long a source of high-skilled immigrants to the United States, and the Philippines and Vietnam, which supply immigrants at both low- and high-education levels. The two regions from Latin America and the Carib-

2. Since 1990, nearly all of the growth in US immigration from China, Hong Kong, and Taiwan is due to immigration from mainland China.

bean are the predominant sources of low-skilled immigrants to the United States, making them of interest in terms of their less studied, high-skilled labor outflows. Although we leave Africa and the Middle East out of the figures in this section, we will include these regions in the analysis presented in the following section.

1.3.1   College-Educated Males

Figure 1.1 shows the share of the foreign born in total US male employment of college graduates, as measured by hours worked, for six immigrant source regions in each of the six occupational groups. It displays the well-known pattern of a growing presence of highly educated immigrants in the US labor force. Across all origin countries, the foreign-born share of total hours worked by prime-age male college graduates increases from 6.6 percent in 1960 to 28.1 percent in 2010–2012 in STEM occupations; from 4.1 percent to 14.9 percent in management and finance; from 10.7 percent to 24.7 percent in health-related occupations; from 4.2 percent to 11.6 percent in education, law, and social work; from 3.8 percent to 13.1 percent in technical, sales, and administrative support; and from 7.8 percent to 18.8 percent in manual occupations.

In 1960, Europe was by far and away the major origin region for high-skilled immigrants to the United States. Whereas Europe's share of occu-

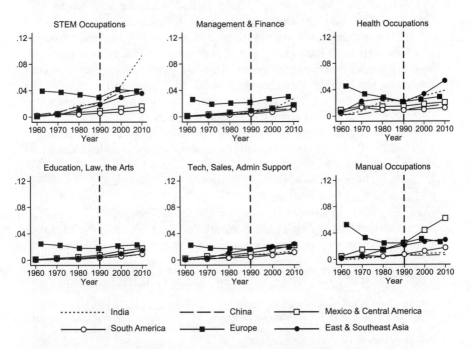

Fig. 1.1   **Share of immigrants in US occupational employment, males**

pational employment in 1960 ranged between 2 and 6 percent, no other region even topped 1 percent. Europe's importance reflects historical US immigration policies, which between 1924 and 1965 allocated visas based on national quotas that favored European countries (Ngai 1999; Udansky and Espenshade 2000).

In the decades since 1960, Europe's role as the primary source for newly arrived high-skilled US immigrants has been supplanted by Asia. By the period 2010 to 2012, immigrants from India, at 9.3 percent of college-educated US employment, were the largest foreign-born group in US STEM occupations, and immigrants from East and Southeast Asia, at 5.4 percent of employment, were the largest foreign-born group in US health-related occupations. Among the six occupational categories in figure 1.1, Europe remained the top immigrant-supply region in 2010–2012 in just two, management and finance, where it held a slim lead over India at 3.1 percent versus 2.7 percent of US employment of the college educated, and education, law, social work, and the arts, where it held another slim lead in this case over Mexico and Central America at 2.3 percent versus 1.8 percent of US employment.

Asia's rise as a source of high-skilled immigrants is the result of multiple factors. The Immigration and Nationality Act of 1965 replaced national-origin quotas with a quota-allocation scheme that favored family members of US residents, and, to a lesser degree, skilled workers demanded by US employers. Over time, this change in policy allowed non-European countries to join the queue for US immigration visas. One common route through which foreign-born individuals gain a permanent residence or temporary work visa is by first completing undergraduate or graduate study in the United States (Kato and Sparber 2013; Salzman, Kuehn, and Lowell 2013). Being a student at a US university facilitates contact with US employers (Bound et al. 2015) and creates opportunities to meet and to marry a US resident (Jasso et al. 2000), either of which earns one a place in the queue for a green card. Due in part to its rapidly expanding supply of college students, Asia has become a leading source of foreign students in US universities. As of the 2013/14 academic year, six of the top ten source countries for foreign students in the United States were from Asia (Institute of International Education 2015).[3] These countries accounted for 57.4 percent of the 886,052 foreign students studying at US institutions.[4] The four highest-ranking European countries on the list accounted for just 3.6 percent of US foreign

3. These countries in descending rank order are China, India, Korea, Taiwan, Japan, and Vietnam.
4. This total includes undergraduate students, graduate students, nondegree students, and students in Optional Practical Training. Together, undergraduate and graduate students accounted for an average of 88.3 percent of foreign students in the United States in the 1990s and first decade of the twenty-first century.

students in that year.[5] Within Asia, China and India stand out as leading origin countries for foreign students. Their shares of the US foreign-student population grew from 8.7 percent and 6.9 percent, respectively, in 1989–1990 to 31.2 percent and 13.6 percent, respectively, in 2013–2014.

In addition to geographic diversification in source regions for US high-skilled immigration, two other patterns in figure 1.1 call one's attention. One is that 1990 is an inflection point for immigrant presence in US employment. It is after 1990 when India's and China's presence in STEM occupations rises most dramatically and when Southeast Asia's and India's presence in health-related occupations begins to take off. One contributing factor to this growth is the H-1B program for temporary high-skilled, foreign-born workers, which Congress created as part of the Immigration Act of 1990.[6] The US government first allocated 65,000 H-1B visas per year, which it raised to 115,000 per year in 1999 and to 195,000 in 2001, before settling at 85,000 per year in 2006 (General Accounting Office 2011).[7] Since these visas are for a period of three years and are renewable once, a single visa expands the supply of high-skilled US immigrants by up to six person years. If all visa recipients stay for a full three-year term, in steady state a supply of 85,000 temporary visas would accommodate a rotating stock of 255,000 immigrants. If these recipients in turn each renew their visas and stay for a full additional three-year term, the initial visa allocation would accommodate a rotating stock of 510,000 visa holders.

Of course, far from all H-1B visa recipients extend their visas or even stay for their complete initial three-year terms.[8] Nevertheless, given that the total stock of US immigrants in 2010–2012 age twenty-one to fifty-four years old with a college education was 5.8 million, a temporary visa program of the magnitude of the H-1B is capable of bringing about a sizable increase in immigrant labor supply. In practice, the H-1B visa appears to operate as a queue for a green card (Lowell 2000). Congress allocates 140,000 employer-sponsored green cards each year. It is common for employers to first seek

5. These countries in descending rank order are the United Kingdom, Germany, France, and Spain.

6. The H-1B program is the largest and most well known source of temporary work visas for high-skilled US workers, but it is far from the only such program. Other programs that supply high-skilled immigrants with temporary work visas include the L-1 visa (for intracompany transferees, which allows foreign workers of US multinational companies to work in the United States), the O visa (for individuals of extraordinary ability or achievement), the P visa (for artists, athletes, and entertainers), and the TN visa (for professional workers from NAFTA countries). To give a sense of the relative scale of these programs, in 2008 the United States issued 129,000 H-1B visas (the sum of new visas and visa extensions) and 84,000 L-1 visas.

7. The current level of 85,000 H-1B visas includes 65,000 visas for temporary immigrant workers in specialty occupations and 20,000 visas for foreign-born individuals who have earned an advanced degree from a US institution of higher education.

8. Clemens (2010) finds that for an Indian software company in the middle of the first decade of the twenty-first century, just 44.8 percent of H-1B visa recipients were in the United States two years after obtaining a visa.

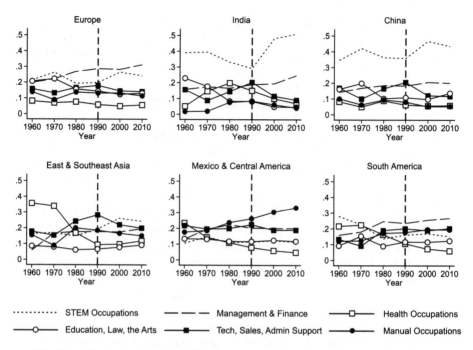

Fig. 1.2   Share of occupation in immigrant employment by national origin, males

H-1B visas for foreign employees, and later, depending on their performance and desire to stay in the United States, to apply for a green card on their behalf. The two largest recipient countries for H-1B visas are India and China. Over the 2000–2009 period, they accounted for 46.9 percent and 8.9 percent, respectively, of approved H-1B workers (General Accounting Office 2011).

A second pattern evident in figure 1.1 is variation in occupational specialization patterns by immigrants from different origin regions. To see these details more clearly, in figure 1.2 we plot the share of total labor hours worked by male college graduates from each of the six immigrant origin regions in each of the six occupational categories. India's and China's specialization in STEM is strongly apparent in figure 1.2, with occupations in this group in 2010–2012 accounting for 51.0 percent of Indian immigrant employment and 43.5 percent of Chinese immigrant employment. Although STEM occupations are also the top employment category for immigrants from East and Southeast Asia, the sector's dominance is much less pronounced for this region than for India and China. For immigrants from Europe and South America, management and finance is the top occupation for male college graduates, whereas for immigrants from Mexico and Central America, the top category is health-related professions. These patterns are a first indication of differences in occupational comparative advantage for immigrants from difference source countries. In the following section, we examine occupational specialization by immigrants in more detail.

1.3.2 College-Educated Females

We next examine high-skilled immigration among women and occupational specialization by female immigrants according to their region of birth. Analogous to figure 1.1 for males, figure 1.3 shows the share of the foreign born in total US female employment of college graduates for six immigrant source regions in each of the six occupational groups. Similar to patterns for men, immigrant presence in high-skilled female employment has increased substantially over time. Across all origin countries, the foreign-born share of total hours worked by prime-age female college graduates increases from 9.2 percent in 1960 to 31.1 percent in 2010–2012 in STEM occupations; from 4.6 percent to 14.5 percent in management and finance; from 8.5 percent to 17.9 percent in health-related occupations; from 2.3 percent to 8.7 percent in education, law, social work, and the arts; from 6.8 percent to 13.9 percent in technical, sales, and administrative support; and from 17.3 percent to 21.4 percent in manual occupations.

As with men, in 1960 Europe begins as the dominant source region for college-educated immigrant women and by the first decade of the twenty-first century is replaced by another region in all six occupational categories.

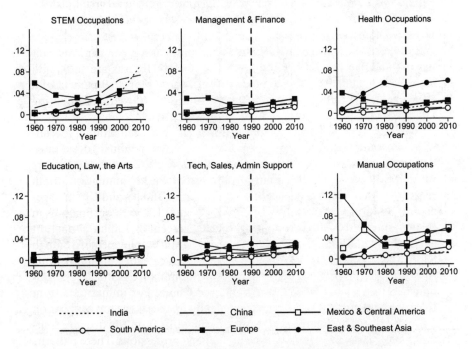

Fig. 1.3   Share of immigrants in US occupational employment, females

India and China become the largest immigrant-origin regions in STEM occupations; Southeast Asia becomes the largest immigrant-origin region in health-related occupations; and Mexico and Central America become the largest immigrant-origin regions in manual occupations. In 2010–2012, female immigrants from India and China represent 9.1 percent and 7.3 percent of US female STEM employment, compared to 9.3 percent and 4.2 percent for these regions, respectively, among men. Immigrant women from East and Southeast Asia account for 6.1 percent of female employment in health-related occupations, compared to 5.4 percent for this region among men. And immigrant women from Mexico and Central America account for 5.8 percent of female employment in manual occupations, compared to 6.2 percent for this region among men. These findings are broadly suggestive that occupational specialization patterns are more country-of-origin specific than gender specific.

To explore occupational specialization in more detail, figure 1.4, similar to figure 1.2, plots the share of total labor hours worked by female college graduates from each of the six immigrant origin regions in each of the six occupational categories. Although occupational specialization among female immigrants is less extreme than among men, male and female immigrants from some origin regions tend to specialize in similar lines of work. For immigrants from Europe, the top category for both men and women is

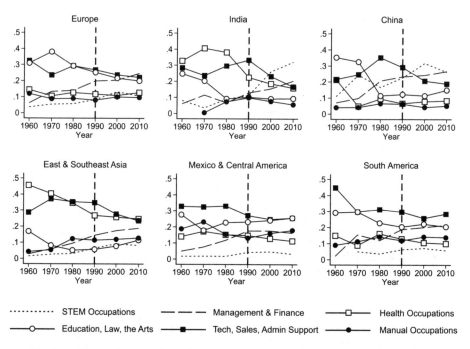

Fig. 1.4   **Share of occupation in immigrant employment by national origin, females**

management and finance, and for immigrants from India and China, it is STEM occupations. For Southeast Asia and Latin America, however, the less skill-intensive activities of technical, sales, and administrative support and manual occupations are the largest categories of female employment, distinct for patterns for men from these regions.

Entering the United States on a student visa and later transitioning to a green card appears to be a common path for settlement in the United States among high-skilled immigrant women, as it is for high-skilled immigrant men. Yet, the large majority of H-1B visas appear to go to men, suggesting that the student-visa-to-H-1B-to-green-card transition path is primarily open to male workers (and in particular those in the technology sector). The literature contains little information about differences by gender in how immigrants enter and remain in the United States.

1.4 Comparative Advantage of Foreign-Born Workers

The previous section reveals that immigrant presence in the US high-skilled labor force has grown over time, that immigrant presence has risen much more strongly in some occupations (STEM, management, and finance) than in others (education, law, social work, and the arts), and that the propensity to specialize in particular occupations varies by region of birth. In this section, we define, measure, and evaluate comparative advantage across broad occupations for high-skilled immigrants, where we allow advantage to vary both over time and by origin country.

1.4.1 Defining Comparative Advantage

We consider the possibility that specialization patterns arise from occupation-specific differences in worker productivity across source countries. As a result of cross-country variation in the quality of higher education, traditions of excellence in particular academic disciplines, or other institutions through which individuals acquire occupation-specific skills, workers from particular countries may be relatively likely to develop aptitudes that are highly valued in particular occupations. Russia's long tradition of excellence in mathematics, for instance, may result in college graduates from Russia being relatively likely to pursue careers in engineering, mathematics, or physics.

Consider a Roy model of occupational sorting, as in Lagakos and Waugh (2013), Hsieh et al. (2013), or Burstein, Morales, and Vogel (2015). Suppose that college-educated workers from origin-country and gender groups, indexed by λ, choose the country in which to reside, indexed by κ, and an occupation in which to work, indexed by σ. Suppose also that productivity for an individual from origin country λ (e.g., India) working in occupation σ (e.g., software programming) in destination κ (e.g., the United States) is determined by a random draw from a Fréchet distribution, with location parameter $T_{\lambda,\kappa,\sigma}$. We allow productivity to be $\lambda - \kappa$ specific, as may result from variation across origin countries λ in the portability of human capital to destination country κ, $\lambda - \sigma$ specific, as may result from variation across origin countries λ in the aptitude for occupation σ (e.g., the excellence of Russian mathematicians), and $\kappa - \sigma$ specific, as may result from variation across destination countries κ in the productivity of workers in occupation σ (e.g., the success of the United States in software services). We can then derive a simple expression for comparative advantage in which the productivity for a worker from origin country λ in occupation σ relative to some base occupation σ' (e.g., software programming versus manual work) is compared to relative productivity in the same two occupations for a worker from a base country (λ_{us} = United States), where these productivities are evaluated in a common destination market (κ_{us} = United States). This expression is given by,

$$(1) \qquad \frac{T_{\lambda,\kappa_{us},\sigma}}{T_{\lambda,\kappa_{us},\sigma'}} \Big/ \frac{T_{\lambda_{us},\kappa_{us}\sigma}}{T_{\lambda_{us},\kappa_{us},\sigma'}} = \frac{\Phi_{\lambda,\kappa_{us},\sigma}}{\Phi_{\lambda,\kappa_{us},\sigma'}} \Big/ \frac{\Phi_{\lambda_{us},\kappa_{us},\sigma}}{\Phi_{\lambda_{us},\kappa_{us},\sigma'}}.$$

where $\Phi_{\lambda,\kappa_{us},\sigma}$ denotes the share of workers from origin-country gender group λ (India, males) working in the United States (κ_{us}) in occupation σ (software programming). Equation (1) states that the employment shares of Indian immigrants relative to US native-born workers in software programming relative to manual jobs reveals the comparative advantage of Indian immigrants in programming. By comparing employment shares for workers from a common origin-country gender group (India, males) in two distinct occupations (software programming vs. manual work) in the United States, we neutralize the average productivity loss incurred by immigrants from India when working in the United States. Similarly, by comparing employment shares for workers from two distinct origin countries (India vs. the United States) in the same occupation, we neutralize productivity effects specific to the occupation in the destination market.

We evaluate the revealed comparative advantage of immigrants from different origin countries working in the United States using the log of the expression on the right of equation (1). Throughout the analysis, we treat US-born workers as the base demographic group and manual work support as the base occupational category. Although equation (1) suppresses time subscripts, we will allow comparative advantage to evolve freely over time. Because of the double differencing in equation (1), the evolution of comparative advantage will be free of the effects of changes in the average productivity of Indian immigrants or in average labor productivity in US software programming.

1.4.2 Comparative Advantage of Foreign-Born Relative to Native-Born Workers

In figure 1.5, we plot $\log(\Phi_{\lambda,\kappa_{us},\sigma}/\Phi_{\lambda,\kappa_{us},\sigma'}) - \log(\Phi_{\lambda_{us},\kappa_{us},\sigma}/\Phi_{\lambda_{us},\kappa_{us},\sigma'})$, log comparative advantage for foreign-born workers relative to native-born workers

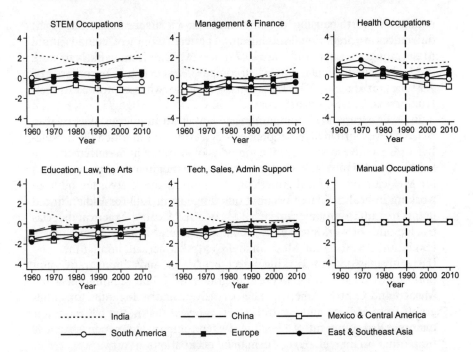

Fig. 1.5   Log comparative advantage by occupation, males relative to US counterparts

in an occupation using manual jobs as the base category, for each nonbase occupation in the six origin regions over time, where the sample is male prime-working-age college graduates. Given the double log difference form, a positive value of log comparative advantage for an origin group in an occupation indicates comparative advantage relative to US workers and a negative value indicates comparative disadvantage relative to US workers.

It is in STEM occupations that variation in comparative advantage across origin regions is most pronounced. Male college-educated immigrants from India and China exhibit a strong revealed comparative advantage in STEM jobs, whereas immigrants from Europe and Southeast Asia display a modest advantage in the sector, and immigrants from Latin America possess a clear disadvantage in STEM. The direct implication is that US college-educated men have a disadvantage in STEM relative to manual occupations when compared to immigrants from India and China and an advantage when compared to immigrants from Latin America. In 2010–2012, figure 1.5 shows that the log difference in the likelihood of Indian immigrants working in STEM over manual occupations when compared to US native-born men is 2.37, for European immigrants it is 0.59, for Southeast Asian immigrants it is 0.31, for immigrants from South America it is −0.41, and for Mexican and Central American immigrants it is −1.23. This quantity is the relative log odds of working in an occupation for immigrants from a particular origin region. It is worth pausing for a moment to appreciate the magnitude of the differences in occupational specialization patterns that these log odds imply. Male immigrants from India are 10.7 times (exp{2.37}) more likely to work in STEM than in manual jobs, when compared to US native-born men, and 7.9 times (exp{2.37 − 0.31}) more likely to do so, when compared to male immigrants from Southeast Asia.

In other occupations, comparative advantage of immigrant men relative to US native-born men is compressed when evaluated against STEM. Relative to US native-born men, the log odds of working in management and finance (over manual jobs) range from 0.96 for Indian immigrants to −1.35 for Mexican and Central American immigrants, the relative log odds of working in health-related occupations range from 1.43 for Indian immigrants to −1.02 for immigrants from Mexico and Central America, the relative log odds of working in education and law range from 0.65 for Chinese immigrants to −1.33 for Mexican and Central American immigrants, and the relative log odds of working in technical, sales, and administrative support range from 0.23 for Chinese immigrants to −1.12 for immigrants from Mexico and Central America. The pervasive negative log odds for immigrants from Mexico and Central America reveal that in the US economy, their revealed comparative advantage (when compared to college graduates from other origin regions) lies in manual occupations.

In figure 1.6, we show the analogous log comparative advantage plots for women. The patterns are broadly similar to those for men. In STEM, college-educated immigrants from India and China display a strong comparative advantage, whereas immigrants from Mexico and Central America display a comparative disadvantage. STEM is again the sector with the widest variation in comparative advantage. In 2010–2012, the log difference in the likelihood of Indian immigrant women working in STEM over a manual job when compared to US native-born women is 2.13 and for Mexican and Central American immigrants it is −1.31. Relative to US native-born women, the log odds of working in management and finance (over manual jobs) range from 0.54 for Chinese immigrants to −1.21 for Mexican and Central American immigrants, the relative log odds of working in health-related occupations range from 0.48 for Indian immigrants to −1.02 for immigrants from Mexico and Central America, the relative log odds of working in education and law range from −0.44 for Chinese immigrants to −1.62 for Southeast Asian immigrants, and the relative log odds of working in technical, sales, and administrative support range from 0.07 for Chinese immigrants to −0.88 for immigrants from Mexico and Central America.

What explains differences in occupational specialization across US workers according to their country of birth? One possibility is that the quality or availability of education in science varies across countries (Hanushek and Kimko 2000), with differences in math and science perhaps being most important. To obtain a job in STEM generally requires a college or advanced

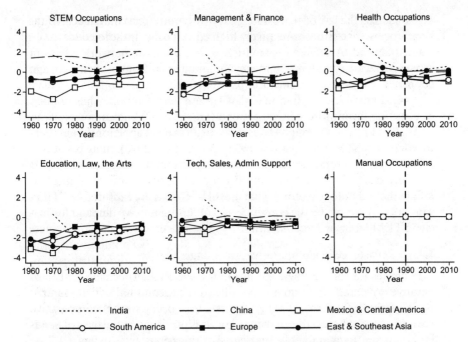

Fig. 1.6   Log comparative advantage by occupation, females relative to US counterparts

degree in a STEM discipline. US students and students from Latin America may begin their undergraduate studies with relatively poor math and science skills, which leaves them ill equipped to complete an engineering or science degree. When it comes to STEM disciplines, US secondary-school students do tend to underperform their peers from other high-income nations. In the 2012 PISA exam, US fifteen-year-olds ranked 36th in math and 28th in science out of sixty-five participating countries.[9] Students from Latin America also underperform on PISA exams relative to countries at similar income levels. Among the eight Latin American countries that participated in the 2012 exam, the highest-ranking country was Chile at 51st in math and 46th in science.

A second possible explanation for immigrant success in obtaining STEM jobs is that these are jobs in which workers educated or trained abroad can signal their skills to employers at relatively low cost. In some non-STEM professional fields, such as insurance and marketing, the foreign born may have an absolute disadvantage because they lack a nuanced understanding of American culture or because subtleties in face-to-face communication are an important feature of interactions in the marketplace. Others of these

9. See www.oecd.org/pisa.

fields, such as the law or real estate, may involve an occupational accreditation process that imposes relatively high entry costs on those educated or trained abroad. A related explanation is that there are network effects in job search, which result in a tendency for immigrants from particular origin countries to cluster in specific occupations (Card 2001).

A third possible explanation is that US immigration policy has implicit screens that favor more-educated immigrants in STEM fields over those in non-STEM fields. Although H-1B visas do go in disproportionate numbers to workers in STEM occupations (Kerr and Lincoln 2010), there is nothing preordained about this outcome in terms of US immigration policy. H-1B visas are designated for "specialty occupations," which are not limited to jobs in the technology sector.[10] That most H-1B visas are captured by STEM workers may simply be the consequences of strong relative demand for foreign STEM labor by US companies.

1.4.3 Persistence in Comparative Advantage

In figures 1.5 and 1.6, there is only modest variation in occupational comparative advantage over time, especially in the second half of the sample period from 1990 forward. This suggests that occupational comparative advantage for college-educated immigrants is persistent at the level of sending countries. To characterize the degree of this persistence, in figure 1.7 we plot log immigrant comparative advantage in STEM occupations (relative to manual occupations) in 2010 versus 1990. The 45-degree schedule is shown as a solid line and the regression plot as a dashed line. We expand the sample to include all origin regions for US immigrants. We present data for the thirty largest sending countries for immigrants and for remaining countries aggregated into ten regional groups.[11] To make within-country comparisons as precise as possible, we control for differences in the age composition of immigrants by restricting the sample to be individuals twenty-one to thirty-seven years old (as compared to the full sample of individuals twenty-one to fifty-four years old used in previous sections).

In figure 1.7, panel A, which displays results for college-educated males,

---

10. Specialty occupations are ones in which (a) a bachelor's or higher degree or its equivalent is normally the minimum entry requirement for the position, (b) the degree requirement is common to the industry in parallel positions among similar organizations, (c) the employer normally requires a degree or its equivalent for the position, or (d) the nature of the specific duties is so specialized and complex that the knowledge required to perform the duties is usually associated with attainment of a bachelor's or higher degree. See http://www.uscis.gov/eir/visa -guide/h-1b-specialty-occupation/understanding-h-1b-requirements.

11. The twenty-nine largest sending countries for college-educated immigrants are Bangladesh, Brazil, Canada, China, Colombia, Cuba, the Dominican Republic, Egypt, France, Germany, Great Britain, Haiti, Hong Kong, India, Iran, Japan, Jamaica, Korea, Mexico, Nigeria, Peru, the Philippines, Pakistan, Poland, Russia, Spain, Taiwan, Venezuela, and Vietnam. The ten regional groups are Central America, South America, Western Europe, Southern Europe, Eastern Europe, South Asia, Southeast Asia, Middle East and North Africa, sub-Saharan Africa, and Oceania.

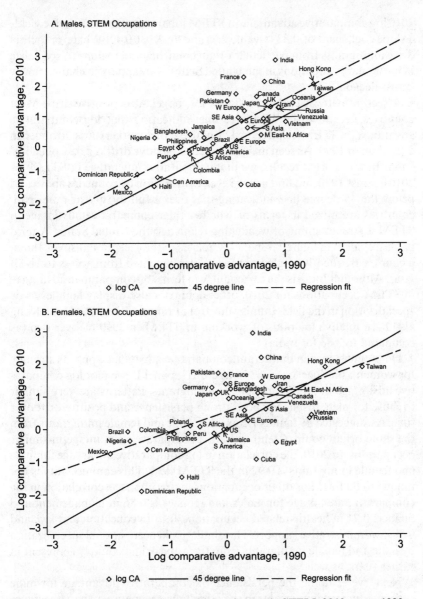

Fig. 1.7 Log comparative advantage for immigrants in STEM, 2010 versus 1990

we see evidence of strong persistence over time in comparative advantage in STEM occupations for immigrants by country of origin. The regression of log comparative advantage in STEM for 2010 against the 1990 value yields a slope coefficient estimate of 0.99 (t-value 7.5) and an R^2 of 0.60 ($N = 40$). Further evidence reveals that this persistence is not a new phenomenon in the US labor market. In unreported results, a regression of

2010 log comparative advantage in STEM jobs against the 1970 value yields a slope coefficient of 0.53 (*t*-value 2.7) and an R^2 of 0.42. Whatever factors drive immigrants from particular origin countries and regions to specialize in particular occupations in the United States, they appear to change slowly across decades.

A second pattern evident in figure 1.7, panel A, is positive drift. Most countries lie above the 45-degree line, indicating that log comparative advantage in STEM relative to US native-born workers was stronger in 2010 than in 1990. As seen in figure 1.5, this positive drift is a new phenomenon. In unreported results, we plot comparative advantage in STEM for 2010 against 1970 and find a more even distribution of countries above and below the 45-degree line, indicating that over a full forty-year time span, countries are mixed in terms of whether their comparative advantage in STEM is strengthening or weakening relative to the United States. A third pattern evident in figure 1.7, panel A, relates to the exceptionalism of India, a country frequently singled out for having benefited from access to H-1B visas. Although India is the top country in terms of comparative advantage in STEM occupations for 2010, other countries also display high levels of specialization in the field. Immigrants from France, China, and Hong Kong also have relative log odds of working in STEM in 2010 of over two (as compared to 2.86 for India).

Does persistence in immigrant comparative advantage apply as strongly for women as it does for men? In figure 1.7, panel B, we plot log comparative advantage in STEM for female immigrants. Patterns are very similar to those for men, displaying both strong persistence and positive drift over time. As suggested by figures 1.5 and 1.6, male and female immigrants from the same origin country tend to have a comparative advantage in similar occupations. In 2010, the correlation in log comparative advantage for male and female immigrants is 0.92 in the STEM field. This commonality is not unique to STEM. For other occupations in that year, the correlation in log comparative advantage for males and females is 0.86 in management and finance, 0.71 in health-related occupations, 0.67 in education and law, and 0.59 in administrative support. This similarity in occupational specialization by male and female immigrants from the same origin country is present in earlier years, as well.[12]

Next, we examine the persistence of comparative advantage for male college-educated immigrants in the other four occupations, shown in figure 1.8. Similar to STEM, these occupations display strong persistence over time in comparative advantage by immigrant origin country and a tendency for positive drift in comparative relative to US native-born workers, as indicated

---

12. In 1990, the correlation in log comparative advantage across origin countries for male and female immigrants is 0.82 in STEM, 0.73 in management and finance, 0.62 in health-related occupations, 0.66 in education and law, and 0.75 in administrative support.

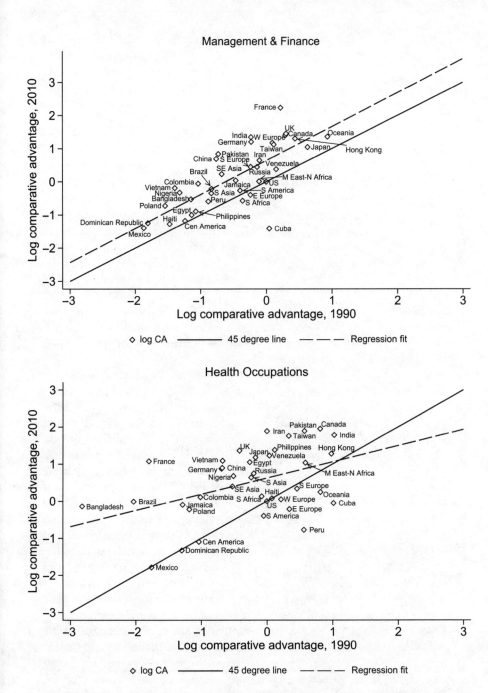

Fig. 1.8 Log comparative advantage for male immigrants, 2010 versus 1990

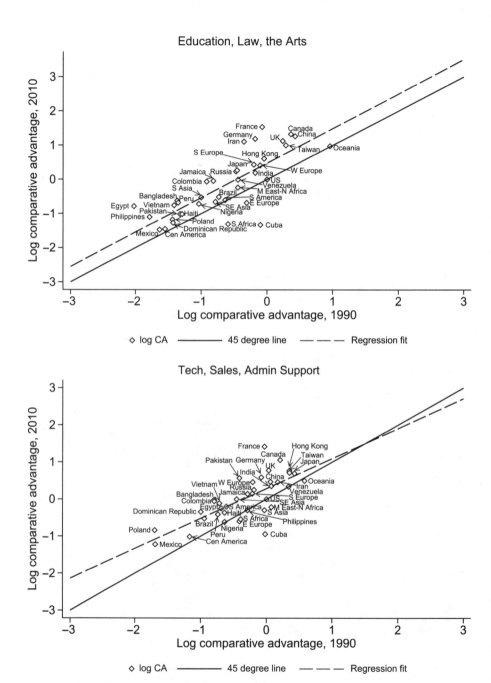

Fig. 1.8 (cont.)

by the mass of points lying above the 45-degree line. The slope coefficient (*t*-value) for a regression of log comparative advantage in 2010 on 1990 values is 1.02 (6.8) in management and finance, 0.43 (2.9) in health-related occupations, 1.01 (7.7) in education and law, and 0.81 (6.4) in administrative support. Persistence in comparative advantage appears to be weakest in health-related occupations. In unreported results, we find patterns in comparative advantage in these occupations for women that are similar to those for men, though for women, persistence in comparative advantage appears to be somewhat weaker.[13]

What explains the persistence in occupational comparative advantage for immigrants across time? One possibility is long-standing differences between countries in the quality of educational institutions or occupational training. Russia's preeminence in mathematics dates back to the eighteenth century, which may have helped create a long-lived tendency for Russian migrants abroad to pursue occupations that are intensive in the use of quantitative reasoning. If differences in educational quality are a root cause of comparative advantage, we should observe differences in occupational choice between immigrants from Russia who arrive in the United States as adults, thus having completed their education in the origin country, and immigrants who arrive in the United States as children, who complete their education in US schools. In figure 1.9, we plot comparative advantage for two groups of male immigrants twenty-one to thirty-seven years old: one group that arrived in the United States at age eighteen or older, whose comparative advantage is given by values on the vertical axis, and a second group that arrived in the United States before age eighteen, whose comparative advantage is given by values on the horizontal axis. For all occupations, the slope coefficient is near one. Occupational comparative advantage for immigrants who arrive as children is nearly identical to that for immigrants who arrive as adults. We find similarly strong positive correlations in comparative advantage between immigrants who arrive as adults and immigrants who arrive as young children (age twelve or younger). These results suggest that the origin of immigrant comparative advantage by occupation is not the country in which one completes tertiary education or even the country in which one completes secondary education. The transmission of occupational skills to a nation's workers (or at least to the workers who migrate abroad) appears to operate through mechanisms other than direct learning in school.

A second explanation for persistence in immigrant occupational comparative advantage is the presence of job networks that are specific to

13. For the sample of female workers, the slope coefficient (*t*-value) for a regression of log comparative advantage in 2010 on the 1990 value is .62 (4.3) in STEM occupations, 0.48 (3.24) in management and finance, 0.60 (4.22) in health-related occupations, 0.49 (4.42) in education and law, and 0.26 (1.84) in administrative support.

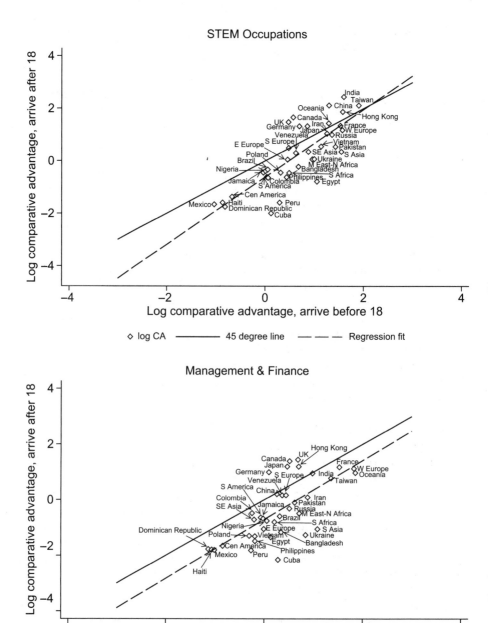

Fig. 1.9 **Log comparative advantage for male immigrants in 2010–2012, US arrivals at age birth to seventeen versus US arrivals at age eighteen or older**

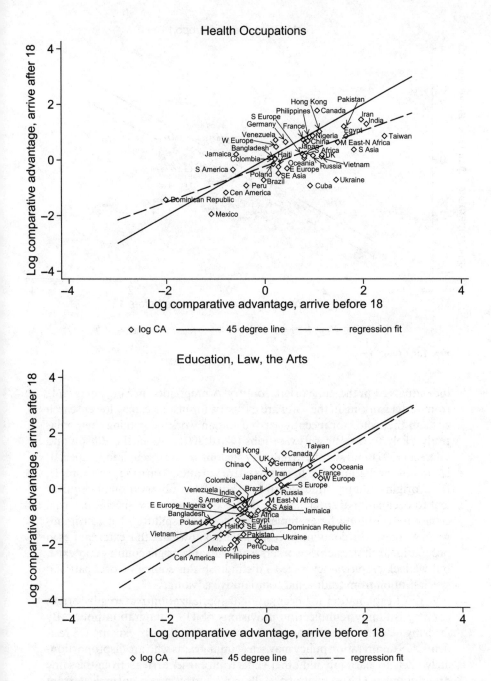

Fig. 1.9 (cont.)

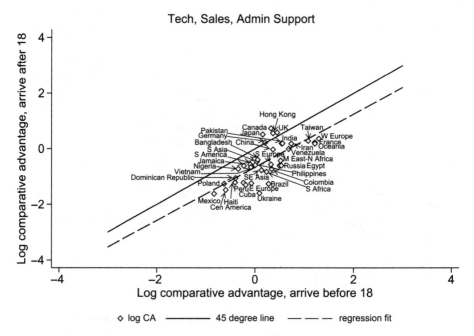

Fig. 1.9   (cont.)

individuals from the same origin country. A preponderance of immigrants from India working in the software industry, for instance, may lower search costs in the sector for recently arrived Indian workers, making them relatively likely to take up software jobs (Card 2001). As in the Ellison and Glaeser (1997) analysis of US industry agglomeration, occupational specialization of immigrants due to comparative advantage (arising, for example, from origin-country educational institutions) is observationally equivalent to occupational specialization due to origin-country-specific external economies (resulting, for example, from knowledge spillovers between immigrant workers with common ancestry). We acknowledge that externalities in occupational choice across workers from the same origin country may exist, but we lack empirical leverage to distinguish this source of occupational specialization from traditional comparative advantage.

A third explanation for occupational specialization patterns by origin country is family reunification provisions of US immigration policy. By favoring new immigrants who have kinship connections to existing US residents, US immigration policy may select immigrants who are disproportionately likely to learn job and other skills from earlier arrivals from the same origin country. The occupational skills picked up by immigrant arrivals from China in the 1980s may then transmit to immigrant arrivals from China in the 1990s and early in the twenty-first century, due in part to the earlier arrivals consisting of many of their relatives.

1.4.4   Ancestry Analysis

A further way to identify the types of mechanisms that may transmit occupational skills across individuals with a given nationality is to compare job choice by immigrants from a particular origin country with native-born workers who have ancestral ties to that origin nation. If transmission mechanisms (e.g., job-search networks) operate on the basis of country of birth, then we would expect to see immigrants from a particular origin country (e.g., India) choosing common occupations in the United States, regardless of whether they arrived in the country as children or as adults. But there is no reason occupational choice among Indian immigrants, say, will overlap with that for native-born US residents of Indian heritage unless these job-search networks are spread broadly throughout the Indian community in the United States.

Our final exercise is to examine comparative advantage for three groups of workers: immigrants from a given origin country who arrive in the United States at or after age eighteen, immigrants from a given origin country who arrive in the United States before age eighteen, and individuals born in the United States (or abroad to US citizens) who claim ancestry from a given origin country. We define ancestry according to the first country of ancestry an individual selects in census or ACS surveys. It is important to note that these surveys do not distinguish ancestry according to the number of generations from which an individual is removed from immigration. Sharing a common ancestry thus may combine those whose parents were born abroad with those who families have resided in the United States for many generations. We again define origin countries (and now ancestral countries) using the forty country/region groups defined in the previous section. The sample is college-educated males between twenty-one to forty-four years old. (See table 1.1.)

Figure 1.10 plots log comparative advantage in STEM occupations for immigrants who arrived in the United States as adults (y-axis of the top panel) and for immigrants who arrived as children (y-axis of the bottom panel) against that for US native-born individuals with the same ancestry (x-axis). In both panels, there is a strong positive correlation between immigrant comparative advantage in STEM and comparative advantage in STEM for US native-born individuals with common ancestry. In the left panel (immigrants who arrived as adults), the slope coefficient is 0.92 (t-value 3.43) with an R^2 of 0.25, while in the right panel (immigrants who arrived as children) the slope coefficient is 0.68 (t-value 4.23) with an R^2 of 0.32. The persistence in comparative advantage in STEM thus applies across generations: current generations of immigrants show a tendency to

Table 1.1   Dispersion of log comparative advantages by occupations and groups

Group	Occupation	Standard deviation
Immigrants arrival after 18	STEM	1.34
Immigrants arrival before 17	STEM	0.85
Native, same ancestry	STEM	0.68
Immigrants arrival after 18	Management & finance	1.15
Immigrants arrival before 17	Management & finance	0.75
Native, same ancestry	Management & finance	0.59
Immigrants arrival after 18	Health occupations	1.15
Immigrants arrival before 17	Health occupations	1.09
Native, same ancestry	Health occupations	0.97
Immigrants arrival after 18	Education, law, the arts	1.13
Immigrants arrival before 17	Education, law, the arts	0.81
Native, same ancestry	Education, law, the arts	0.55
Immigrants arrival after 18	Tech, sales, admin support	0.76
Immigrants arrival before 17	Tech, sales, admin support	0.63
Native, same ancestry	Tech, sales, admin support	0.48

specialize in STEM jobs that is strongly related to the tendency of current descendants of earlier immigrants.

Next, in figure 1.11 we display the analogous comparative advantage plots for immigrants and common-ancestry, native-born workers in other occupations. These plots also reveal positive correlations in comparative advantages for immigrants and common-ancestry natives, but these correlations are weaker than for STEM. Slope coefficients in the left panels (for immigrants who arrived in the United States as adults) are 0.53 (t-value 1.80) in management and finance; 0.60 (t-value 3.76) in health occupations; 0.41 (t-value 1.28) in education, law, and the arts; and 0.31 (t-value 1.31) in technical, sales, and administrative support. Corresponding slope coefficients for immigrants who arrived as children are slightly smaller in all cases.

One pattern that is evident in figures 1.10 and 1.11 is that dispersion in comparative advantage tends to be higher among immigrant workers than among common-ancestry, native-born workers. In table 1.1, we summarize dispersion in comparative advantage across origin countries for each nativity group (immigrants who arrived as adults, immigrants who arrived as children, and common-ancestry, native-born workers) in each of the five occupation groups. For each occupation, dispersion in comparative advantage decreases with time in the United States: it is highest among immigrants who arrived in the United States as adults, second highest among immigrants who arrived in the United States as children, and lowest among common-ancestry, native-born individuals. Accumulated time in the United States thus seems to be associated with attenuation in the impact of origin-country factors that create occupational comparative advantage.

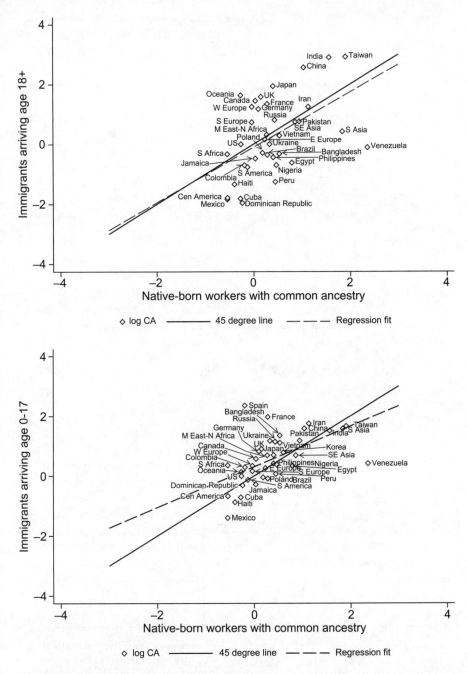

Fig. 1.10   Log comparative advantage in STEM for immigrants versus native-born workers with common ancestry, males 2010–2012

Management & Finance

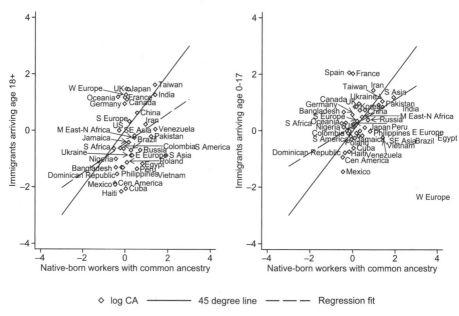

◇ log CA ——— 45 degree line — — — Regression fit

Health Occupations

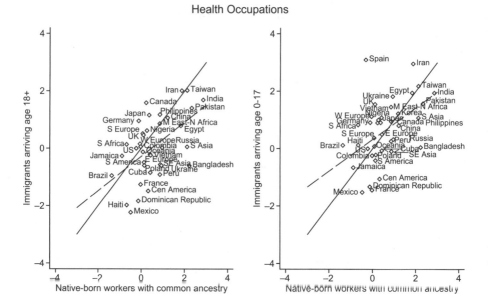

◇ log CA ——— 45 degree line — — — Regression fit

Fig. 1.11 Log comparative advantage in other occupations for immigrants versus native-born workers with common ancestry, males 2010–2012

Education, Law, the Arts

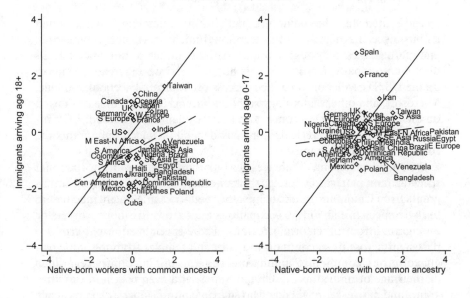

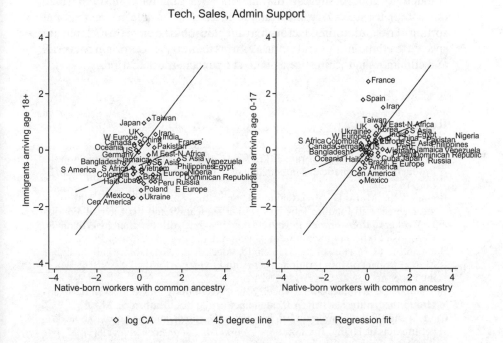

Fig. 1.11 (cont.)

1.5   Discussion

The United States has built its strength in high technology in part through its businesses having access to exceptional talent in science, engineering, and mathematics. Although US universities continue to dominate STEM disciplines globally, it is individuals born abroad who increasingly make up the US STEM labor force. The success of Amazon, Facebook, Google, Microsoft, and other technology standouts seems to hinge, at least in part, on the ability of the US economy to import talent from abroad. US continued success in STEM fields thus may depend on which immigrants the country chooses to admit.

We document strong differences across origin countries in occupational specialization patterns by foreign-born workers in the US economy. Immigrants from China, India, and some other countries in Asia are much more likely to specialize in STEM occupations than are native-born workers or immigrants from other origin regions. These specialization patterns are persistent across time, common to males and females from the same origin countries, common to immigrants from an origin country regardless of their age of arrival in the United States, and even common to immigrants and native-born workers who share a common ancestry. Persistence in occupational specialization patterns across age cohorts, arrival cohorts, and nativity cohorts suggests that factors other than the country in which one completes secondary or tertiary schooling play a role in occupational sorting. These additional factors may include job-search networks that are specific to ethnic groups and cultural norms that vary across origin countries and ethnicities in the prestige assigned to particular occupations.

References

Borjas, George, and Kirk Doran. 2012. "The Collapse of the Soviet Union and the Productivity of American Mathematicians." *Quarterly Journal of Economics* 127 (3): 1143–203.

Bound, John, Murat Demirci, Gaurav Khanna, and Sarah Turner. 2015. "Finishing Degrees and Finding Jobs: US Higher Education and the Flow of Foreign IT Workers." In *Innovation Policy and the Economy*, vol. 15, edited by William R. Kerr, Josh Lerner, and Scott Stern. Chicago: University of Chicago Press.

Burstein, A., G. H. Hanson, L. Tian, and J. Vogel. 2017. "Tradability and the Labor Market Impact of Immigration: Theory and Evidence for the US" NBER Working Paper no. 23330, Cambridge, MA.

Burstein, A., E. Morales, and J. Vogel. 2015. "Accounting for Changes in Between-Group Inequality." NBER Working Paper no. 20855, Cambridge, MA.

Card, David. 2001. "Immigrant Inflows, Native Outflows, and the Local Labor Market Impacts of Higher Immigration." *Journal of Labor Economics* 19 (1): 22–64.

Clemens, Michael. 2010. "The Roots of Global Wage Gaps: Evidence from Randomized Processing of US Visas." Center for Global Development Working Paper no. 212. https://www.cgdev.org/publication/roots-global-wage-gaps-evidence-randomized-processing-us-visas-working-paper-212.

Eaton, Jonathan, and Samuel Kortum. 2002. "Technology, Geography, and Trade." *Econometrica* 70 (5): 1741–79.

Ellison, Glenn, and Edward L. Glaeser. 1997. "Geographic Concentration in US Manufacturing Industries: A Dartboard Approach." *Journal of Political Economy* 105 (5): 889–927.

Freeman, Richard. 2005. "Does Globalization of the Scientific/Engineering Workforce Threaten US Economic Leadership?" NBER Working Paper no. 11457, Cambridge, MA.

General Accounting Office. 2011. "H-1B Visa Program: Reforms Are Needed to Minimize the Risks and Costs of Current Program." GAO Report no. 11-26, Washington, DC, General Accounting Office. http://www.gao.gov/products /GAO-11-26.

Goldin, Claudia, and Lawrence F. Katz. 2008. *The Race between Education and Technology*. Cambridge, MA: Harvard University Press.

Grogger, Jeffrey, and Gordon H. Hanson. 2015. "Attracting Talent: Location Choices of Foreign-Born PhDs in the United States." *Journal of Labor Economics* 33 (S1): S5–38.

Hanushek, Eric A., and Dennis D. Kimko. 2000. "Schooling, Labor-Force Quality, and the Growth of Nations." *American Economic Review* 90 (5): 1184–208.

Hsieh, C.-T., E. Hurst, C. I. Jones, and P. J. Klenow. 2013. "The Allocation of Talent and US Economic Growth." NBER Working Paper no. 18693, Cambridge, MA.

Hunt, Jennifer. 2011. "Which Immigrants Are Most Innovative and Entrepreneurial? Distinctions by Entry Visa." *Journal of Labor Economics* 29 (3): 417–57.

Hunt, Jennifer, and Marjolaine Gauthier-Loiselle. 2010. "How Much Does Immigration Boost Innovation?" *American Economic Journal: Macroeconomics* 2 (2): 31–56.

Institute of International Education. 2015. "Top 25 Places of Origin of International Students, 2013/14–2014/15." Open Doors Report on International Educational Exchange. http://www.iie.org/opendoors.

Jasso, Guillermina, Douglas S. Massey, Mark R. Rosenzweig, and James P. Smith. 2000. "Assortative Mating among Married New Legal Immigrants to the United States: Evidence from the New Immigrant Survey Pilot." *International Migration Review* 34 (2): 443–59.

Jones, Charles I. 2002. "Sources of US Economic Growth in a World of Ideas." *American Economic Review* 92 (1): 220–39.

Kato, Takao, and Chad Sparber. 2013. "Quotas and Quality: The Effect of H-1B Visa Restrictions on the Pool of Prospective Undergraduate Students from Abroad." *Review of Economics and Statistics* 95 (1): 109–26.

Katz, L. F., and David H. Autor. 1999. "Changes in the Wage Structure and Earnings Inequality." *Handbook of Labor Economics* 3:1463–555.

Kerr, William R., and William F. Lincoln. 2010. "The Supply Side of Innovation: H-1B Visa Reforms and US Ethnic Invention." *Journal of Labor Economics* 28 (3): 473–508.

Lagakos, David, and Michael E. Waugh. 2013. "Selection, Agriculture, and Cross-Country Productivity Differences." *American Economic Review* 103 (2): 948–80.

Lowell, B. Lindsay. 2000. "H-1B Temporary Workers: Estimating the Population." CCIS Working Paper no. 12, Center for Comparative Immigration Studies, University of California, San Diego. http://escholarship.org/uc/item/4ms039dc.

Ngai, Mae M. 1999. "The Architecture of Race in American Immigration Law: A

Reexamination of the Immigration Act of 1924." *Journal of American History* 86 (1): 67–92.

Peri, Giovanni. 2012. "The Effect of Immigration on Productivity: Evidence from US States." *Review of Economics and Statistics* 94 (1): 348–58.

Rosenzweig, Mark. 2006. "Global Wage Differences and International Student Flows." *Brookings Trade Forum* 2006:57–86.

———. 2007. "Education and Migration: A Global Perspective." Working Paper, Yale University. http://siteresources.worldbank.org/EXTPREMNET/Resources /489960-1338997241035/Growth_Commission_Workshops_Equity_Rosenzweig _Presentation.pdf.

Roy, Andrew Donald. 1951. "Some Thoughts on the Distribution of Earnings." *Oxford Economic Papers* 3 (2): 135–46.

Ruggles, Steven, Matthew Sobek, Trent Alexander, Catherine A. Fitch, Ronald Goeken, Patricia Kelly Hall, Miriam King, and Chad Ronnander. 2010. Integrated Public Use Microdata Series: Version 3.0. Minneapolis: Minnesota Population Center.

Salzman, Hal, Daniel Kuehn, and B. Lindsay Lowell. 2013. "Guestworkers in the High-Skill US Labor Market." EPI Briefing Paper no. 359, Economic Policy Institute.

Udansky, Margaret L., and Thomas J. Espenshade. 2000. "The H-1B Debate in Historical Perspective: The Evolution of US Policy toward Foreign-Born Workers." CCIS Working Paper no. 11, Center for Comparative Immigration Studies, University of California, San Diego. https://ccis.ucsd.edu/_files/wp11.pdf.

2

The Innovation Activities of Multinational Enterprises and the Demand for Skilled-Worker, Nonimmigrant Visas

Stephen Ross Yeaple

Multinational enterprises, those firms that operate productive facilities in multiple countries, engage in the lion's share of both international commerce and formal innovative activities such as research and development (R&D). An almost universally held view is that the nature of knowledge creation and its usage leads to the development of these firms (e.g., Helpman 1984; Markusen 1984). Knowledge is a public good that can be used in many places by many people simultaneously, and so the firms that create knowledge have difficulty extracting rents from it. These market imperfections give rise to multinationals.

While the use of existing technology has been integrated into the theory of the multinational enterprise, the international flows of labor that facilitate its creation have received less attention. The development and management of new technologies within the firm require the most highly trained and capable minds. Moreover, while the world has seen the rapid fragmentation of production processes, which have allowed individual countries to specialize in particular stages of the physical production process, the fragmentation of the production of technology remains limited. Despite some diffusion in recent years, most formal R&D remains highly concentrated in a few firms' headquarters that are located in even fewer countries. Yet, it is likely that raw intellectual talent is not nearly as concentrated globally as the location of multinationals' headquarters.

A growing literature (e.g., Kerr and Kerr 2015) suggests that there are substantial frictions to international collaboration that can only be fully

Stephen Ross Yeaple is professor of economics at Pennsylvania State University and a research associate of the National Bureau of Economic Research.

For acknowledgments, sources of research support, and disclosure of the author's material financial relationships, if any, please see http://www.nber.org/chapters/c13844.ack.

overcome by allowing researchers to work in close physical proximity for an extended period of time. Hence, international relocation costs, many of which are driven by government policies, that impede the flow of the world's most talented workers from low- to high-innovation locations may have substantial negative consequences for global welfare. Indeed, in testimony before Congress, Bill Gates has argued that US limits on skilled-worker inflows could lead to innovative activities moving out of the United States to places where there is less competition for the most highly skilled workers.

The United States accommodates some of this need for labor movements within firms through its H-1B and L-1 nonimmigrant visa programs. The H-1B program is highly visible and so is well known. Every year the US Citizen and Immigration service accepts applications by US-based firms for temporary work visas that number 65,000 for workers with specialized skills and an additional 20,000 visas for recent graduates of American universities.[1] The annual number of petitions for these visas usually exceeds the allowed number of visas, so that the cap is binding.

The L-1 visa program, which came into being in the 1970 amendments of the Immigration and Nationality Act, is less well known. It has two components. The L-1A program is designed to offer temporary work visas with a typical duration of three years for the managers and executives that are being transferred within the firm, but across the border. The L-1B program is designed for workers being transferred within the firm, but across the border, who have specialized knowledge of the company's products/services, research, systems, proprietary techniques, management, or procedures. Both cases are relevant for the international movement of the labor to develop and to manage new technology.

This chapter presents an analysis of the industrial structure of international labor flows that are made possible by the L-1 and H-1B visa programs. We begin by providing a simple model of firm sourcing of skilled labor based on recent advances in the quantitative literature on differentiated intermediate input sourcing (e.g., Antras, Fort, and Tintelnot 2017). In the model the welfare effects of temporary work visas may be much like the welfare effects of sourcing intermediate inputs: they lead to increased innovative activities at the firm level and an expansion of the domestic workforce at those firms that actually use foreign workers. According to this framework, it may be the firms that do not use temporary skilled foreign workers who suffer the most and whose contraction may adversely affect the welfare of domestic US workers. Further, it is shown that under reasonable parameter values skilled US workers may benefit from the existence of these programs!

---

1. Many more are given without restriction to university professors and employees of nonprofits. Surely without this exception, US universities would be hard pressed to maintain their world-leading reputation for research!

We then turn to data on L-1 and H-1B visa programs to assess whether the qualitative implications of our model are consistent with the facts. As our model points to a complementarity between multinational production and worker visa usage, we focus on the role played by multinational enterprises in these flows. Using firm-level data of the users of these programs, we show that it is the most R&D-intensive firms in the most R&D-intensive industries that rely most heavily on temporary visas. Our results provide support for the hypothesis that international flows of specialized workers are important because these workers are highly complementary to the use and to the development of innovative technologies.

Going further, we demonstrate that the structure of sourcing of labor across the types of visas differs dramatically across industries and countries. For instance, H-1B visas are fairly evenly distributed over high-tech industries while L-1 visas and all temporary work visas are more skewed toward the industries in which US multinationals operate the most aggressively abroad. This suggests that the L-1 visa program plays the role of a substitute for the H-1B program. Supporting this hypothesis is the observation that after controlling for the relevant firm-level characteristics, multinational firms are still granted a large number of temporary work visas than nonmultinational firms. This suggests that these firms are better able to overcome the frictions, both driven by US policies and by the natural difficulties associated with identifying and acquiring the proper skills in distant labor markets.

Temporary work visas are the source of much controversy in the United States. As noted above, employers in high-tech areas argue that the program is too restrictive and so reduces the size of the high-tech sector in the United States to the ultimate detriment of all. Others argue that despite its relatively small size, both programs allow US firms to substitute lower-cost workers from abroad for comparable workers in the United States. Further, assert many critics, the program facilitates the offshoring of skilled activities as foreign workers can be efficiently "trained" in the United States. In an analysis of the L-1 program, the Department of Homeland Security describes the controversy: "Opponents of the L-1 visa program feel that it drives down salaries, reduces employment opportunities for domestic technology workers, and allows unscrupulous petitioners to exploit foreign beneficiaries. However, proponents of the L-1 visa argue that this program allows US firms to remain innovative and to recruit and to retain the 'best and brightest'" (Office of the Inspector General 2013, 5).

Within the vast academic literature on immigration, the role played by temporary work visas for skilled labor has received less attention. To the extent that it has, the key questions have been (a) whether the expansion of H-1B visa programs has had the effect of increasing or decreasing demand for competing American workers, and (b) has the program had the effect of spurring additional innovation (see, e.g., Kerr and Lincoln 2010; Kerr, Kerr, and Lincoln 2015). Our contribution is to look at the cross-firm structure of skilled-labor temporary work visa usage by individual firms for patterns that shed light on precisely these issues. We provide a portrait of which industries use these visas intensively, which firms within industries use these visas most, and which countries are the sources of these workers. We show that the foreign investment activities of US firms predict much of the variation in these sourcing patterns. This suggests that the expansion of multinational enterprises may lead to greater integration of the labor markets for high-skilled labor.

The conceptual framework that we believe is most appropriate for analyzing the welfare consequences of temporary work visas is the import-sourcing work of Antras, Fort, and Tintelnot (2017), who analyze the firm-level decisions to import differentiated intermediate inputs. In the activities associated with the development and management of new technologies, sourcing individual talents may be even more critical than sourcing individual components. Human specialization in high-technology industries is perhaps greater than in any other activity associated with mass production as there may only be a handful of candidates who are truly qualified for particular jobs. Further, given the nature of the activities involved, actual worker mobility, rather than remote communication, may be critical.[2]

In the context of sourcing foreign inputs, multinationals are important for two reasons. The first reason is that the L-1 visa program makes it possible for these firms to avoid the H-1B visa cap. This is a source of a competitive advantage of multinationals that has not been considered in the literature. It is still true, however, that this advantage is limited to sourcing workers only from countries in which it has affiliates, and so represents only a partial solution to sourcing problems. Second, because workers are, in large part, experience goods, multinationals may have a sourcing advantage in identifying, obtaining, and nurturing qualified workers relative to firms with no facilities on the ground.[3]

The remainder of the chapter is organized into six sections. In the next section we briefly describe the L-1 visa program, as it is relatively unfamiliar in the literature. In section 2.2, we provide a model of the international sourcing of skilled labor by firms engaged in innovation. In the model, firms gain from access to foreign workers for two reasons: they may be able to pay a low wage and they benefit from a diversity of skills from different locations. In sourcing such labor, multinationals have improved access because of their proximity to foreign labor markets. We also show how this framework can be used to measure the welfare impact of foreign investment and the availability of temporary work visas.

2. See Keller and Nune Hovhannisyan (2015) for the role of businessman mobility in the related context of international trade.

3. It may be the case that workers and firms need to make relationship-specific investments in order for the worker to be able to adequately implement an important task. In this context, L-1 intracompany transfer visas and H-1B visas may then be different animals for different firms depending on which type of investment is most important. In this case, Antras (2003, 2005) becomes relevant.

In section 2.3, we describe the data. In section 2.4, we provide simple econometric analyses. We first describe the cross-industry structure of temporary visa usage pointing out the similarities and differences between the usage of L-1 and H-1B programs. We then conduct a firm-level analysis in order to understand which firm characteristics are most associated with temporary visa usage. Finally, we look at the cross-country pattern in the origin of temporary visa usages. We argue that the results suggest that our model would be worth calibrating as its first-order implications are consistent with the data. Section 2.5 provides additional detail on what data would allow the full model to be estimated and used to do policy analyses were employer-employee visa data to be merged with data on the activities of US multinationals. The final section concludes.

2.1   The L-1 Program

Like the H-1B visa program, the L-1A visa and L-1B visa programs allow firms to sponsor specific workers for specific jobs for a temporary period of time. The L-1A visa covers workers who enter the United States in order to provide service in an executive or managerial capacity for an American branch, subsidiary, affiliate, or office of the same employer. An executive capacity refers to the employee's ability to make decisions of wide latitude and autonomy, while managerial capacity refers to the ability of the employee to supervise and control the work of professional employees and to manage the organization or a department, subdivision, function, or component of the organization.[4] The L-1B visa covers workers who have a specialized knowledge of a company's product, service, research, equipment, techniques, management, or other interests and its application in international markets, or an advanced level of knowledge or expertise in the organization's processes and procedures.

To qualify for an L-1 visa a worker must have been working for a qualifying organization abroad for one continuous year within the three years immediately preceding his or her admission to the United States. Qualified employees entering the United States to establish a new office will be allowed a maximum initial stay of one year. All other qualified employees will be allowed a maximum initial stay of three years. For all L-1B employees, requests for extension of stay may be granted in increments of up to an additional two years, until the employee has reached the maximum limit of five years. For all L-1A employees, requests for extension of stay may be granted in increments of up to an additional two years, until the employee has reached the maximum limit of seven years.

To obtain a visa for a qualified employee, an employer must file a Form I-129, Petition for a Nonimmigrant Worker, and pay a fee. Certain organi-

---

4. In the absence of an existing affiliate, a firm may use this visa program to send a worker to the United States to open a new affiliate.

zations may establish the required intracompany relationship in advance of filing individual L-1 petitions by filing a blanket petition. Eligibility for blanket L certification may be established if: (a) the petitioner and each of the qualifying organizations are engaged in commercial trade or services; (b) the petitioner has an office in the United States that has been doing business for one year or more; (c) the petitioner has three or more domestic and foreign branches, subsidiaries, and affiliates and the petitioner, along with the other qualifying organizations, meet one of the following criteria: have obtained at least ten L-1 approvals during the previous twelve-month period; have US subsidiaries or affiliates with combined annual sales of at least $25 million; or (d) have a US workforce of at least 1,000 employees. Blanket petitions offer employers the flexibility to transfer eligible employees to the United States quickly and with short notice without having to file an individual petition with the United States Citizenship and Immigration Service.

Aside from offering access to skilled foreign workers to US employers, the L-1 program has other features in common with the better-known H-1B program. In terms of its scope, the L-1 program is smaller but of a similar order of magnitude as the H-1B program. According to the Department of Homeland Security, the number of L-1 visa petitions approved or renewed in 2015 stood at 78,537 compared with 172, 748 for the H-1B program. Both programs are dual-intent programs that can act as a stepping-stone to a green card.[5]

In other respects, the visas offered by the two programs are not perfect substitutes. First, the ability of heavy users of the program to file blanket petitions and the lack of a cap on the number of employees that could be hired makes the L-1 program relatively more flexible so that firms can better smooth demand shocks than with the H-1B program. Furthermore, because H-1B visas may be denied due to the cap in such a way that specific skills cannot be prioritized, the L-1 program eliminates another source of uncertainty facing the firm. Yet another advantage of the program is that it gives firms better incentives to make long-term investments in the skills of their employees. A weakness of the program, however, is that unlike the H-1B program, the L-1 program does not provide firms the ability to recruit new graduates.[6]

2.2   Visas, Multinationals, and Innovation in General Equilibrium

In this section, we provide a simple model to analyze the effect of temporary visa programs on the innovation activities of firms. The key idea

---

5. The data can be found at https://travel.state.gov/content/visas/en/law-and-policy/statistics/non-immigrant-visas.html.

6. Another subtle difference between H-1B and L-1 programs is that most spouses of workers with an L-1 visa will qualify for an L-2 visa that allows the spouse to work in the United States. In 2015, the number of L-2 visas was over 86,000.

is that the high-skilled labor that is necessary to provide advertising and R&D services and to manage complex corporations labor inputs are at least as highly differentiated as intermediate inputs. Nevertheless, laborers from given countries will have some common features such as cultural and educational background and industrial experience. Multinational firms will have lower cost of hiring foreign workers than firms without global operations because they are more likely to be able to identify, to train, and to attract talented individuals abroad.

We show how the model could be estimated using data that exists, but is not readily available. We also show how the elasticities to be estimated determine the welfare implications of temporary visa programs. For instance, under reasonable parameter values, the elimination of skilled-worker temporary visa programs would have a negative impact on the relative wage of skilled labor as it would shrink research-intensive activities.

2.2.1   Assumptions

Consider a world in which there are I countries that are indexed by i and j. These countries are endowed with skilled (L_i^s) and unskilled labor (L_i^u). In each country, there is a representative consumer with preferences defined over a differentiated good (X) and a homogeneous good (Y). These preferences are given by

$$(1) \qquad U_i = \frac{\sigma}{\sigma - 1} X_i^{(\sigma-1)/\sigma} + Y_i, \sigma > 1,$$

where σ is the elasticity of substitution across goods, the aggregator of varieties of the differentiated good is constant elasticity of substitution (CES),

$$(2) \qquad X_i = \left(\int_{\omega \in \Omega_i} x(\omega)^{(\varepsilon-1)/\varepsilon} d\omega \right)^{\varepsilon/(\varepsilon-1)},$$

$\varepsilon > \sigma$ is the elasticity of substitution across varieties of the differentiated good, and Ω_i is the set of available varieties in country i. We assume that good Y is freely traded between countries, produced using exclusively unskilled labor, and is the numeraire. Assuming that Y is produced everywhere, the wage of unskilled labor (not our interest in this chapter) is the same everywhere, and we choose units so that its price is one.

Consumer maximization of equations (1) and (2) yield demand for variety ω in country i of

$$(3) \qquad x_i(\omega) = (P_i)^{\varepsilon-\sigma} p_i^{-\varepsilon}(\omega),$$

where p_i is the price in i, and the price index of differentiated goods in country i is

$$P_i^{1-\varepsilon} = \int_{\omega' \in \Omega_i} p_i(\omega')^{1-\varepsilon} d\omega'.$$

Note that because $\varepsilon > \sigma$ an increase in the aggregate price index for the differentiated good raises demand for an individual variety but lowers aggregate demand for the composite differentiated good.

Differentiated goods are not traded and their production requires both skilled and unskilled labor. Skilled labor is used in management and innovation functions to lower marginal costs of production, while unskilled labor physically creates output. In country i there is a measure of N_i firms indexed by ω. Each firm produces a distinct variety of the differentiated good according to a firm-specific production function given by

$$(4) \qquad x_i(\omega) = \varphi(\omega) r_i(\omega) l_i^u(\omega),$$

where $\varphi(\omega)$ is the inherent productivity of the firm and $l_i^u(\omega)$ is the quantity of unskilled labor employed by the firm in country i and $r_i(\omega)$ is an endogenous component of firm productivity that is due to the firm's conscious R&D effort. Firms are heterogeneous in their inherent productivity φ, which is distributed according to the cumulative distribution function G. Firms from country i are also heterogeneously endowed with foreign affiliates with firm ω assumed to own an affiliate in set $J(\omega)$ of countries.[7] These firms may produce in any country in which they have an affiliate, but more importantly, as we describe below, they are better able to access skilled-labor markets from countries in which they own an affiliate.[8]

The endogenous component of firm ω's productivity in country i, $r_i(\omega)$, depends on management and R&D services provided by the firm at that location. These services take the form of a bundle of tasks that require skilled labor such as managers, marketing professionals, computer programmers, and scientists. These tasks lie on the unit interval and have an elasticity of substitution between them of ρ. Formally, the production function for this bundle of tasks is

$$M_i = \left(\int_0^1 s_i(t)^\rho \, dt \right)^{1/\rho},$$

where $s_i(t)$ is the effective quantity of labor services of task t provided in country i. Crucially, we assume that all workers contributing to the production of this bundle must share the same location. Finally, in order for a firm with inherent productivity φ to obtain a productivity level of φr requires the firm to produce $f r^\phi$ units of these bundles, where $\phi > \varepsilon - 1$ guarantees an interior solution to R&D.

Skilled workers in country i have productivities, z, across tasks that are drawn independently from the Fréchet distribution,

$$\Pr(Z < z) = \exp\left(-T_i z^{-\theta}\right),$$

where the parameter $\theta > \rho - 1 > 0$ captures the extent of skilled task comparative advantage across countries, and the parameter T_i captures the general quality of education, and hence skilled-labor capability, in country i. The endogenous wage of skilled labor in country j is given by w_j^s.

---

7. We choose not to endogenize the location choice of firms given the lack of data and the complexity involved. This is an area where further work would be desirable.

8. We are not taking any stand in the model on asymmetries between a firm's headquarters and its various plants.

Moving workers across countries is costly. This is either because the workers do not have experience with the workings of the particular firm, because cultural differences make workers less effective abroad, or simply because compensating differentials must be paid to induce labor to move to unfamiliar and isolated environments. We assume that the size of these moving costs depends on whether the firm owns an affiliate in the worker's country. If the firm owns an affiliate in country j, then it faces iceberg-type costs $\tau_{ji} \geq 1$ that vary across country pairs so that the realized cost of employing l_j^s skilled workers from country j for an operation in country i incurs the cost $w_j^s \tau_{ji} l_j^s$.[9] If a firm does not operate an affiliate in country j, then it has a higher cost of obtaining labor from that country and it faces the additional cost of sourcing labor $\delta_{ji} \geq 1$ so that its cost of sourcing labor is given by $\delta_{ji}\tau_{ji}$.[10]

The market structure is perfect competition in the labor markets for skilled and unskilled labor and for the homogeneous good industry. The market structure in the differentiated good industry is one of monopolistic competition.

The timing is as follows. First, firms hire skilled workers globally. Next, the firms engage in innovation and marketing efforts. Finally, the firm hires unskilled labor locally, produces, and sells its product in the local market.

2.2.2 Firm-Level Implications

In this subsection we solve for firms' innovation decisions (R&D and skilled-labor sourcing) as a function of the firms' productivity φ and set of affiliate locations J. We focus on a firm of arbitrary characteristics from a single country and characterize how variation in firm characteristics in this country gives rise to different behavior in sourcing of skilled labor and in total innovation effort.

We solve the model backward. We first derive the variable profit associated with production at a given level of productivity. Second, we determine the optimal level of productivity chosen by the firm given the cost of management and innovation. Finally, we derive the optimal sourcing of workers internationally.

The profit associated with our representative firm of inherent productivity φ that is located in country i, that is associated with an affiliate network J, that charges price p, and that implements innovation effort r is

$$(5) \qquad \Pi_i(\varphi, J) = \max_{p,r} \left\{ \left(p - \frac{1}{\varphi_i r} \right) x_i(p) - C_i(J) f r^\phi \right\},$$

where demand $x_i(p)$ is given by equation (3) and $C_i(J)$ is the cost of a bundle of managerial and R&D inputs in country i for a firm with affiliate network

9. For simplicity, we assume that there are no fixed costs associated with sourcing labor from abroad. This has the unrealistic implication that a firm sources workers from every country. We leave this extension to future work.

10. For evidence that the internal labor markets of large firms may be more efficient at matching workers and tasks, see Papageorgiou (2016).

J. The first-order condition for profit maximization with respect to the price of output has the solution

(6)
$$p(\varphi, r_i) = \frac{\varepsilon}{\varepsilon - 1} \frac{1}{\varphi r_i(\varphi, J)},$$

which together with the first-order condition for the optimal choice of productivity in country i yields the optimal productivity level of

(7)
$$r_i(\varphi, J) = \left(\frac{B_i \varphi}{f C_i(J)} \right)^{1/(\phi - \varepsilon + 1)},$$

where

(8)
$$B_i = \frac{1}{\phi} \left(\frac{\varepsilon}{\varepsilon - 1} \right)^{-\varepsilon} (P_i)^{\varepsilon - \sigma}$$

is the markup adjusted demand level in country i. It is immediately clear from equation (7) that a firm's choice of innovation intensity is increasing in the size of the market that it serves, is increasing in inherent productivity, and is decreasing in the cost of a bundle of management tasks. Equation (7) further implies that the total spending on skilled labor by the firm in country i is

(9)
$$S_i(\varphi_i, J) = \left(f C_i(J) \right)^{-(\varepsilon-1)/(\phi-\varepsilon+1)} \left(B_i \varphi \right)^{\phi/(\phi-\varepsilon+1)}.$$

We now turn to the cost minimization problem of the firm with respect to its sourcing of skilled labor. For a given task, the firm will employ skilled labor from country j if

$$\frac{w_j^s}{z_j} d_{ji} \leq \frac{w_k^s}{z_k} d_{ki} \text{ for all } k,$$

where $d_{ji} = \tau_{ji}$ if $j \in J$ and $d_{ji} = \tau_{ji} \delta_{ji}$ otherwise. Following the calculations made in Eaton and Kortum (2002), it follows that the share of tasks performed for firm from country i with affiliate network J that are filled with skilled workers from country j is

(10)
$$\pi_{ji}(J) = \begin{cases} \dfrac{T_j \left(w_j^s \tau_{ji} \right)^{-\theta}}{\Theta_i(J)} & \text{if } j \in J \\[4mm] \dfrac{T_j \left(w_j^s \left(\tau_{ji} \delta_{ji} \right) \right)^{-\theta}}{\Theta_i(J)} & \text{if } j \notin J \end{cases},$$

where

(11)
$$\Theta_i(J) \equiv \sum_{j \in J} T_j \left(w_j^s \tau_{ji} \right)^{-\theta} + \sum_{j \notin J} T_j \left(w_j^s \left(\tau_{ji} \delta_{ji} \right) \right)^{-\theta}$$

is the human resource "sourcing potential" of the firm with affiliate network J.

Following the algebra presented in Eaton and Kortum (2002), the cost of bundle of managerial inputs for a firm with affiliates in the set J of countries can be shown to be

$$(12) \qquad C_i(J) = \left(\gamma\Theta_i(J)\right)^{-1/\theta},$$

where γ is a constant.

We now tease out some of the qualitative implications of the model, beginning with two of the most immediate. First, note that by using equations (3), (6), (7), and (9) that we can solve for the share of skilled labor in total firm revenues (R), which is given by $(S_i/R_i) = (C_i f \varphi_i^\phi) / (p_i x_i) = (\varepsilon - 1)/\varepsilon\phi$. The first proposition follows from this observation.

PROPOSITION 1. *Absolute demand for temporary skilled-worker visas is higher in R&D-intensive industries (i.e., those with high $(\varepsilon - 1)/\varepsilon\phi$).*

Firms in industries in which the return to management and/or R&D will hire more skilled labor and so will also use more skilled-labor visas.

Turning to the next firm-level implication, it follows immediately from equations (10) and (11) that as a firm becomes more multinational in the sense that it owns an affiliate in a larger number of locations that it substitutes away from both domestic employment and from H-1B visa workers. By construction the model implies that at *the level of the task*, L-1 visa holders displace domestic workers. This does NOT mean, however, that as a group the employment of domestic, or H-1B visa holders, becomes less commonplace as the firm opens more foreign affiliates. To see this, consider an increase in the number of countries in which a firm invests. From equation (11), adding a country to the set J of countries with an affiliate increases the firm's sourcing potential, which in turn reduces its cost of innovation through equation (12). Hence, an increase in multinational production induces the firm to increase its innovation efforts and so expands the firm's scale of operations.[11] The following proposition follows from equations (9) and (14):

PROPOSITION 2. *A firm that opens an additional foreign affiliate reduces the share of domestic workers employed in innovation activities, but expands the absolute employment of skilled workers from all existing locations if*

$$(13) \qquad \frac{1}{1+1/\theta} < \frac{\varepsilon-1}{\phi}.$$

When demand for final varieties is elastic relative to the elasticity of innovation costs, a reduction in the costs of innovation labor leads to a large

---

11. This expansion may come at the expense of other firms in the industry or firms in other industries. The aggregate impact on demand for domestic skill depends on the details of the full general equilibrium that we do not address here.

increase in a firm's market share. If, in addition, workers across countries are not very substitutable (low θ), then skilled workers are net complements at the level of the firm. Note that the right-hand side of equation (13) is monotonic in the R&D/managerial intensity of a firm so that, everything else equal, more R&D-intensive firms are more likely to expand their total employment of all types of skilled labor when increasing their sorting potential. Another implication is that holding fixed the elasticity of innovation costs with respect to productivity, φ, greater sourcing potential leads to an increase in the absolute number of all worker types if the extent of heterogeneity of worker types across countries is high (so that θ is low) relative to the extent of heterogeneity across consumption goods (captured by ε).

Note also that this implication of the model is consistent with the findings of Kerr, Kerr, and Lincoln (2015), who find that increased H-1B usage made possible by increases in the visa cap had the effect of increasing net employment of skilled workers at those firms.

2.2.3   Parameter Estimation

In this subsection, we sketch how the model parameters could be estimated were we in possession of firm-level data that included the payments to L-1 and H-1B visa holders by the country of origin of the employee, the size of domestic employment by firm, and the location of production by country. This data would allow the estimation of a gravity equation that identifies many of the model's key parameters.

Equations (9)–(10) can be manipulated to obtain an expression for the total wage payments made by headquarters in country i to workers from country j for a firm of type (φ, J):

$$(14) \qquad S_{ji}(\varphi, J) = \begin{cases} \dfrac{T_j \left(w_j^s \tau_{ji} \right)^{-\theta}}{\Theta(J)} S_i(\varphi, J) & \text{if } j \in J \\[2em] \dfrac{T_j \left(w_j^s \left(\tau_{ji} \delta_{ji} \right) \right)^{-\theta}}{\Theta(J)} S_i(\varphi, J) & \text{if } j \notin J \end{cases}.$$

Expression (14) illustrates how the employee-sourcing part of the model can be estimated as a gravity equation using data on firm-level payments to temporary visa holders.[12] As in Antras, Fort, and Tintelnot (2017), the model implies the equation

---

12. To connect our model to data we need to assume that the worker inflows associated with countries in which a firm owns an affiliate occur using L-1 visas issued for the purpose of intercompany transfers, while the worker inflows associated with countries in which a firm does not own an affiliate occur as H-1B visas. Of course, a firm with an affiliate in a given country might identify a worker who is not currently an employee in that country and so use the H-1B program, such a situation might be an intermediate case in which δ_{ji} is lower for firms with a

$$\log \frac{S_{ji}(\varphi, J)}{S_{ii}(\varphi, J)} = \xi_{ji} + \xi_{ji}^{wa} + e_{ij},$$

where the country sourcing potential dummies $\xi_{ji} = \log[T_j(\tau_{ji})^\theta / T_i(w_i^s)^{-\theta}]$ for firms with a local affiliate in country j and $\xi_{ji}^{wa} = \log[T_j(w_j^s \tau_{ji} \delta_{ji})^{-\theta} / T_i(w_i^w)^{-\theta}]$ for firms without an affiliate. Regressing the sum of these country-level dummy coefficients on country controls for distance and efficiency would then allow instrumented skilled wage data to reveal θ.

From the coefficient estimates of θ, and estimates of T_j backed out from the data using equation (14), the cost reduction enjoyed by individual firms made possible by their multinational network and to the visa program can be calculated. To infer whether these firms are induced to hire more American workers in the model, we can compare the estimate of θ to the R&D intensity of American firms, which is $(\varepsilon - 1)/\phi$ in the model. In the most-R&D-intensive industries we would expect multinational firms to be most aggressive in hiring skilled labor from all countries.

2.2.4   Temporary Work Visas and Domestic Skilled-Worker Wages

Proposition 2 suggests that at the level of the individual firm foreign skilled workers and domestic skilled workers can be net complements. This outcome is consistent with some of the existing evidence. In this section, we show that this complementarity could be so strong that in the aggregate restrictions on skilled-worker visas could lower the welfare of a country's skilled workforce. The mechanism through which this would work in our model lines up well with the concerns of skilled-worker employers in the United States. If costs of innovation become very high because of restrictions on skilled foreign workers then the entire industry could shrink, leaving domestic skilled workers worse off.

In our special case we consider a world with two countries, now called H and F. In this world, both countries share the same number of workers and skilled workers have the same average productivity, determined by common T. Countries differ in that H has more demand for skilled labor, that is, $N_H > N_F = 0$. We assume that in a regime in which international sourcing of labor is allowed that it occurs frictionlessly (i.e., $\tau_{FH} = \delta_{FH} = 1$). Finally, all firms are identical in their productivity ($\varphi = 1$ for all firms) and no firm owns a foreign affiliate ($J = 0$).

In this setting, skilled workers from H are as vulnerable as possible to competition from immigrants from F and, as such, are most likely to be harmed by skilled-worker inflows.

We first characterize the equilibrium in which labor flows are unimpeded.

---

local affiliate but greater than one given the lack of experience with that worker. Further, it is also possible that a firm might choose to use the H-1B program for an employee were H-1B visas available.

Associating the worker-mobility equilibrium variables with a subscript m, the representative firm in H pays $C_m fr_m^\phi$ units of the numeraire to skilled workers to fund its R&D efforts. Of this spending, fraction $(w_H^s)^{-\theta}/[(w_H^s)^{-\theta} + (w_F^s)^{-\theta}]$ is paid to domestic skilled workers while the rest is paid to foreign skilled workers. It is easily confirmed that the free flow of skilled labor in this setting, in which countries that are identical except for the presence of local differentiated goods producers, implies factor price equalization.[13]

Given factor price equalization, the shares of domestic and foreign workers equally split domestic employment and the wage is determined by the single skilled-labor market-clearing condition:

$$(15) \qquad w_m^s 2L^s = N_H C_m fr_m^\phi,$$

This expression shows that the cost of innovation activities of the N_H firms in H given the endogenous choice of productivity r_m is paid out to the skilled workers from both countries.

Using factor price equalization and equations (12) and (11), it is straightforward to show that the cost of a bundle of innovation inputs is linear in the wage paid for a unit of skilled labor:

$$(16) \qquad C_m = (2\gamma T)^{-1/\theta} w_m^s.$$

Finally, homogeneity among firms implies that the price index in H[14] is always given by

$$(17) \qquad P = \frac{\varepsilon}{\varepsilon - 1} (N_H)^{1/(1-\varepsilon)} \frac{1}{r}.$$

These three expressions combined with equations (7) and (8) completely characterize the worker-mobility equilibrium.

Now consider the equilibrium that obtains when workers are not able to move. We denote this "autarky" equilibrium with subscript α on the endogenous variables. Now the skilled-labor market-clearing condition becomes

$$(18) \qquad w_a^s L^s = N_H C_a fr_a^\phi,$$

and the cost of a bundle of innovation inputs becomes

$$(19) \qquad C_a = (\gamma T)^{-1/\theta} w_a^s.$$

The key difference in expressions (18) and (19) from (15) and (16) is the factor by which L^s and T are multiplied. This reflects the fact that there is only half

13. Although skilled workers are differentiated by their source, they have identical average productivities and they are in equal supplies given the symmetry assumption. Therefore, factor prices must equalize.

14. Because $M_F = 0$ and because there is no trade in final goods and no local foreign affiliates, the differentiated good is not available in F.

the skilled-labor supply in this equilibrium, and there is a lack of intellectual diversity as only one country's labor type is available.

These expressions, when combined with (7) and (8), imply the following price differences between the two equilibria:

$$\frac{P_m}{P_a} = 2^{-(1+\theta)/\theta\phi},$$

$$\frac{w_m^s}{w_a^s} = 2^{(1/\theta)-[(1+\theta)/\theta][1-(\sigma-1)/\phi]}.$$

These expressions imply the following proposition:

PROPOSITION 3. *Home's skilled workers have higher income under perfect skilled-labor mobility than with no skilled-labor mobility if*

(20)
$$\frac{1}{1+1/\theta} < \frac{\sigma-1}{\phi}.$$

The proposition establishes a sufficient condition for skilled workers in the "protected" country to lose from that protection. Intuitively, if workers internationally are poor substitutes for one another (θ low), then international labor mobility will substantially lower the cost of innovation. If, in addition, lower innovation costs induce a substantial increase in demand for differentiated goods (high σ), then allowing skilled-labor migration from a country with excess supply of skilled labor may increase aggregate demand for skilled labor by so much that the real income of domestic skilled workers increases relative to the price of homogeneous goods. Moreover, more innovation lowers the marginal cost of production and so lowers the relative price of differentiated goods. Were the condition in the proposition not to hold, skilled workers might yet gain because skilled immigration lowers the price of differentiated goods through increased innovation. In this sense, condition (20) is sufficient but is not necessary.

That the conditions (13) and (20) are so similar is not surprising. At the firm level, opening an affiliate yields better access to foreign workers and so allows the firm to benefit from the increased diversity and the productivity gain associated with that cost reduction depends on the elasticity of innovation costs with respect to productivity. At the firm level, the key issue is how this cost reduction shifts market share away from competitors, whereas at the industry level this is about how lower marginal costs induced by productivity gains induces a shift in consumption toward the innovative industry.

This model presented in this section has interesting implications regarding how skilled-labor welfare is affected by the existence of a skilled-labor temporary visa program. The discussion in the previous subsection showed how with the right data set the relevant elasticities and international mobility frictions could be estimated in a manner similar to that of Antras, Fort, and Tintelnot (2017).

2.2.5   Summary of Model Implications

We have discussed how existing, but hard to access, data could be used to estimate the model. The data to which we do have access includes components of the ideal data set but lacks the detail necessary for estimation. Hence, we instead explore in our data whether the model is consistent with the key assumptions and implications of our model.

The model is built upon several premises. Among these is the premise that L-1 and H-1B visas are substitutes at the level of the task, the premise that sourcing frictions induce a gravity structure to worker flows, and that multinational firms can source L-1 employees more freely than they can source H-1B visa holders. Implications of the model are that in the aggregate that multinationals will not only hire more L-1 visa employees but also more H-1B employees and domestic workers because skilled workers from different backgrounds can be complements in aggregate employment. This is especially true in R&D-intensive sectors. The remainder of this chapter will explore variation in the publicly available data.

2.3   Data

The key data used in this study is built from a listing of firm name, US state of location, and the number of L-1 and H-1B visa petitions approved by the United States Citizenship and Immigration Service (USCIS) in the year 2007.[15] While these data are only flows for a single year, the largest users of this program reliably petition a similar number each year and so it is likely to be reasonably representative of the stock. These petitions reflect a subset of the actual petitions as the USCIS has substantial leeway in its approval of these visas and a visa can be rejected because a worker does not fit the description of a long-term employee of the foreign operations of the firm operating in the United States. As a result, up to a quarter of petitions each year are rejected.

We matched the USCIS data to the Compustat database using the name-matching algorithm written by Wasi and Flaaen (2014). This allowed us to associate the operating characteristics of the petitioner provided by the Compustat database. As many of the heaviest users of the L-1 visa program are not publicly listed companies, and so do not appear in the Compustat database, we conducted Internet searches for all petitioners who had more than twenty petitions and recorded country of incorporation, main line of business, and global employment in the year closest to 2007. The final match rate accounted for slightly more than 51 percent of petitions approved or nearly 26,000 petitions approved for nearly 1,000 firms. We are confident that we have identified almost all the visa usage by the firms in Compustat

15. I thank Will Kerr for providing these data to me.

and have a reasonably representative picture of the cross-industry aggregate usages of these visas as well. Nevertheless, with respect to our firm-level data, the fact that so many firms are not public means that we cannot be absolutely sure that our coverage is entirely representative of the US population of firms.

As these data do not reveal the country source of the workers entering the United States, we also used the aggregate statistics provided by the USCIS, which breaks out the number of petitions filed by country for each year.

In our analysis below, we make use of the publicly available data on the activities of US multinationals abroad and in the United States. These data come from the 2007 Benchmark Survey of the affiliates of foreign firms operating in the United States and the 2007 annual survey of the domestic and foreign operation of US-based multinationals. We use these data to measure the cross-industry and cross-country structure of employment by parents and affiliates and the cross-industry R&D and management intensity of parent-firm operations.

2.4 Facts

This section has three parts. In the first, we aggregate the matched data to the level of the industry to investigate the cross-industry characteristics associated with temporary skilled-worker visas. In the second, we consider purely within-industry, cross-firm variation. We find that R&D-intensive, multinational firms in R&D-intensive sectors dominated by multinational firms are the heaviest users of the visa programs.

In the third subsection, we consider a different dimension of the data: the cross-country variation in the two programs. We find that visa usage follows a "gravity" equation: bilateral visa flows are proportional to the size of the economy and decay with physical and cultural differences between countries. However, this relation is weaker for the L-1 program where visa flows are instead skewed toward those countries that are favored locations for US firms' foreign affiliates. As a whole, the aggregate data suggests that the model presented in the chapter is worthy of serious estimation.

As our data is in the form of counts that display evidence of overdispersion, we use negative binomial regression analysis. The results are qualitatively similar when Poisson regression is used and so we report only the negative binomial regression results below.

2.4.1   Cross-Industry Temporary Work Visa Usage by US-Based Firms

In this section, we aggregate our approved visa petition data across all firms that are incorporated in the United States according to their main line of business. This gives us a snapshot of the cross-industry structure of temporary skilled-worker visas by US firms by industry. We then regress these counts on the logarithm of the aggregate employment of these firms

Table 2.1   Industry-level descriptive statistics

$N = 56$	Mean	Standard deviation
L-1 visas	202	458
H-1B visas	225	378
Total visas	427	782
R&D Intensity		
Logarithm	−3.27	1.65
Level (share of sales)	0.08	0.09
Managerial wage		
Logarithm	4.51	0.31
Level ($ thousands)	95.72	30.13
US employment		
Logarithm	5.63	1.40
Level (thousands)	584.2	1,057
Affiliate employment abroad		
Logarithm	4.61	1.08
Level (thousands)	173.24	209.8

Notes: All data is for the year 2007. Visa counts have been aggregated to the industry level on the basis of the main line of business of the firm. Industry data for employment is from Compustat while R&D, managerial wage, and affiliate employment are from the Bureau of Economic Analysis.

(US employment), the logarithm of the employment of R&D personnel (R&D employment in total employment), the logarithm of the average wage paid to managerial and technical staff at US multinationals (managerial wage), and the logarithm of the employment of the foreign affiliates of US-based multinationals (affiliate employment abroad). Bringing the North American Industry Classification System (NAICS) industry classification used in Compustat into concordance with the Bureau of Economic Analysis (BEA) industry classification required some industrial aggregation, and so we are left with fifty-six traded and nontraded industries. The descriptive statistics are shown in table 2.1. Note that variables that enter the regression in logarithms have their descriptive statistics shown in both logarithms and levels.

As a first pass, we plot the logarithm of the number of new L-1 visas per 1,000 employees by industry against the logarithm of R&D intensity (R&D employment by total employment) by industry in figure 2.1. We label only a handful of interesting observations in the scatter diagram to prevent the figure from becoming too busy. Table 2.2 shows the top ten and bottom ten industries.

The data plotted in figure 2.1 shows that the most R&D-intensive industries use the L-1 visa program most thoroughly. There are, however, substantial deviations from the best linear predictor. Looking at table 2.2, we see that many of the intensive users of L-1 visas are in service industries such as computer design, publishing (which contains software develop-

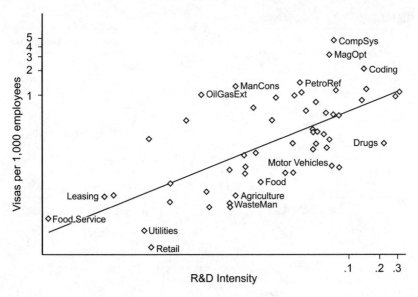

Fig. 2.1   US firms' L-1 visa usage by industry

Table 2.2   Top and bottom L-1 intensities

Rank	Name	Rank	Name
1	Computer systems design	47	Retail trade
2	Wholesale, petroleum	48	Beverages & tobacco
3	Publishing	49	Telecommunications
4	Computers & peripheral	50	Printing
5	Management consulting	51	Misc. services
6	Industrial machinery	52	Furniture
7	Petroleum refining	53	Real estate
8	Communication equipment	54	Rental & leasing
9	Fabricated metal products	55	Utilities
10	Mining, other	56	Agriculture, forestry, fishing

ment), and management consulting. Interestingly, in addition to high-tech manufacturing industries such as semiconductors, computer equipment, and industrial machinery, a number of extraction industries appear as well. These include mining, petroleum refining, and petroleum wholesaling. It is industries such as these that most represent the big deviations from the best linear predictor in figure 2.1.

The results of the regression analyses are shown in table 2.3. Column (1) of table 2.3 reports the coefficient estimates when the dependent variable is the number of L-1 visas by industry, column (2) reports the coefficient estimates when the dependent variable is the number of H-1B visas by indus-

Table 2.3   Cross-industry patterns

	L-1 visas	H-1B visas	Sum of visas
R&D employment	0.167*	0.270***	0.171**
	(0.091)	(0.074)	(0.080)
Managerial wage	2.402***	2.226***	2.520***
	(0.572)	(0.413)	(0.482)
US employment	0.208*	1.225***	0.371***
	(0.115)	(0.183)	(0.107)
Affiliate employment abroad	0.455***	0.252	0.467**
	(0.158)	(0.196)	(0.159)
Constant	−8.641***	−14.5***	−9.498***
	(2.933)	(2.26)	(2.524)
Alpha	0.906***	0.854***	0.838***
	(0.155)	(0.152)	(0.144)
N	56	56	56
Chi-squared	35.5	72.1	51.1

Notes: The estimation is by negative binomial regression. Standard errors are shown in parentheses. All independent variables enter the specifications in logarithms.
***Significant at the 1 percent level.
**Significant at the 5 percent level.
*Significant at the 10 percent level.

try, and column (3) shows the results when the total number of visas is the dependent variable.

Looking across the first row of table 2.3, we see that controlling for industry employment, higher R&D employment is associated with higher expected number of visas of both types. The effect is particularly strong for H-1B visas. This supports the premise of our model that temporary skilled-worker visas are an important feature of supporting innovation. Turning to the second row, we see that a high average wage paid to managerial and technical workers is also associated with greater visa usage for both types of visas. Ceteris paribus, an industry with a 10 percent higher managerial wage is associated with an almost 25 percent increase in the expected number of visas of both types.

The coefficient estimates in rows three and four provide evidence that there are differences in the effect of US industry employment and US multinational employment abroad on different visa counts. The third row suggests that the size of US employment by industry does not predict the number of L-1 visas issued, while H-1B visas issued by industries rise so quickly with industry employment that the total number of visas issued rise moderately with industry size. The fourth row suggests that it is the size of an industry's foreign employment that predicts the expected number of L-1 visa issued, but this measure of industry size has no predictive power whatsoever with regard to H-1B visas issued. When the total count (the sum of H-1B and

L-1 visas) is considered as the dependent variable in the third column, we see that industries that employ large numbers of people in foreign affiliates receive more visas.

These results suggest that the motives for applying for both L-1 and H-1B visas are indeed to hire specialized personnel but that the fact that there is no cap on the number of L-1 visas has the impact of skewing the total number of visas issued toward industries with a significant multinational presence abroad.

2.4.2   The Propensity of Firms to Use Temporary Work Visas

Having documented the structure of temporary work visas by industry, we now focus on the firm-level characteristics associated with visa usage. We consider a negative binomial regression model with conditional fixed effects by the NAICS three-digit industry code.

As we will be interested in the differences in the behavior of multinational firms relative to those that are not, we define an indicator variable (MNE) that takes the value of one if at least one of four conditions are satisfied: (a) the firm has successfully received an L-1 visa, (b) the firm is incorporated in a country other than the United States, (c) the firm reported foreign income, and (d) the firm reported paying foreign income taxes. Of the 4,227 firms for which we have data, just shy of half met the criteria of being a multinational enterprise. Among the publicly listed firms that are in the Compustat database, multinationals account for over 90 percent of visa petition approvals. Of these, half of multinationals' visa approvals are H-1B.

To measure a firm's size and its (rough) productivity, we measured a firm's employment (employment) and its sales (sales). These data were available for most firms in the Compustat database. We also measured the extent to which specialized employees are needed using the advertising expenditures (advert) and R&D expenditures (R&D) reported by the firm. All of these continuous variables are in logarithms, and to construct advert and R&D we first add one to the raw data to keep the zero observations. When data is missing we simply drop the observation. Finally, as it is widely believed that Indian-based firms tend to be much more aggressive in applying for H-1B visas for potentially strategic reasons, we include a dummy variable (INDIA), which takes the value of one if the firm is incorporated in India. The descriptive statistics are to be found in table 2.4 and the firm-level patterns in table 2.5.

In columns (1)–(3) we first consider a more limited set of independent variables in order to not lose observations. In column (1) where the dependent variable is the count of L-1 visas by firm, we restrict the sample to only multinational firms as nonmultinationals cannot apply. The full set of firms is present when the dependent variable is H-1B visa (column [2]) or the total number of visa approvals (column [3]).

Looking across row three, we see that an increase in sales per worker is

Table 2.4 **Descriptive statistics, firm-level patterns**

	Mean	Standard deviation
L-1 visas	4.6	32.3
H-1B visas	7.4	62.9
Total visas	12	85
Advert		
Logarithm	2.0	4
Level ($ millions)	107	478
R&D		
Logarithm	2.0	2.1
Level ($ millions)	105	550
Sales		
Logarithm	5.5	2.7
Level ($ millions)	4,824	19,150
Employment		
Logarithm	0.22	2.5
Level (thousands)	13	52
MNE	0.60	0.50

Note: Visa counts are for only those visas that were matched to Compustat data and so are not in the same proportion to visa totals for 2007.

Table 2.5 **Firm-level patterns**

	(1) L-1 visas	(2) H-1B visas	(3) Sum	(4) L-1 visas	(5) H-1B visas	(6) Sum
Advert				0.095*	0.140***	0.153***
				(0.054)	(0.051)	(0.042)
R&D				0.183***	0.305***	0.284***
				(0.049)	(0.044)	(0.037)
Sales	0.282***	0.215***	0.215***	0.119	−0.068	0.003
	(0.037)	(0.030)	(0.030)	(0.140)	(0.099)	(0.091)
Employment	0.071*	0.089**	0.089**	0.136	0.145	0.110
	(0.039)	(0.031)	(0.031)	(0.631)	(0.096)	(0.084)
India	0.777*	1.090***	1.093***	3.03***	5.10***	4.57***
	(0.411)	(0.35)	(0.35)	(0.63)	(0.542)	(0.442)
MNE		1.170***	1.170***		0.039	0.600***
		(0.078)	(0.078)		(0.196)	(0.175)
N	2,059	4,210	4,227	480	771	792
Chi-square	439	1,124	1,123	229	354	554

Notes: Estimation is by conditional fixed effect (by NAICS's three-digit industry codes) negative binomial regression. All independent variables are from Compustat and are in logarithms. The number of observations varies with the number of firms reporting the full set of covariates. L-1 visas only included only multinational firms, whereas H-1B and sum include all firms. Standard errors are shown in parentheses.

***Significant at the 1 percent level.
**Significant at the 5 percent level.
*Significant at the 10 percent level.

associated with higher levels of visas of both types, while rows three and four indicate that larger firms also receive a larger number of visas. Indian firms are indeed much more likely to receive visas, including L-1 type, than non-Indian firms.[16] Finally, there is some evidence that multinational firms are more likely as a whole to obtain H-1B visas than nonmultinationals as shown in column (2) and more visas in total as shown in column (3). These results suggest that larger, more productive multinationals are more heavily engaged in obtaining all types of visas. This result is consistent with workers from all locations being complements.

We now expand our variable set to include direct measures of the importance of skilled workers to firms in columns (4)–(6). Doing so reduces the sample substantially. The coefficients on the common variables are very different across data sets, but this appears to be because of the inclusion of the additional variables and not because of selection.[17]

In all three columns, the coefficients on advertising expenditure (row 1) and R&D spending (row 2) are positive and statistically significant. Hence, even within industry, it is the most R&D-intensive firms that are engaged in hiring temporary skilled workers from abroad. Moreover, the actual magnitudes are roughly similar across specifications. At the same time, the coefficients on sales (row 3) and employment (row 4) all become statistically indistinguishable from zero. Looking at the coefficient on R&D in column (6), we see that economic magnitude is quite large: a 10 percent increase in a firm's R&D spending relative to its industry peers is associated with an almost 3 percent increase in the expected number of visas.

Even after controlling for firm characteristics associated with demand for skilled labor (i.e., R&D and advertising), the coefficient on MNE in column (6) is large and statistically significant. Everything else equal, a multinational will expect to get 60 percent more visas per year than a nonmultinational. This is consistent with the foundations on which the model is built: ceteris paribus, multinationality confers a talent-sourcing advantage.

These results shape our view of who demands and who has access to skilled foreign workers. First, the fact that R&D and advertising expenditures predict visa counts, while firm productivity or size does not, suggests that it is skilled-labor intensity rather than inherent productivity per se that influences firms' petitioning behavior. Second, the similarity in the coefficients on firm characteristics (excluding multinationality) across columns suggests that the firms that demand skilled workers do not perceive funda-

16. We have experimented with adding dummies for other countries and have found that this proclivity to obtain visas is not universally prevalent across foreign firms operating in the United States.
17. When the smaller coefficient set model is run on a sample restricted to only those observations with both advertising and R&D data, the coefficients are roughly unchanged with the exception of the coefficient on MNE when the dependent variable is H-1B counts. In that case, it is considerably smaller.

mental differences in the type of visa program used. Third, within multinationals there is no tendency to favor one type of visa program over another as is suggested by the zero coefficient on MNE in column (5). Finally, the fact that MNE coefficient is positive in column (6), where the dependent variable is the sum of the two counts tells us that multinational firms do have an inherent advantage obtaining access to talented foreign labor. These stark results are consistent with a simple explanation: the L-1 visa program gives multinational firms an advantage over nonmultinationals in recruiting foreign talent by allowing these firms to at least partially *escape the H-1B visa cap.*

2.4.3   Cross-Country Pattern of Visa Issuance

Our data affords substantial information about the nature of the firms that are making use of the temporary work program but are less informative about the nature of the workers. For instance, the country of origin of the workers is not available at the firm level in our L-1 visa data.[18]

In order to make inferences about the types of countries that are sending the workers, we turn to a different data set from the US Department of State,[19] that compiles the total numbers of new and renewed L-1 and H-1B visas by country of origin. Unfortunately, the data does not break out whether these visas are issued to US or foreign firms operating in the United States. In addition, the data does not allow us to distinguish between multinational enterprises and purely domestic firms.

The breakdown by country is shown in figure 2.2, which graphs the (logarithm of the) number of L-1 visas against the (logarithm of the) number of H-1B visas issued to workers from each country. The figure shows a high correlation between the sources of workers for each skilled-labor visa program. As is well known, India is an enormous outlier in both programs. The other important sources of workers are an interesting mixture of developed countries (e.g., Japan, Great Britain, and Germany), and developing countries (e.g., Mexico, the Philippines, Korea, and China).

In our analysis we estimate a negative binomial regression with a gravity structure that has been augmented to include the logarithms of the employment of the US affiliates of the foreign country and the logarithm of the foreign affiliates employment of US firms operating in that country.[20] We include a dummy for India as it is a substantial outlier. The descriptive statistics are shown in table 2.6 and the coefficient estimates are shown in table 2.7.

---

18. Unlike the H-1B program, the L-1 program does not require a petitioner to submit a local labor conditions form and so this source of information is lacking.
19. The data can be found at https://travel.state.gov/content/visas/en/law-and-policy/statistics/non-immigrant-visas.html. Note that we use data for 2004 in order to expand the number of countries for which publically available multinational affiliate is available.
20. We first add one to the levels of employment to avoid dropping observations for which there are no employees.

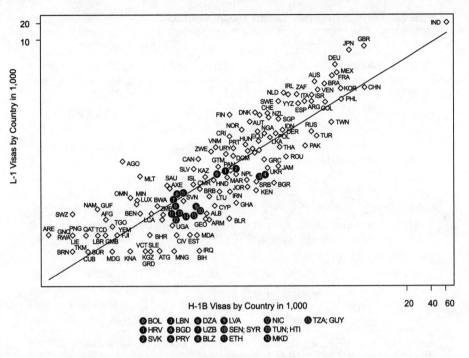

Fig. 2.2 Country composition of skilled-labor visas
Source: US Department of State.

Table 2.7 is organized into three columns for L-1, H-1B, and total visas. Looking across the first two rows, we see that higher log gross domestic product (GDP) is associated with more temporary worker flows under these programs. As this result obtains controlling for log employment, this can be interpreted as temporary worker visas coming primarily from more developed countries. This is consistent with these countries being abundant in the skilled labor for which the program is intended. The positive and statistically significant coefficients on GDP and population tell us that larger countries send more workers.

Looking at the effect of log distance in row 3, we see that distance powerfully discourages H-1B visas (a 10 percent increase in distance is associated with a 10 percent reduction in the expected number of visas), but it has no impact on L-1 visas: L-1 visa flows are more "weightless" than H-1B flows. This is evidence that experience with foreign labor markets confers an advantage on multinational firms in sourcing global talent. This advantage does not extend to language barriers, however, as the coefficients on the dummy variable for shared language for the two visa counts of similar size.

Looking at row 6 (inward employment), we see that the employment by

Table 2.6   Descriptive statistics, country-level analyses

	Mean	Standard deviation
L-1 visas	333	1,684
H-1B visas	738	4,715
Total visas	1,072	6,327
Language	0.430	0.500
Contig.	0.006	0.075
GDP		
Logarithm	23	2.4
Level ($ billions)	1,700	5,520
Population		
Logarithm	1.5	2.2
Level (millions)	32.2	129.7
Distance		
Logarithm	9.1	0.49
Level (km)	9,522	3,466
Inward employment		
Logarithm	0.078	1.6
Level (thousands)	29	116
Outward employment		
Logarithm	1.7	1.9
Level (thousands)	51	146

Notes: Affiliate employment data are from BEA surveys, gravity variables are from the CEPII data set, and visa data are from the US Department of State.

foreign multinational affiliates in the United States does not predict any of the visa counts (with the exception of India). This is interesting because it suggests that after controlling for log GDP and log population there is no greater propensity of firms from multinational affiliates in the United States to source labor from their home countries.

When we consider the coefficients in row 7 (outward employment), we see that more L-1 visas are granted to workers from countries in which US affiliates employ many workers, but there is no such pattern with respect to H-1B visas. As in the case of the very different coefficients on distance, this result is consistent with similar roles for the visas themselves in practice, but the lack of a cap on L-1 visas shifts the total number of visa awards toward those countries in which US firms have affiliates.

Overall, these results suggest that multinationals are better able to overcome distance-related costs associated with recruiting talented foreign workers.

2.5   Feasibility of Full Model Estimation

In this section, we discuss how improved access to firm-level, nonimmigrant visa data could be used to extend the preliminary analyses presented

Table 2.7   Cross-country patterns

	L-1 visas	H-1B visas	Sum
GDP	0.776***	0.796***	0.803***
	(0.098)	(0.104)	(0.098)
Population	0.132*	0.276**	0.260***
	(0.073)	(0.078)	(0.075)
Distance	−0.187	−1.041***	−0.951***
	(0.204)	(0.233)	(0.220)
Language	1.052***	0.880***	0.894***
	(0.188)	(0.195)	(0.186)
Contig.	−4.982***	−5.219***	−5.287***
	(1.007)	(1.113)	(1.077)
Inward employment	0.072	−0.118	−0.048
	(0.256)	(0.087)	(0.088)
Outward employment	0.256***	−0.052	−0.012
	(0.088)	(0.105)	(0.104)
INDIA	1.845*	2.377*	2.201***
	(0.965)	(1.075)	(1.025)
Alpha	0.859	1.071	0.972***
	(0.106)	(0.113)	(0.103)
N	172	172	172
Chi-squared	363	314	341

Notes: The estimation is by negative binomial regression. Standard errors are shown in parentheses. All independent variables enter the specifications in logarithms.

***Significant at the 1 percent level.
**Significant at the 5 percent level.
*Significant at the 10 percent level.

in this chapter to the full model estimation strategy sketched in section 2.2.3. A data-sharing agreement between government agencies that would allow the matching of H-1B and L-1 visa firm-level data to the multinational enterprise data collected by the BEA would allow several questions to be addressed.

All approved petitions of H-1B and L-1 visas provide information on the employer identification number, name, and geographic location of the petitioner as well as the country from which the approved employee resides. This visa data could then be matched with the BEA's surveys of US-based multinational enterprises and foreign multinational affiliates operating in the United States, as both BEA surveys collect this information to identify firms. Given many years of visa approval data, a stock of current L-1 and H-1B visa holders by firm and country of origin could be assembled.

The confidential BEA data from the Direct Investment Abroad surveys identifies the location, operating data, and degree of parent ownership for each of the American firms' foreign affiliates. For the confidential BEA data for US affiliates of foreign multinationals, collected by the Foreign Direct

Investment in the United States surveys, less data is collected about their parents' foreign operations, but the country of the ultimate beneficial owner of each firm is known. For the US operations of these firms, the survey provides information on the local employment of the firm (both managerial and production workers), the level of R&D expenditure, the industry, and the volume of exports and sales in the United States.

Given this information, the key parameters (i.e., T_i, τ_{ji}, δ_{ji}, and θ) can be estimated via the firm-level gravity equations (14). Moreover, the volume of H-1B visas obtained by US multinational affiliates in countries in which they have affiliates can be contrasted with the H-1B visas obtained by the same firms in countries in which they do not own an affiliate. This information would shed light on how improved access to foreign skilled-labor markets afforded by local production induces greater worker flows. Combined with measures of firm's R&D intensities, the estimated parameters and firm-level investment patterns have two implications. First, they would reveal how an expansion in a firm's foreign production activities affect its sourcing potential and hence the cost of doing R&D and management activities. Second, they could be compared to R&D intensities to determine whether increased multinational activity raises or lowers demand for skilled US labor, and whether, as Bill Gates has asserted, tighter restrictions on temporary worker visas would lower American innovation and ultimately hurt skilled Americans.

2.6 Conclusion

This chapter has provided a first look at the structure of temporary worker flows at the firm, industry, and country level. It has documented a tendency for these flows to be concentrated in high-tech and high-wage industries and within industries in high-tech, multinational corporations. Controlling for their size and technical intensity, multinational firms use foreign workers more intensively than do nonmultinationals. At the firm level, there is no evidence that on net L-1 visas are a substitute for H-1B visas, because multinational status does not reduce the absolute level of H-1B visas but rather expands the total number of visas.

These facts are consistent with a framework built on firm sourcing of differentiated intermediate inputs. A key feature of this sort of model is that it can reconcile diverse sourcing behavior of firms. In industries with highly differentiated inputs and high R&D intensities, greater access to foreign workers can increase firm-level and country-level demand for domestic workers. Hence, while individual workers might find specific tasks are reallocated to foreigners, the total employment of firms accessing foreign workers may actually increase.

The chapter concluded with a blueprint for the future work that would be made possible were it possible to match administrative L-1 individual petition data to BEA firm-level data on multinational activity. Combined with the structural model sketched in this chapter, matched petition firm data of this sort would allow the size of migration frictions to be estimated and the welfare implications backed out from the model. Creating such a matching is technically feasible, but challenging, given that the government agencies that collect the data are part of very different bureaucracies.

References

Antras, Pol. 2003. "Firms, Contracts, and Trade Structure." *Quarterly Journal of Economics* 118 (4): 1375–418.

———. 2005. "Incomplete Contracts and the Product Cycle." *American Economic Review* 95 (4): 1054–73.

Antras, Pol, Teresa Fort, and Felix Tintelnot. 2017. "The Margins of Global Sourcing: Evidence from U.S. Firms." *American Economic Review* 10 (9). https://scholar.harvard.edu/antras/publications/margins-global-sourcing-theory-and-evidence-us-firms.

Bureau of Economic Analysis. *Foreign Direct Investment in the United States.* Various volumes.

———. *US Direct Investment Abroad.* Various volumes.

Eaton, Jonathan, and Samuel Kortum. 2002. "Trade, Geography, and Trade Costs." *Econometrica* 70 (5): 1741–779.

Helpman, Elhanan. 1984. "A Simple Theory of International Trade with Multinational Corporations." *Journal of Political Economy* 92 (3): 451–71.

Keller, Wolfgang, and Nune Hovhannisyan. 2015. "International Business Travel: An Engine of Innovation?" *Journal of Economic Growth* 20 (1): 75–104.

Kerr, Sari, and William Kerr. 2015. "Global Collaborative Patents." NBER Working Paper no. 21735, Cambridge, MA.

Kerr, Sari, William Kerr, and William Lincoln. 2015. "Skilled Immigration and the Employment Structure of US Firms." *Journal of Labor Economics* 33 (3): 147–86.

Kerr, William, and William Lincoln. 2010. "The Supplyside of Innovation: H-1B Visa Reforms and US Ethnic Invention." *Journal of Labor Economics* 28 (3): 473–79.

Markusen, James. 1984. "Multinationals, Multi-Plant Economies, and the Gains from Trade." *Journal of International Economics* 16:205–26.

Office of the Inspector General. 2013. "Implementation of L-1 Visa Regulation." Washington, DC, Department of Homeland Security.

Papageorgiou, Theodore. 2016. "Large Firms and Within Firm Occupational Reallocation." Unpublished Manuscript, McGill University.

Wasi, Nada, and Aaron Flaaen. 2014. "Record Linkage Using STATA: Preprocessing, Linking and Reviewing Utilities." Working Paper, University of Michigan.

Digital Labor Markets and Global Talent Flows

John Horton, William R. Kerr, and Christopher Stanton

3.1 Introduction

Globalization has been a mighty force over the last few decades. Compared to the movements of material goods and financial capital across countries, however, labor and talent have been much slower to globalize. This greater localization of labor and talent is perhaps not surprising given that it is easier to transmit financial capital in a disembodied form or build/ship a physical good for an exact purpose. People and their labor, however, have typically come as a collective and fully integrated package, so to speak, that makes location decisions more complex. If one seeks to access labor inputs available abroad, one option is to attract and host the individual, temporarily or permanently, near the location of the work to be performed. For a variety of reasons this has proven politically unpopular, and nearly all countries place restrictions on migrations. As a result, only about 3 percent of the world's population lives outside of their country of birth.[1]

A second option is to identify how the required task can be exchanged

John Horton is assistant professor of information, operations and management sciences at New York University's Stern School of Business. William R. Kerr is the Dimitri V. D'Arbeloff–MBA Class of 1955 Professor of Business Administration at Harvard Business School and a research associate of the National Bureau of Economic Research. Christopher Stanton is assistant professor of business administration at Harvard Business School and a faculty research fellow of the National Bureau of Economic Research.

This chapter is a revision of the paper prepared for the NBER Global Talent Summer Institute Conference meeting on July 10, 2016. Comments are most welcome. For acknowledgments, sources of research support, and disclosure of the authors' material financial relationships, if any, please see http://www.nber.org/chapters/c13840.ack.

1. Kerr et al. (2016, 2017) review the literature, data, and policy environments for global talent flows. Clemens (2011) emphasizes the "trillion-dollar bills" that remain on the sidewalk due to this low rate of migration in light of productivity differences across countries.

at a distance, without necessitating a person's physical migration. Offshoring—the performance of a specified task in another country—has become a substantial force in certain business functions where the tasks can be effectively located at a geographic distance. Thus, the focus shifts from "trade in goods" to "trade in tasks" needing to be performed (Grossman and Rossi-Hansberg 2008). Prominent examples include low-end data entry and high-end, back-office information technology (IT) in India for US and European companies. In a prominent study, Blinder and Krueger (2013) estimate that around one-quarter of jobs could be offshored from the United States.[2]

Offshoring was initially best suited for large corporations due to the substantial fixed costs in establishing an overseas presence. Even if using an external outsourcing vendor, it only made sense for organizations to engage in trade in tasks if they had a sufficiently large ongoing volume of work to justify learning about overseas options, vetting contractors, negotiating terms and prices, and reorienting their own business processes to fit around the overseas work. Similar to the Melitz (2003) model for international trade, firms entered into these overseas efforts when a large and sustained improvement that exceeded a threshold requirement was feasible. Helpman, Melitz, and Yeaple (2004) develop a framework where the most productive firms launch overseas facilities, those with intermediate productivity engage in trade, and the least productive firms serve domestic markets only. Helpman (2014) provides a review.

Digital labor markets have the potential to radically alter this picture. These Internet-based platforms connect workers worldwide with companies seeking to have tasks completed. This chapter describes digital labor markets, evaluating their dramatic rise and global span, and reviews academic studies of how these markets function. We first discuss the persistent information frictions that have been a barrier to offline global labor sourcing and how digital labor platforms address these barriers. Sections 3.2 and 3.3 provide both micro- and macro-level perspectives, respectively, and we present some new empirical analyses that link these two perspectives together with respect to cross-border contract placement over countries. Our empirical discussion uses data from Upwork, the world's largest digital labor platform, and its predecessor oDesk.[3] We extend prior

2. Offshoring closely relates to outsourcing—the performance of a specified task by an external party to the purchasing company—and the two terms are often used interchangeably in the press. Outsourcing is possible without offshoring (e.g., purchasing services from an external company in one's own country), and offshoring is possible without outsourcing (e.g., setting up a company-owned data center or manufacturing plant abroad). For most of this chapter's discussion of digital labor markets, the two concepts overlap completely as the contracts are both externally sourced and abroad.

3. Upwork is the result of a merger in 2014 of Elance and oDesk, which were founded in 1999 and 2003, respectively. In 2016, Upwork reports annually servicing over three million jobs that represent more than $1 billion in work. Projects range from simple transcription work to high-end services, and Upwork records over twelve million registered freelancers and five million companies (https://www.upwork.com/about/, accessed June 21, 2016).

work by Ghani, Kerr, and Stanton (2014) on ethnic contract placement, and we provide new evidence regarding flows and substitution across countries.

Section 3.4 then considers the evolution of digital labor markets and provides case-based examples of other ways that digitization is extending the spatial reach of labor and talent inputs. For example, many corporations and governments are rushing to build "open innovation" platforms that expose their organizations to valuable external ideas. We discuss examples from Procter & Gamble (P&G), the National Aeronautics and Space Administration (NASA), and similar large organizations on how they are using open collaboration concepts for solving thorny innovation challenges. Digital platforms are also extending the use of global labor to many smaller start-ups, and overseas tech development has become the norm for many US and European entrepreneurs given the cost savings possible.

Only time will tell the ultimate impact of digital labor markets, online innovation contests, and similar collaborative activities for the globalization of labor markets and talent, but their strong potential is now evident. Moreover, they are becoming a powerful tool for researchers seeking to understand the functioning of labor markets. It is exceptional, for example, to observe a recorded history of the bids given for contracts, the traits of accepted bids versus the competition, the performance outcomes of projects, the prior and subsequent longitudinal history of workers and contracting firms, and so on. See Horton and Tambe (2015) for an overview of the research potential of computer-mediated labor markets. These platforms have also been the site for multiple experimental studies of labor market behavior. Building on our research experience, the fifth section provides some perspectives for researchers about the advantages and pitfalls of using these types of data and platforms for economic studies, and we close with some open questions for the future about these platforms and the digitization of work.

3.2   The Environment of Digital Labor Markets

3.2.1   Upwork

Upwork is an online platform that connects workers who supply services with buyers who pay for and receive these services from afar. Examples include data entry and programming tasks. The platform is the result of a 2014 merger between Elance and oDesk, and the merged entity was rebranded as Upwork in 2015. In 2016, Upwork is the world's largest platform for online outsourcing, and oDesk and Elance were the two largest platforms before the merger. To be consistent and reduce confusion, we favor using the name Upwork even when describing a period before the company was known by this name. When discussing and extending studies of earlier periods that use oDesk-specific data, we mention this alternative sample. The data used in this study were obtained directly from oDesk and Upwork for research purposes.

On the Upwork platform, any worker can contract with any firm directly, and all work takes place and is monitored via a proprietary online system.[4] In exchange for a 10 percent transaction fee from the total wage bill,[5] Upwork provides a comprehensive management and billing system that records the time spent by the worker on the job, allows easy communication between workers and employers about scheduled tasks, facilitates simple document uploading and transfer, and takes random screenshots of workers' computer terminals to allow electronic monitoring.[6]

These features facilitate easy, standardized contracting, and any company and any worker can form electronic relationships with very little effort. More advanced features provide tools for teams to collaborate on projects.

A worker who wants to provide labor services on Upwork fills out an online profile describing his/her skills, education level, and experience. A worker's entire history of Upwork employment, including wages and hours, is publicly observable to potential employers. For contracts that have been completed, a feedback measure from the employer is publicly displayed. Figure 3.1 provides an example of a worker profile.

Companies and individuals looking to hire on Upwork fill out a job description, including the skills required, the expected contract duration, and some preferred worker characteristics. In the first few years after the platform's founding, most of the jobs posted were hourly positions for technology-related or programming tasks (e.g., web development), but postings for administrative assistance, data entry, graphic design, and smaller categories have become more prevalent as the platform has grown. Advanced tasks include search engine optimization, data analytics, and mobile app programming. Table 3.1 provides a distribution of contracts over job category. After a company posts a position opening, workers apply for the job and bid an hourly rate. Firms can interview workers via Upwork, and ultimately form a contract if both parties agree. In the past, this process was largely decentralized, but in more recent years, Upwork has invested heavily in making algorithmic recommendations to both employers and workers about which worker to hire or which job to apply to, respectively. See Horton (2017) for evidence on the effectiveness of these algorithmic recommendations in increasing the quantity of matches formed in the market.

---

4. This section draws from Ghani, Kerr, and Stanton (2014).
5. Upwork recently announced a new nonlinear pricing structure in which fees would be gradually reduced as the match-specific wage bill increased.
6. We use the terms "employer" and "employment" for consistency with the existing labor literature rather than as a comment on the precise legal nature of the relationships created on these sites.

Fig. 3.1   Example of a worker profile from a digital labor platform
Source: oDesk.

3.2.2   Microevidence on Information Frictions

Most past studies of oDesk/Upwork are micro-based studies that tend to focus on matching or information frictions. Evidence of the existence of these frictions is present in the data used here. The literature's focus on these micro-based frictions is perhaps surprising at first glance, given that the core power of these platforms and their rising economic importance is the global information access and firm-worker matching process that the platforms enable, often for the first time. Yet, even though these platforms have removed many frictions from their labor markets (e.g., information access, document transfer, billing, etc.), some classic issues remain and perhaps become more evident, such as uncaptured externalities for the development

Table 3.1 Summary statistics by job category

Job category (1)	Number of job openings (2)	Number of unique applicants (3)	Number of contracts (4)	Number of cross-border contracts (5)	Cross-border contract share (%) (6)	Wage bill ($ millions) (7)	Wage bill from cross-border contracts ($ millions) (8)	Cross-border wage bill share (%) (9)
Administrative support	3,741,563	22,443,920	484,244	435,450	90	184.7	155.5	84
Business services	853,436	2,741,608	95,699	79,552	83	78.3	59.4	76
Customer service	436,211	2,232,582	50,541	43,665	86	89.3	70.9	79
Design & multimedia	5,339,055	14,267,825	498,949	457,700	92	106.2	92.9	87
Networking & info. systems	646,733	1,431,241	47,445	43,108	91	39.3	31.8	81
Sales & marketing	2,797,382	15,416,597	376,295	342,496	91	141.8	121.0	85
Software development	2,736,048	8,886,761	230,407	217,343	94	307.5	285.0	93
Web development	7,918,424	30,365,649	772,828	724,107	94	607.6	561.5	92
Writing & translation	4,163,107	10,566,662	598,715	480,517	80	167.4	107.2	64
Total	28,631,959	108,352,845	3,155,123	2,823,938	90	1,722	1,485	86

Notes: Data come from oDesk/Upwork from the launch of the platform through 2014. Wage bill is in millions of US dollars at the time of recording.

of information about workers and firms or ethnic/racial biases people have in contract selection. Also, similar to other online environments like auction sites or e-commerce platforms, new issues can arise due to the platform's features and aggregation of many buyers and sellers that are hard to antici-pate. Here we review several studies and tie together what they mean for our understanding of matching frictions.

Many of the matching frictions that have previously been documented arise because employers hire discrete workers into particular slots (see Lazear, Shaw, and Stanton 2016). Table 3.1 shows that there are many more applicants than slots available to contract. That there are many applicants relative to openings suggests that it may be hard for workers to determine what employers are looking for or how an applicant will be assessed against other workers. On oDesk/Upwork, because of unobserved capacity to take on new projects, employers have the same problems when they pursue work-ers (see Horton 2016a). These and other forms of information frictions result in sunk effort on both sides of the market before a successful match is formed.

Several factors contribute to these frictions, and many are also present in traditional labor markets. These include uncertainty and difficulty in assess-ing worker quality, leading to concerns about adverse selection. Other ques-tions around direct contract enforcement are potentially relevant as well. For larger projects, team aggregation challenges appear to be compounded in the online setting.

Over time, the Upwork market has evolved to better provide features that mitigate these sources of friction. Reputation systems, prevalent in many peer-to-peer and electronic markets, were early features designed to mitigate adverse selection. However, these systems often provide only coarse information that results in "bunching" of scores either at the top or bottom of the rating scale. Many employers are reluctant to leave negative feedback, and so only "good" feedback is reported. It also appears that what is considered "good" has increased over time, leading to a kind of reputation inflation. As such, would-be employers have difficulty assessing ability ex ante (though this is far from a challenge unique to online set-tings). As a reaction to this problem, Upwork has moved to utilize the fact that experienced workers often transact with many employers, enabling the display of private feedback ratings that are not linked to an individual transaction. This has reduced the effect of bunching on market frictions by providing additional gradation between workers.

While reputation systems provide information about past performance, new workers face the problem of how to break into the market. Hiring a nov-ice worker produces two outputs: the direct work product and information about that worker's quality. However, because these are spot markets with somewhat limited full-time repeated contracting, the information about worker output is not particularly valuable to an employer. As a result, there is underhiring of unknown workers because employers do not internalize the value of generating knowledge about workers that is revealed once they start work (Tervio 2009). In the data, very few novice workers are hired relative to the experienced cohort. Pallais (2014) demonstrates through an experiment that a major contributing factor to the low share of novice hires is the Tervio mechanism where employers do not internalize the value of information. To do so, she randomly hires novice workers and leaves them honest feedback. This initial feedback has profound effects on treated workers' online careers. Future employers are much more likely to hire workers in the treatment group who receive a rating than control workers who did not receive the rating.

Stanton and Thomas (2016b) then show that the market has evolved to include intermediation as a response to the worker start-up problem. Intermediaries, called agencies, have entered online labor markets and have altered hiring patterns for novice workers. These agencies tend to be small groups consisting of several online workers, and employers can observe agency affiliation and an agency-level feedback score on each affiliated worker's profile. Most agency workers are colocated, suggesting some role for offline ties in the formation of these groups. A key factor for overcoming the information problem is an incentive to invest, and intermediaries are provided with this incentive because they own the reputation of their affiliated workers. Stanton and Thomas show that novice workers who enter the market with intermediary affiliation are much more likely to find work than workers who enter without affiliation. They identify the information effect of intermediation by comparing outcomes over workers' careers; the initial intermediary advantage fades out as workers gain experience. The entry of intermediary agencies has improved the prospects of novice affiliated workers and has reduced frictions for novice affiliated workers who seek to enter the market.

The earliest frictions explored in the literature were due to adverse selection concerns because of employers' difficulty distinguishing worker quality. More recent literature explores the consequences either of uncertainty about the environment that employers face or switching frictions when changing from a familiar offline environment. Stanton and Thomas (2016a) explore uncertainty about the market as the result of employers being unfamiliar with the value of the market. Because employers' interviews are observed in the data, a measure of search effort is available. Stanton and Thomas document that employer interviewing falls dramatically with experience, suggesting an important role for learning about the distribution of matches through the process of hiring. If some factors cause new employers to forgo initial hiring, strong experience effects suggest that these factors limit market size by the failure to move new users along the experience curve. Stanton and Thomas suggest that the nature of how workers bid for jobs is a significant factor that has limited the take up of new users. Because workers can observe employer inexperience, it is possible for them to tailor wage bids to what employers are likely to know about the market. In most markets inexperienced users receive lower prices to draw them in, but in online labor markets inexperienced employers receive wage bids that are approximately 7 percent higher than their experienced alter egos. The spot nature of contracting means that workers do not participate in the employer gains from learning the market. Workers' higher bids limit take up of the market and hinder the expansion of online work. The failure of decentralized actors to internalize the consequences of how their own behavior affects information for trading partners has the potential to limit the growth of online exchange. Differences in pricing policy may be necessary to counteract some of these incentives.

Other work suggests that offline familiarity influences online hiring behavior. For example, Ghani, Kerr, and Stanton (2014) document the prevalence of ethnic-linked exchanges online by studying the hiring patterns of the Indian diaspora on oDesk/Upwork. Importantly for identification, applicants do not know the ethnic identity of the employer; this minimizes concerns about sorting as a confounding factor. Even with access to workers from all over the world, they find that the ethnic Indian diaspora is much more likely to hire in India than employers of other ethnicities. Whether due to preferences or information problems, this may limit the amount of trade conducted through opening labor markets online. On the other hand, the reliance on familiarity may, in theory, grease the wheels of transactions and help employers to overcome uncertainty about workers. In the Upwork context, the size of the Indian diaspora hiring online suggests this role for encouraging the sourcing of online work is likely to be a small factor in encouraging market growth.

For those employers who do take an initial jump, several strategies may be used to deal with an uncertain environment. For example, many employers appear to use hiring tournaments in which small pieces of a project are done by multiple workers; the best workers are retained. This process can be repeated until a satisfactory set is found. This strategy is likely to make sense for production processes like software engineering where there are multiple ways to solve a problem. For tasks where accuracy is important, sourcing redundant projects and using error checking across workers to find mistakes may be more appropriate. Both of these strategies help to resolve uncertainty. Employers also appear to use pattern matching after successful outcomes. For example, Ghani, Kerr, and Stanton (2014) report that employers who initially choose to source work in India are more than 11.5 percent more likely to choose India on their next contract upon success compared to employers with unsuccessful first contracts.

That employers use workers' countries as an important source of information has been documented in several sources. Mill (2013) studies statistical discrimination and employer learning through experience with hiring in particular countries. Xu (2016), using data from an early online labor market called rentacoder, shows that employers update their beliefs about all workers from a country after hiring from that country. Agrawal, Lacetera, and Lyons (2014) examine the structure of information and how this affects workers differently depending on their country. An interesting and important finding of this paper is that although at least some employers behave in a way consistent with statistical discrimination, information about actual worker productivity seems to be a remedy: with more information, employers engage in less crude statistical discrimination. Using an experiment, Lyons (2016) also examines cross-country versus intracountry differences in team production when hiring online, extending many of these results to more complicated production.

3.2.3   Ethnic Diasporas and Contract Placement

While microfrictions have been the literature's main focus, we turn in the next section toward a more macro-oriented analysis of contract placement, providing some first evidence regarding flows and substitution across countries. In preparation for the macro perspective, we first provide an example of how the micro and macro lens connect with each other. We do this by extending the work of Ghani, Kerr, and Stanton (2014), who quantify how members of the Indian diaspora are more likely to place an outsourcing contract into India, compared to non-Indians, and have some important differences as to how these contracts are structured. While this analysis shows microconnectivity, it differs from the standard analysis in the macro literature. Rauch and Trindade (2002), for example, relate trade flows to the distribution of the ethnic Chinese population across countries, rather than the greater likelihood that two observed traders are Chinese. We thus extend our earlier work to now mirror the approach of Rauch and Trindade (2002). To keep the analysis in line with Ghani, Kerr, and Stanton (2014), we use oDesk data covering 2005–2010.[7]

In this analysis, as well as the one to come in section 3.3, we use the gravity framework from the international trade literature to guide our work.

---

7. The oDesk data do not record a person's ethnicity or country of birth, so Ghani, Kerr, and Stanton (2014) use the names of company contacts to probabilistically assign ethnicities. This matching approach exploits the fact that individuals with surnames like Chatterjee or Patel are significantly more likely to be ethnically Indian than individuals with surnames like Wang, Martinez, or Johnson. The matching procedure exploits two databases originally developed for marketing purposes, common naming conventions, and hand-collected frequent names from multiple sources like population censuses and baby registries. The process assigns individuals a likelihood of being Indian or one of eight other ethnic groups. Kerr (2007, 2008) and Kerr and Lincoln (2010) provide extended details on the matching process, list frequent ethnic names, and provide descriptive statistics and quality assurance exercises. Ghani, Kerr, and Stanton (2014) provide an extended discussion and analysis of this match in the oDesk-specific context.

More broadly, recent research emphasizes the importance of immigrants in frontier economies for the diffusion of technologies and ideas to their home countries (e.g., Saxenian 2002, 2006; Kerr 2008; Agrawal et al. 2011). Kerr (2016) reviews this literature and its connection to trade more completely and provides appropriate references.

Similar to planetary pull, these trade models suggest that countries should engage more in trade to the degree that they are larger and also closer together. There are several theoretical ways that one can derive a gravity model, and the appendix to this chapter outlines the Eaton and Kortum (2002) model that is most aligned with our work. The Eaton and Kortum (2002) model considers countries having a range of technological productivities for various activities. Each country purchases the activity from the country that can be the lowest cost provider of the activity, including the purchasing country itself. This cost considers the price levels and wage rates in countries, the productivity of countries for tasks, and distances between nations. Thinking of these activities as tasks on a digital labor platform is a natural extension, and our empirical analysis relates the volume of contracting between countries. The appendix provides a more rigorous introduction.

The dependent variable in columns (1)–(7) of table 3.2 is the share of contracts originating from a country on oDesk that are outsourced to India. We focus on shares of contracts, rather than contract volumes, as the adoption of oDesk across countries as a platform for e-commerce is still under way and somewhat idiosyncratic to date. Shares allow us to consider the choice of India for outsourcing independent of this overall penetration of oDesk. The core regressor is taken from the World Bank's Bilateral Migration and Remittances 2010 database. This database builds upon the initial work of Ratha and Shaw (2007) to provide estimates of migrant stocks by country. We form the Indian diaspora share of each country's population by dividing these stocks by the population levels of the country. We complement this diaspora measure with distances to India calculated using the great circle method, population and gross domestic product (GDP) per capita levels taken from the United Nations, and telephone lines per capita in 2007 taken from World Development Indicators. We also calculate a control variable of the overall fit of the country's outsourcing needs with the typical worker in India.[8]

Column (1) presents our base estimation. We have ninety-two observations, and we weight by the log number of worldwide contracts formed on oDesk. The first row shows the connection of digital outsourcing to the diaspora population share, which is quite strong. A 1 percent increase in the Indian diaspora share of a country is associated with a 1 percent increase in the share of oDesk contracts outsourced to India. The country-level placement of digital contracts in India systematically followed the preexisting

---

8. We calculate this control by first measuring the share of contracts outsourced from the country in nine job categories indicated. We likewise measure the distribution of oDesk work performed in India across the nine job categories, independent of where the company contact is located. We then calculate the sum of the squared deviations of these two distributions to measure how closely the work typically filled in India matches the needs of a given country. We subtract this sum of deviations from one, so that positive values represent a better fit, and we transform the measure to have unit standard deviation to aid interpretation.

Table 3.2   Estimates of contract volumes formed on oDesk with workers in India

	Dependent variable is share of oDesk contracts formed with workers in India							DV is India's share of dollar value of contracts for country	DV is share of company contacts with Indian ethnic name
	Base estimation (1)	Including distance covariates only (2)	Weighting by log population (3)	Unweighted estimation (4)	Adding worldwide oDesk contracts (5)	Adding trade with India control (6)	Excluding UAE outlier firm (7)	(8)	(9)
Indian diaspora share of country population	1.090*** (0.197)	0.728*** (0.156)	0.969*** (0.364)	0.850* (0.429)	1.135*** (0.218)	1.004*** (0.236)	0.531** (0.204)	0.694* (0.360)	2.577*** (0.188)
Indicator for geographical distance to India of 5,000–10,000 kilometers	0.071** (0.030)	0.041 (0.026)	0.090** (0.043)	0.087** (0.044)	0.069** (0.031)	0.077** (0.033)	0.059* (0.030)	−0.033 (0.056)	0.004 (0.058)
Indicator for geographical distance to India of >10,000 kilometers	0.095*** (0.029)	0.088*** (0.030)	0.100** (0.039)	0.092** (0.041)	0.119*** (0.027)	0.102*** (0.033)	0.087*** (0.028)	0.058 (0.063)	−0.074 (0.047)
Log population	−0.009 (0.007)		−0.016* (0.009)	−0.017* (0.010)	0.010 (0.008)	−0.009 (0.007)	−0.010 (0.006)	0.011 (0.013)	0.000 (0.007)
Log GDP per capita	−0.042** (0.022)		−0.051* (0.027)	−0.045 (0.029)	−0.008 (0.025)	−0.041* (0.023)	−0.034 (0.022)	0.010 (0.039)	−0.078** (0.035)
Log telephone lines per capita	0.004 (0.034)		0.002 (0.039)	−0.004 (0.038)	0.005 (0.030)	0.004 (0.034)	−0.005 (0.034)	−0.056 (0.055)	0.052 (0.041)
Overall fit of project profile with India's worker profile	0.078** (0.039)		0.070 (0.047)	0.054 (0.054)	0.085** (0.039)	0.076* (0.040)	0.074* (0.039)	0.015 (0.057)	−0.032 (0.083)
Log count of oDesk contracts worldwide					−0.027*** (0.009)				
Trade with India as share of GDP						0.660 (1.046)			
Observations	92	92	92	92	92	92	92	92	92
Mean of DV	0.341	0.341	0.341	0.341	0.341	0.341	0.338	0.372	0.096
Relative effect (1% diaspora share)	0.032	0.021	0.028	0.025	0.033	0.029	0.016	0.019	0.268

Notes: Country-level regressions in columns (1)–(7) estimate traits associated with a larger share of work being contracted to India. Column (8) considers shares based upon dollar values. Column (9) considers the share of company contacts placing contracts that have an ethnically Indian name. Regressions weight by log number of worldwide contracts formed on oDesk, unless otherwise noted, and report robust standard errors.

***Significant at the 1 percent level.

**Significant at the 5 percent level.

*Significant at the 10 percent level.

levels of Indian diaspora communities. Looking at the other covariates, spatial distance does not matter in the digital labor context like it does in many estimates of economic exchanges. In fact, the share of contracts sent to India increases with spatial distance.[9] The overall fit of a country's outsourcing needs with the skill sets of Indian workers predicts that greater shares of work are sent to India. On the other hand, country population levels and telephone penetration do not play an important role. We likewise find similar weakness in Internet-penetration measures, but they are not as uniformly available. Finally, countries with higher GDP per capita send less of their work to India conditional on the other covariates.

Many countries have been slower to develop on digital labor platforms, and nations with very few contracts can generate noisy share estimates. Our main estimations thus weight by contract volume to focus attention on better measured data and more meaningful observations; we utilize log weights to not overly emphasize the United States experience in particular. Columns (3) and (4) show similar results when we weight by log country population or when we exclude the weights. In both cases, the coefficients decline somewhat and the standard errors grow given the greater emphasis placed on noisy outcomes, but the role of diasporas remains economically and statistically significant. Column (5) shows similar results when adding a control for the total worldwide count of contracts on oDesk by a country. This variable picks up the negative effect earlier associated with GDP per capita. Column (6) tests whether this connection is simply following on existing business relationships that countries have with India. We measure the extent to which India is a trading partner of the focal country by the total volume of trade in 2007 between India and the country divided by the country's GDP. Introducing this as a control does not affect our results.

Column (7) shows that the elasticity declines when excluding an outlier firm in the United Arab Emirates that outsourced an enormous number of contracts to India, but overall the pattern remains similar and statistically significant.[10] Column (8) finds similar results when examining the

9. Unreported estimations also find that time zones do not play a strong role in contract placement. The coefficient values suggest a negative effect of being further apart in terms of time zone, but these results are very small in magnitude and not statistically significant. Two important details to note are (a) many digital contracts (e.g., data entry) do not require extensive synchronous interaction, and (b) for those that do, many Indian workers are willing to work the originating country's business day if that is needed for securing the job. Appendix figure 3A.1 provides a more detailed application time-zone analysis taken from Horton (2016a). This figure shows the shifting of schedules more broadly.

10. The results are not overly dependent upon a single country, and we find very similar results when excluding the United States, Pakistan, and similar. Excluding the UAE has the largest effect, resulting in a point estimate of 0.878 (0.660), which is not very surprising given that the Indian diaspora's share of 35 percent in the UAE is by far the largest, twice that of the next-highest states of Qatar (18 percent) and Oman (17 percent). As a second approach, we find a point estimate of 1.629 (0.654) when winsorizing outlier diaspora shares to Oman's value to cap the UAE's extreme value. The role of the diaspora community is also very similar when including a control for English language proficiency, which we are able to assemble for about half of the countries in our sample.

dollar share of contracts being sent to India rather than the count share. This estimation naturally puts more weight on contracts that have higher wages and longer durations. The coefficient declines compared to column (1) but remains economically important and statistically significant. Finally, column (9) provides an important connection to our earlier estimation approaches. The dependent variable is the share of company contacts using oDesk in the focal country that are of ethnic Indian origin (independent of whether or not the work is contracted with India). Larger Indian diaspora shares in a country's general population are highly correlated with a larger share of oDesk company contacts for the country being of ethnic Indian origin. The coefficient measures that a 1 percent increase in the relative size of the India diaspora to host country population (e.g., from 1 percent to 2 percent) is correlated with a 2.6 percent increase in the share of oDesk company contracts in that host country who have Indian ethnic names (e.g., from 10 percent to 13 percent).[11]

To summarize, in a spirit similar to Rauch and Trindade's (2002) analysis of Chinese diaspora and flows of trade in manufactured goods, we find clear evidence linking the Indian diaspora to the placement of digital outsourcing contracts into India. This complements the micro-level perspective taken by Ghani, Kerr, and Stanton (2014). This is encouraging more broadly, as it provides greater assurance that micro- and macro-level approaches are providing complementary perspectives on the functioning of digital labor markets.

3.3   Macro-Level Perspective

3.3.1   Contract Flows on Digital Labor Platforms

Figure 3.2 displays the asymmetric distribution of contract flows on Upwork. The most striking features of contract flow on Upwork are (a) the North-South nature of placements, and (b) the very limited degree that countries provide services to themselves, with the United States being a major exception.

Table 3.3A ranks the top twenty hiring countries by aggregate wage bill from cross-border contracts from the launch of the platform through 2015. The United States is by far the largest hiring economy, with a cumulative wage bill for cross-border contracts that is almost seven times higher than second-ranked Australia. In addition to placing more jobs abroad, US

---

11. Considering partitions of the data, the diaspora coefficient is 0.893 (0.263) for 2008 and prior, 1.085 (0.240) for 2009 and later, 0.798 (0.238) for high-end contracts, 0.592 (0.113) for low-end contracts, 0.448 (0.232) for initial contracts, and 1.134 (0.334) for subsequent contracts. Ghani, Kerr, and Stanton (2014) analyze further how overseas ethnic Indians show higher rates than other ethnic groups of outsourcing initial contracts to workers in India and the path dependence that follows for subsequent contracts.

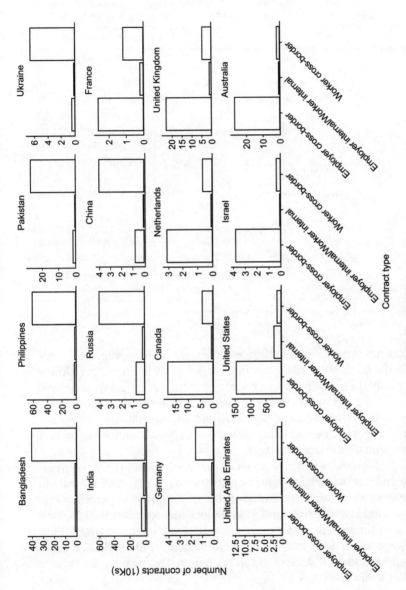

Fig. 3.2   The asymmetric nature of Upwork global contract flows

Notes: The figure quantifies the number of contracts for selected countries by their cross-border nature. The vertical axis is specific to each country and measured in tens of thousands. The first bar in each triplet captures outbound contracts made by employers in the country to workers in another country. The second bar reflects contracts made by employers to workers in their own country. The third bar measures the contracts completed by workers in the country where the employer is in another country.

Table 3.3A   **Hiring and working patterns for top hiring countries on oDesk/Upwork**

Country (1)	Employer wage-bill rank from cross-border contracts (2)	Worker wage-bill rank from cross-border contracts (3)	Number of cross-border hiring contracts (4)	Wage bill from cross-border hiring ($ millions) (5)	Number of cross-border worker supply contracts (6)	Wage bill from cross-border worker supply ($ millions) (7)
United States	1	7	1,468,476	964.6	123,157	56.0
Australia	2	24	269,941	138.0	17,499	8.5
United Kingdom	3	11	229,056	92.6	44,201	23.0
Canada	4	9	183,206	86.6	42,332	30.4
United Arab Emirates	5	45	122,343	69.7	10,939	3.5
Germany	6	19	40,392	19.1	15,456	10.7
France	7	33	26,494	18.5	11,356	5.7
Netherlands	8	40	30,933	14.8	6,379	4.6
Israel	9	57	38,285	13.3	3,202	2.3
Ireland	10	58	17,984	13.0	4,525	2.2
Denmark	11	72	13,119	11.4	2,179	1.4
Switzerland	12	64	18,428	11.1	1,532	1.7
Sweden	13	46	13,980	10.0	6,045	3.4
Spain	14	23	19,295	9.1	12,803	8.9
Singapore	15	56	31,820	9.0	4,713	2.3
New Zealand	16	55	16,772	8.4	4,422	2.4
Hong Kong	17	60	15,320	8.2	3,013	2.0
Norway	18	66	9,344	7.4	2,075	1.7
Belgium	19	61	11,263	6.1	2,547	2.0
Italy	20	27	13,373	4.3	12,039	6.9

Notes: See table 3.1. The top twenty countries by hiring employer wage bill are displayed.

employers have contracts that average 35 percent more in wage bills compared to the other countries given in table 3.3A. By contrast, the United States is only the seventh-ranked country from a worker perspective, and only four of the top twenty worker countries are present on this employer country list (i.e., United States, United Kingdom, Canada, and Germany). This emphasizes the exceptionally strong North-South nature of contract placements on digital labor markets.

Table 3.3B provides a mirror image of table 3.3A from the worker perspective. India is the largest country by worker wage bill, with $340 million in cumulative wages received through 2014. This is about 19 percent larger than the cumulative wage bill for the Philippines, the second-ranked country. After the Philippines, the gap is more dramatic; the Ukraine is ranked third, with a wage bill of $118 million, or about 35 percent of the Indian total. Figures 3.3A and 3.3B depict the top bilateral routes by contract volume and dollar value, respectively.

Table 3.4 ranks the top suppliers of contract labor to the United States, again using cumulative wage bills over the oDesk/Upwork history. The United States edges out India and the Philippines as the largest provider of contract labor to itself. Behind this aggregate statistic, India and the Philip-

Table 3.3B   **Hiring and working patterns for top working countries on oDesk/Upwork**

Country (1)	Employer wage-bill rank from cross-border contracts (2)	Worker wage-bill rank from cross-border contracts (3)	Number of cross-border hiring contracts (4)	Wage bill from cross-border hiring ($ millions) (5)	Number of cross-border worker supply contracts (6)	Wage bill from cross-border worker supply ($ millions) (7)
India	22	1	48,236	3.4	595,980	340.3
Philippines	41	2	20,573	1.2	627,497	286.9
Ukraine	37	3	4,526	1.4	66,436	118.3
Russia	25	4	7,292	3.1	39,754	89.2
Pakistan	45	5	15,480	0.9	265,127	87.3
Bangladesh	75	6	11,078	0.3	399,845	62.5
United States	1	7	1,468,476	964.6	123,157	56.0
China	30	8	7,962	2.2	40,153	38.1
Canada	4	9	183,206	86.6	42,332	30.4
Poland	38	10	3,967	1.4	13,529	25.5
United Kingdom	3	11	229,056	92.6	44,201	23.0
Belarus	119	12	356	0.1	9,799	18.6
Romania	46	13	5,523	0.9	32,769	17.8
Vietnam	89	14	1,832	0.2	16,929	13.3
Indonesia	55	15	2,941	0.6	26,272	11.5
Argentina	64	16	2,043	0.5	10,228	10.9
Serbia	78	17	2,253	0.3	20,196	10.8
Armenia	100	18	734	0.1	8,918	10.7
Germany	6	19	40,392	19.1	15,456	10.7
Egypt	56	20	5,288	0.6	26,445	10.1

Notes: See table 3.1. The top twenty countries by worker wage bill are displayed.

pines record greater contract volume in column (3), but the average wage bill for US-sourced work has been higher ($943 vs. $666 for India and $538 for Philippines, respectively). Two other South Asian countries (Pakistan and Bangladesh), Russia, and Ukraine round out the next largest providers of digital labor and talent for US employers.

The pattern of flows is quite unique to digital labor markets. Excluding the United States, there is a −0.08 correlation among the remaining nineteen countries in terms of aggregate wage bill supplied (column [4]) and total US imports of manufactured goods (column [7]). China is the eighth-ranked provider of services, at only 10 percent of the level of India or the Philippines. Quite noticeably, Japan and Mexico are not even listed on table 3.4, suggesting the negative correlation would further strengthen in their presence. The correlation is a similar −0.09 when comparing column (4) against the total US imports of services in column (8). While not shown in this table, it is again quickly evident upon reflection that the global sourcing of Upwork contracts is also quite different from global sources for immigrants to the United States.

Figure 3.4 provides a summary statistic of the distribution of US source countries for workers on Upwork compared to America's distribution of

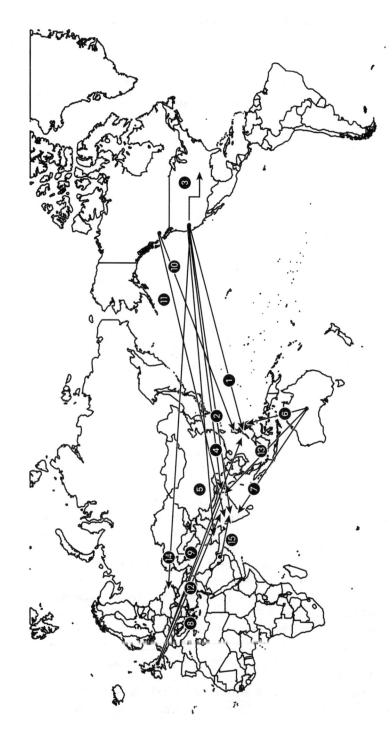

Fig. 3.3A   Top employer-worker contract flows on Upwork platform by contract volume

Notes: The figure shows the top fifteen employer-worker contract flows on oDesk/Upwork by contract volume through 2014. The arrow points to the location of the worker. The number indicates the rank of the flow, and appendix table 3A.1 provides values. For the no. 3 case, the third-largest flow is the United States to itself.

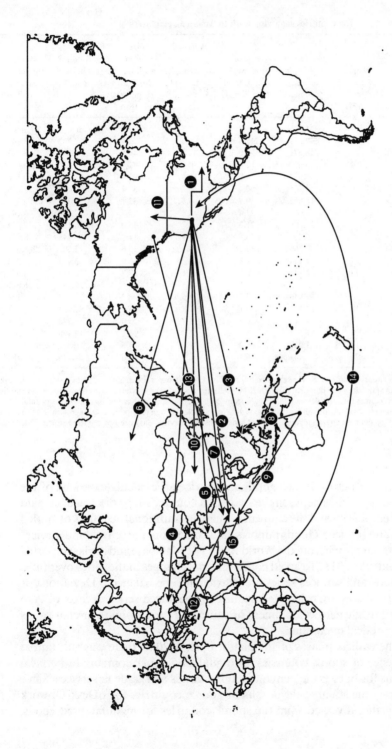

Fig. 3.3B Top employer-worker contract flows on Upwork platform by wage bill

Notes: The figure shows the top fifteen employer-worker contract flows on oDesk/Upwork by wage bill through 2014. The arrow points to the location of the worker. The number indicates the rank of the flow, and appendix table 3A.1 provides values. For the no. 1 case, the largest flow is the United States to itself.

Table 3.4   Top countries supplying work to American employers

Country (1)	Worker wage-bill rank (2)	Number of work supply contracts, total (3)	Wage bill from work supply, total ($ millions) (4)	Wage bill from work supply, 2005–2011 ($ millions) (5)	Wage bill from work supply, 2012–2014 ($ millions) (6)	Total US imports of goods ($ millions) (7)	Total US imports of services ($ millions) (8)
United States	1	235,225	221.7	67.7	154.0	n/a	n/a
India	2	317,731	211.6	59.2	152.4	158,462	53,945
Philippines	3	358,671	193.0	48.4	144.6	51,737	8,362
Ukraine	4	30,612	67.4	20.0	47.4	8,230	n/r
Pakistan	5	140,552	58.4	15.4	42.9	21,345	10,118
Russia	6	19,305	50.1	16.7	33.4	144,435	17,658
Bangladesh	7	218,882	39.7	6.5	33.1	23,322	n/r
China	8	20,055	23.4	3.8	19.7	2,007,688	46,240
Canada	9	25,264	21.2	6.3	15.0	1,778,196	177,874
Poland	10	6,208	16.5	4.8	11.7	16,446	9,476
United Kingdom	11	22,265	14.2	3.5	10.6	317,506	286,063
Belarus	12	4,444	9.8	2.9	6.9	3,753	275
Romania	13	14,447	9.8	2.1	7.7	6,474	n/r
Argentina	14	5,516	8.1	2.5	5.6	26,484	6,612
Vietnam	15	7,836	7.7	1.5	6.2	76,744	198
Indonesia	16	12,735	7.1	1.8	5.3	92,053	1,598
Brazil	17	4,773	6.6	1.7	5.0	158,228	21,621
Egypt	18	11,534	6.4	1.3	5.1	13,498	n/r
Armenia	19	3,949	6.2	1.8	4.5	368	n/r
Australia	20	9,444	6.1	2.1	4.0	54,245	28,384

Notes: The top twenty countries by worker wage bill paid by US employers are displayed. Data come from oDesk/Upwork from the launch of the platform through 2014. Columns (7) and (8) use external data from the census and the World Bank TSD database and take totals over data from 2006 to 2011. The last year of services imports data with a country breakdown is 2011. Although trade in goods data is available through later periods, data ends in 2011 to maintain comparability between the goods and services series. Missing services data are not reported in the TSD database (n/r).

source countries for traded goods and services. We calculate the sum of the squared deviations between the share of a country's Upwork wage bill paid by US employers and the equivalent share in traditional accounts of traded goods and services. Goods imports data come from the census, and services imports data come from the World Bank TSD database and are last reported by country in 2011. To avoid compositional changes in the series over time, the goods and services series are restricted to be balanced. Deviations of Upwork shares are calculated against the balanced series. A level of zero would indicate perfect alignment of source countries, while a level of two is the theoretical maximum.

In the earliest phases of the platform, circa 2006, there was substantial divergence of source countries for digital labor work compared to typical patterns for both trade in manufactured goods and trade in services. Since this time, the squared deviations of source countries for oDesk/Upwork have further diverged from the source countries for manufactured goods,

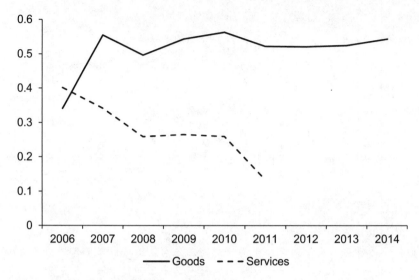

Fig. 3.4   Comparison of Upwork's global sourcing distribution for US employers to that for goods and services imports

Notes: The figure shows squared deviations of the share of Upwork wage bill paid by US employers to a country against the US share of imports of goods and services from that country. Services imports data come from the World Bank TSD database and are last reported by country in 2011. Goods imports data come from the census. To avoid compositional changes in the series over time, the goods and services series are restricted to be balanced. Deviations of Upwork shares are calculated against the balanced series.

while convergence toward source countries for trade in services is evident until 2011. Consistent with earlier tables, the largest deviations for the goods series are for China, India, the Philippines, and Russia. China is a large trading partner offline, but has little online share. For the other countries, their online share exceeds their offline share.

3.3.2   Gravity Models of Contract Flows

Stepping beyond the example of the United States, table 3.5 next examines digital outsourcing patterns across all country pairs using the familiar gravity model. Beyond the information that we derive directly from the Upwork database, most covariates used in this section come from the bilateral gravity and TRADHIST CEPII data sets. We consider a cross-sectional estimation of bilateral country pairs using the pseudo-maximum likelihood estimator of Santos Silva and Tenreyro (2006). This conservative approach also allows us to retain bilateral routes on which zero contract placement occurs on Upwork.

The dependent variable is the wage bill from cross-country contracts paid by the employer country to the worker country. We include employer country and worker country fixed effects in estimations that account for overall

Table 3.5   Estimates of wage-bill volume formed on Upwork

	DV is wage bill from cross-country contracts paid by employer country				
	Estimation without historical trade (1)	Base estimation (2)	Base estimation, pre-2011 (3)	Base estimation, post-2011 (4)	Base estimation, post-2011 with lag (5)
(0,1) Geographic distance, quartile 2	-0.281***	-0.245***	-0.324***	-0.274***	-0.162***
	(0.00150)	(0.00146)	(0.00673)	(0.00242)	(0.00299)
(0,1) Geographic distance, quartile 3	-0.425***	-0.386***	-0.551***	-0.389***	-0.172***
	(0.00184)	(0.00188)	(0.00912)	(0.00323)	(0.00424)
(0,1) Geographic distance, quartile 4 (longest)	-0.539***	-0.449***	-0.752***	-0.438***	-0.142***
	(0.00214)	(0.00243)	(0.0108)	(0.00412)	(0.00528)
(0,1) Employer – worker GDP/cap > $5,000	0.343***	0.367***	1.254***	0.135***	-0.133***
	(0.00368)	(0.00366)	(0.0172)	(0.00464)	(0.00442)
(0,1) Employer – worker GDP/cap > $10,000	1.117***	1.087***	0.419***	1.087***	0.825***
	(0.00498)	(0.00466)	(0.0149)	(0.0112)	(0.00943)
(0,1) Past trade volume, quartile 2		0.0100**	-0.105***	0.0773***	0.194***
		(0.00466)	(0.0370)	(0.00476)	(0.00476)
(0,1) Past trade volume, quartile 3		-0.0836***	-0.328***	0.0145***	0.123***
		(0.00501)	(0.0427)	(0.00515)	(0.00560)
(0,1) Past trade volume, quartile 4 (largest)		0.0867***	-0.0520	0.131***	0.170***
		(0.00491)	(0.0421)	(0.00550)	(0.00563)
(0,1) Zero historical trade		-0.357***	-0.495	-0.324***	-0.0622***
		(0.0197)	(0.309)	(0.0206)	(0.0175)
(0,1) Common-country border	-0.449***	-0.414***	-0.477***	-0.430***	-0.336***
	(0.00555)	(0.00559)	(0.0221)	(0.00864)	(0.00767)

	(1)	(2)	(3)	(4)	(5)
(0,1) Common-country language	0.198***	0.204***	0.295***	0.226***	0.116***
	(0.00319)	(0.00308)	(0.00785)	(0.00478)	(0.00294)
Time zone difference	−0.0114***	−0.0177***	0.0249***	−0.0268***	−0.0381***
	(0.000153)	(0.000137)	(0.000841)	(0.000195)	(0.000172)
(0,1) Both the employer and worker countries are in the WTO	1.645***	1.835***	1.916***	1.828***	1.144***
	(0.266)	(0.127)	(0.529)	(0.173)	(0.108)
Lag of log wage bill for country pair					0.369***
					(0.00237)
Observations	19,430	18,143	13,330	17,485	17,485
Mean of dependent variable ($ millions)	0.0758	0.0811	0.0288	0.0622	0.0622

Notes: Estimates are weighted by total employer country wage bill. Robust standard errors are reported. Estimation is via Poisson pseudo-maximum likelihood and includes employer country and worker country fixed effects. Employer country fixed effects are concentrated out, and worker country fixed effects are included as dummies. All models also include dummies for quartiles of the product of gap between countries (not reported). Historical trade volume is flows taken from the CEPII TRADHIST data set and averaged over 2001 to 2004. Other gravity covariates come from the CEPII Gravity data set. Column (5) includes an indicator for zero trade prior to 2011 in the oDesk data and the lag of log wage bill is set to zero in these cases.

***Significant at the 1 percent level.

**Significant at the 5 percent level.

*Significant at the 10 percent level.

levels evident in tables 3.3A and 3.3B. Employer country fixed effects are concentrated out, and worker country fixed effects are included as unreported indicator variables. Estimations are weighted by total contracts paid by employer country to reflect the global distribution of trade and robust standard errors are used to account for heteroskedasticity.

To allow for nonlinear effects, we model most explanatory variables as indicator variables for various points in the distribution of a covariate. The omitted category for each indicator is the smallest/least category (e.g., shortest bilateral distance or GDP per capita difference between employer and worker country smaller than $5,000). Coefficients for each explanatory factor show the conditional differential compared to the omitted group. All models also include unreported indicator variables for quartiles of the product of GDP between countries.

Column (1) provides a base estimation that does not use recent offline trade flows as an explanatory variable. We first find that distance still matters in shaping the broad distribution of outsourcing contracts. We did not observe this pattern in the special case of India, examined in table 3.2, but it is more systematically present when considering global contract placements. On the other hand, contiguous countries often show stronger links and economic integration, but we do not find evidence of a border effect in these data. A common country language and sharing a time zone also appear to boost contract placement.[12] Finally, we observe that the largest differences in GDP per capita between the employer and worker countries increase the wage bill of contracts.

These basic findings continue to hold in column (2) when also including the level of recent bilateral trade flows. Recent offline trade patterns have modest power for predicting services trade online. We are unable to parse whether the act of trading physical goods has a causal effect in this regard by, for example, boosting business connections and reputations for this work, or whether these past trade relationships reflect more primal determinants that we have not modeled or did not measure well. Potential examples include geographic and economic interactions that are more fine-grained than our gravity covariates could pick up or idiosyncratic relationships across countries (good and bad) that are not included in the framework but affect business interactions.

Columns (3) and (4) compare the periods before and after 2011. The role of distance is becoming less pronounced, while GDP differences are becoming more pronounced. As a whole it looks like a typical trade model performs better after 2011, suggesting that platform maturity is somewhat leading digital labor patterns to look more like those observed for other international exchanges.

---

12. The common country language result, however, is not robust across the multiple language variants developed by Melitz and Toubal (2014) and should be treated with caution. The choice about these language variants does not affect the other coefficients reported in table 3.5.

Finally, column (5) considers persistence in past online trade, which would be expected as a result of the information friction and path-dependence models reviewed earlier in the literature. Does an initial high share of wage bill pre-2011 continue to explain flows in the later period? The answer is a clear yes, even after controlling for offline conditions that may affect the initial distribution. The elasticity is 0.369, so a 10 percent increase in pre-2011 trade implies a 3.7 percent increase in post-2011 digital trade. This connection is consistent with the microresults in Ghani, Kerr, and Stanton (2014), which show that employers replicate their approach to contracting if it works the first time. The estimates may also be consistent with employers who exploit a locale after resolving uncertainty about its fit or after developing some location-specific knowledge.

3.3.3 Substitution Elasticities

The results to this point lead us to ask to what extent changes in relative prices overcome some frictions. The first attempt at addressing this question explores substitution patterns across countries. Table 3.4 suggests that American employers are home biased and are likely to hire US workers despite their high prices. Here we attempt to quantify how variation in relative prices affects substitution by American employers away from US workers and toward workers from the rest of the world. To do so, we restrict the sample to US employers and estimate how contract shares vary with mean wage bids. The regression is

$$\ln\left(s_{jkt}\right) - \ln\left(s_{0kt}\right) = \alpha_0 \bar{W}_{jkt} + \alpha_1 \bar{W}_{jkt} \times \mathrm{US}_j + \mathrm{country}_j + \mathrm{time}_t$$
$$+ \mathrm{jobCategory}_k + \varepsilon_{itk},$$

where s_{jkt} is the share of contracts relative to total job openings posted by US employers in job category k filled by workers from country j in time period t, s_{0kt} is the share of openings without a contract, and $\bar{W}_{jkt}$ is the mean hourly wage bid in that cell. The interaction $\bar{W}_{jkt} \times \mathrm{US}_j$ allows the coefficient on price to differ for workers from the United States. To account for endogeneity of wage bids, we instrument for bids by non-US workers using the z-score of the log of the local currency-to-dollar exchange rate. This instrument comes from Stanton and Thomas (2016a) and exploits the fact that all contracts are in US dollars but non-US workers' outside wages are paid in the local currency. The z-score normalization is necessary to account for different scales relative to the dollar across countries. A second instrument is necessary for US workers. Here we use an instrument that is based on common cost shocks across markets, taking the average wage bid for UK workers interacted with a dummy that the bid in question is from the United States.

The estimating equation is the linear IV analogue of a logit model, but the parameters α_0 and α_1 allow for some additional flexibility in assessing substitution patterns across countries relative to a model where the coefficient on price is constrained to be constant across all alternatives. The own-price elasticity for non-US workers, denoted "row" for "rest of world," is $\alpha_0 (1 - s_{\text{row}}) \bar{W}_{\text{row}}$, where s_{row} is the share of contracts to job openings coming from the rest of the world. The own-price elasticity for US workers is $(\alpha_0 + \alpha_1)(1 - s_{\text{US}}) \bar{W}_{\text{US}}$. The cross-price elasticity for the rest of the world with respect to US bids is $-(\alpha_0 + \alpha_1) s_{\text{US}} \bar{W}_{\text{US}}$, and the cross-price elasticity for the United States with respect to bids from the rest of the world is $-\alpha_0 s_{\text{row}} \bar{W}_{\text{row}}$.

Table 3.6 provides estimates of substitution patterns across countries using these expressions, along with first-stage regressions for the linear IV estimates. In all specifications, demand for workers from the rest of the world is more elastic than for workers from the United States. The base own-bid elasticity for the rest of the world is −4.62. This says that a 1 percent increase in average bids leads to a 4.62 percent decrease in contract share for the rest of the world. Surprisingly, the elasticity is larger in magnitude for technical categories, −8.29, than for nontechnical categories, −3.06. The elasticity has also fallen over time. In contrast, the base own-bid elasticity for US workers is −2.14. It is also larger for technical categories and displays a similar decline over time.

The cross elasticities are of even more interest. We believe this is the first place to document that these elasticities are tiny, suggesting limited substitution across places based on price-related considerations. The cross elasticity for the rest of the world with respect to US bids is 0.039. This says that a 1 percent increase in US bids leads to a 0.039 percent increase in contract share for the rest of the world. This rises to 0.044 in technical categories and has fallen over time. The magnitude of these cross elasticities is even smaller when looking at the elasticity of US share relative to rest of world bids. Figure 3.5 provides a visual comparison.

These results suggest limited substitution between the United States and other countries. This lack of substitution suggests that frictions may be quite persistent. Even in a global labor market with limited switching costs, there is very little substitution between the United States and other countries. Instead, given the magnitude of own-bid elasticities, this suggests employers leave the platform in response to bid increases rather than substitute away from their target search location.

3.4 Additional Digital Collaborations

Our chapter mostly concentrates on an empirical depiction of the Upwork platform, but we now turn to some case examples to describe the range of other ways that digital capabilities are extending access to talent over long distances. First, before leaving digital labor markets, it is important to recognize the multiple types of two-sided labor platforms being developed. Founded in 2013, HourlyNerd (now called Catalant) has built an innovative marketplace for management-consulting work. It focuses on business

Table 3.6   Estimates of contract elasticities for US employers

	Base (1)	Technical categories (2)	Nontechnical categories (3)	Base estimation 2005–2011 (4)	Base estimation 2011–2014 (5)
A. Main regression. Dependent variable is log share of contracts less the no-hire share					
Wage-bid average	-0.316***	-0.416***	-0.261***	-0.629***	-0.268***
	(0.0298)	(0.0596)	(0.0313)	(0.186)	(0.0247)
Wage-bid average × 1(US worker)	0.211***	0.215***	0.204***	0.257***	0.188***
	(0.0189)	(0.0340)	(0.0216)	(0.0682)	(0.0171)
Own-bid elasticity, rest of world	-4.615	-8.291	-3.056	-7.990	-4.140
Own-bid elasticity, US workers	-2.144	-5.557	-0.953	-6.581	-1.808
Cross elasticity, rest of world share and US bids	0.0387	0.0442	0.0222	0.0981	0.0370
Cross elasticity, US share and rest of world bids	0.00685	0.00964	0.00507	0.0135	0.00577
B. First-stage regression for wage-bid average					
Z-score of log local currency to dollar exchange rate	-0.597***	-0.447***	-0.604***	-0.651***	-0.515***
	(0.0525)	(0.0900)	(0.0610)	(0.0870)	(0.0548)
Log wage-bid average in the United Kingdom × worker in United States	0.361***	0.278***	0.423***	0.222***	0.566***
	(0.0379)	(0.0551)	(0.0409)	(0.0489)	(0.0328)
C. First-stage regression for wage bid × 1(US worker)					
Z-score of log local currency to dollar exchange rate	-0.0164***	-0.0289***	-0.00630	-0.0214***	-0.00439***
	(0.00403)	(0.00782)	(0.00383)	(0.00601)	(0.000804)
Log wage-bid average in the United Kingdom × worker in United States	0.556***	0.518***	0.595***	0.336***	0.877***
	(0.0496)	(0.0870)	(0.0438)	(0.0595)	(0.0331)
Observations	33,604	11,862	21,742	10,311	23,293

Notes: Table provides estimations of contract elasticities for US employers. The unit of observation is the country-job category-month of contracts with US employers. Regressions include worker country-by-job category and year-by-month fixed effects. Z-scores of the local currency to US dollar exchange rate are used as instruments for the mean of the bid. The log of the average UK wage bid interacted with a dummy for workers from the United States is an instrument for the wage-bid average for US workers. Robust standard errors reported.

***Significant at the 1 percent level.
**Significant at the 5 percent level.
*Significant at the 10 percent level.

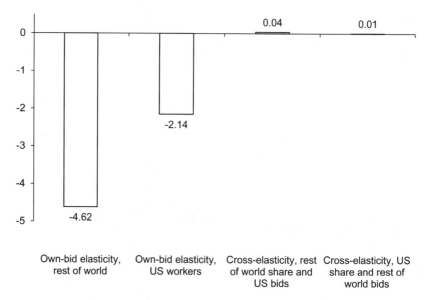

Fig. 3.5   Elasticities of work to own-bid and cross-bids
Notes: See panel A of table 3.6.

consulting and has over 20,000 independent consultants registered for project-based work. Originally targeting ways to connect freelancers with small companies that would not otherwise use consultants, HourlyNerd has grown into fielding enterprise-level solutions that are used by many large companies, too. Like management consulting, many areas that appear today to be protected from digital competition may soon become targets of entrepreneurs seeking to build platforms in these areas. Examples from the legal industry are UpCounsel and InCloudCounsel.

Second, online contests and crowd-based mechanisms provide ways for companies to solicit ideas from many unexpected sources. For instance, pharmaceuticals giant Merck designed an eight-week contest in 2012 to aid its drug development process. It released data on chemical compounds that it had previously tested, and then challenged participants to identify which held the most promise for future testing. The winner would receive $40,000. The contest attracted 238 teams that submitted more than 2,500 proposals. The winning solution came from computer scientists (not professionals in the life sciences) who were using machine-learning approaches previously unknown to Merck. This opened up opportunities for Merck that would not have otherwise been feasible.

Contests held by NASA also illustrate the worldwide span of these human capital inputs (Lakhani, Lifshitz-Assaf, and Tushman 2013). In 2008, NASA launched a set of pilot projects to evaluate the use of global contests and similar crowd-sourced approaches for solving thorny technical challenges that were proving difficult for its internal team. Three for-profit platforms (InnoCentive, TopCoder, yet2.com) were used by NASA during its early phases for challenges like forecasting of solar events, improved food-barrier layers, and compact aerobic-resistive device design. Seven challenges posted on InnoCentive illustrate the global engagement, with 2,900 problem solvers from eighty countries participating. In many cases, the developed crowd-based solutions were twice as good as or better than what the organization had achieved internally. These contests continue to be an important way that NASA sources global talent for its work.

Boudreau and Lakhani (2014) describe further the many ways that contests are used to access far-flung ideas and insights. Similar to Upwork and HourlyNerd, many digital platforms like InnoCentive and TopCoder are positioning themselves to be the platforms for companies to reach talented people with ideas, no matter where they live. This breadth of the crowd-sourcing platforms, moreover, is critically important for the value they can deliver to clients like Merck and NASA. This is because the quality of the outcome depends not on the average quality of the responses assembled, but instead on the extreme tail of the ideas generated. While internal experts may on average deliver better-quality ideas, the extreme values when pulling ideas from a very large external contractor pool are likely to be higher. If it is only the best idea or solution that matters, access to a huge global developer pool can be very advantageous.

Third, as described in the introduction, some companies are seeking to establish porous organizational boundaries directly for their businesses. When P&G developed its Connect + Develop platform, it had 7,500 employees worldwide working on innovation-related activities. But, P&G estimated that there were 200 people outside of P&G working on the same topics for each of its scientists, or about 1.5 million people, and it launched its Connect + Develop to be this global outreach. One of its earliest successes was an important innovation for its Pringles line that came from a technology developed in a small bakery in Italy (Huston and Sakkab 2006). In a similar spirit, companies and developers engaged in open-source software depend upon and contribute to a global common good, where national borders are second order.

3.5   Perspectives for Researchers

Data on digital labor markets provide some special advantages for researchers interested in empirical labor topics. First, they often can provide a unique or rare angle on an important topic through their records of bidders and the outside options of both parties, their record of performance outcomes, the ability to construct longitudinal careers for workers, the conduct of skills assessments for workers, and so on. This often allows researchers to attack very complex problems in new ways, providing a unique edge to papers. For example, studies of discrimination have often been perplexed by how to best determine levels of discrimination when observing realized wage differentials in the market, whereas these platforms could allow one to make inference from the observed bids given to an employer and the characteristics of the chosen worker. On the other hand, weighing against this advantage is the fact that these powerful approaches often bring their own complex problems to solve. Continuing the discrimination example, how do you correctly capture the employer's perceptions of the various performance histories of the bidders?

One limitation of Upwork data for some labor topics is that it is not straightforward to identify corporate firms due to the lack of a unique company identifier. The person hiring within General Motors, for example, could list many variations on the company's name or even the name of the subsidiary that they work for. For researchers familiar with patent data, this structure is operationally quite similar to ambiguities with patent assignee codes/names. This structure limits the ability of researchers to describe outsourcing behavior very well across the firm-size distribution on Upwork, but for most applications this has limited consequence. Longer term, it would be very interesting to match digital labor markets data to confidential administrative sources of employer-employee information, like the Longitudinal Employer-Household Dynamics (LEHD) database that is developed and maintained by the Census Bureau. Another possibility is the VentureXpert records on start-ups backed by venture capital. Obviously, overseas freelancers would not be captured, but such mergers would allow interesting depictions of local hiring versus outsourced contracts.

Third, these platforms allow experiments to be run in labor markets that are not otherwise feasible (e.g., Pallais 2014; Cullen and Pakzad-Hurson 2016). Some of these experiments are conducted at the platform level, changing fundamentally how some aspect of the market "works"—a type of intervention that would be very difficult to conduct in other contexts. For example, Horton (2016b) reports the results of a true minimum wage experiment, while Horton and Johari (2016) report the results of an experiment in which employers were required to publicly signal their relative preferences over price and quality to would-be applicants. They were able to experimentally manipulate whether the employer's preferences were communicated to would-be applicants, allowing them to estimate how much additional sorting of workers to the "right" kind of employer occurs when employer preferences are made explicit.

3.6   Open Questions

The analyses and examples of digital labor markets provided in this review bear witness to an exciting phenomenon in its earliest stage of development. With a focus on high-skilled talent, Freeman (2013) argues increasing globalized knowledge creation and transfer could become the "one ring to rule them all" with respect to international trade in services, financial and capital mobility, and people flows. Perhaps so, and the evidence collected in this review suggests digital labor and talent access could be a central part of such a future. On the other hand, this fate is far from guaranteed, and the ultimate importance of these global forces will only be revealed over the next decade and beyond. We close this review with some open questions to this end (see also the research agenda laid out in Agrawal et al. [2015]).

First, several interesting questions exist about the platforms themselves. Perhaps most important, platforms are still experimenting with the technical designs and algorithms that govern how their labor markets operate, what information is provided to firms and workers, and so on. Many small tweaks are implemented, but some redesigns are quite significant, such as when oDesk began requiring firms and workers to use a similar skill vocabulary, with implications for the matching efficiency of the platform. The digital platforms have clear incentives to make adjustments that improve their efficiency and competitiveness, and researchers likewise may uncover top-notch natural experiments if they can be closely integrated into these adjustments and their design/implementation. On a related note, complementary tools like Dropbox, Slack, Google Docs, and so forth are improving the functioning and accelerating the development of digital labor exchanges. We need to learn more about the symbiotic relationship between other collaborative tools and digital labor markets and how the complementary products coevolve. Ownership of data and privacy have not been major concerns thus far but may take on bigger roles in the future.

Next, many questions exist about how these rapidly expanding digital labor platforms will affect the broader labor markets and economy around them. At present, the modest size of these labor platforms has not delivered local consequences in advanced economies like those associated with Uber and Airbnb. As such, there has been less attention to regulatory structures and tax policies for these markets, especially compared to other parts of the shared economy. It is an open and important question about how the policy environment surrounding these companies will adjust as they scale. Similarly, the future interactions—competitive battles, mergers and acquisitions, and so on—with offline outsourcing or temporary help companies or online platforms in adjacent domains will be intriguing to watch. Recent start-ups that focus on online-to-offline work tasks (e.g., Hello Alfred) suggest the current perceived gaps might close faster than expected.

While small in advanced economies from a contracting perspective, the economic impacts in terms of freelancers and their local economies are already more accentuated in some special settings in developing and emerging economies. For example, some remote Russian towns have an abundance of technical talent due to the Cold War and utilize these digital labor platforms to obtain good-paying work globally when none is available in the local economy. Due to local spillovers and the development of agencies, as discussed in section 3.2, remote places can even become somewhat known for a certain type of outsourced task, similar to the specialized manufacturing towns in China. More research should go into studying the development of these contractor pools and their local operations. Moreover, comparative studies across specialized places in the face of exchange-rate movements and similar shocks will be interesting. On these and similar fronts, studies can be both leading edge in terms of describing an emerging global phenomenon and also on the leading edge in terms of academic insights about important broader economic questions.

Appendix
Conceptual Framework for Gravity Model

This section reviews the Eaton and Kortum (2002) model as a theoretical background for a gravity specification for trade.[13] The world consists of N countries producing and consuming a continuum of goods or services $j \in [0,1]$. In our setting, we think of j as tasks or services that are completed on a digital platform, but we will keep the simple label of "good" throughout this appendix for consistency. Consumers maximize utility in each period by purchasing these goods in quantities $Q(j)$ according to a constant elasticity of substitution (CES) objective function,

$$(A.1) \qquad U = \left(\int_0^1 Q(j)^{(\sigma-1)/\sigma} dj \right)^{\sigma/(\sigma-1)},$$

subject to prices determined below. The elasticity of substitution across goods for the consumers is $\sigma > 0$. Consumers earn wage w and consume their full wages in each period. Accordingly, time subscripts are omitted.

Countries are free to produce or trade all goods. Inputs can move among industries within a country but not across countries. Industries are characterized by identical Cobb-Douglas production functions employing labor with elasticity α and the continuum of produced goods, also aggregated with equation (A.1), with elasticity $1-\alpha$. Factor mobility and identical production functions yield constant input production costs across goods within each country, $c_i(j) = c_i \forall j$.

Technology differences exist across countries, so that country i's efficiency in producing good j is $z_i(j)$. With constant returns to scale in production, the unit cost of producing good j in country i is $c_i/z_i(j)$. While countries are

---

13. Costinot, Donaldson, and Komunjer (2012) extend Eaton and Kortum (2002) to articulate appropriate industry-level estimations of Ricardian advantages as a source of trade among countries.

free to trade, geographic or cultural distance results in "iceberg" transportation costs so that delivering one unit from country i to country n costs $d_{ni} > 1$ units in i. Thus, the delivery to country n of good j made in country i costs

(A.2)
$$p_{ni}(j) = \left(\frac{c_i}{z_i(j)}\right)d_{ni}.$$

An increase in country i's efficiency for good j lowers the price it must charge. Perfect competition allows consumers to buy from producers in the country offering the lowest price inclusive of shipment costs. Thus, the price that consumers in country n pay for good j is

(A.3)
$$p_n(j) = \min\left[p_{ni}(j); i = 1, \dots, N\right].$$

The technology determining the efficiency $z_i(j)$ is modeled as the realization of a random variable Z_i drawn from a country-specific probability distribution $F_i(z) = \Pr[Z_i < z]$. Draws are independent for each industry j within a country. A core innovation of Eaton and Kortum's model is to use the Fréchet functional distribution to model technologies,

(A.4)
$$F_i(z) = e^{-T_i \cdot z^{-\theta}},$$

where $T_i > 0$ and $\theta > 1$. The country-specific parameter T_i determines the location of the distribution, while the common parameter θ determines the variation within each country's distribution. By the law of large numbers, a larger T_i raises the average efficiency of industries for country i, and therefore its absolute advantage for trade. A larger θ, on the other hand, implies a tighter distribution for industries within every country and thereby limits the scope for comparative advantage across nations.

The Fréchet distribution (A.4) allows prices from equations (A.2) and (A.3) to be determined. The probability that country i is the lowest cost producer of an arbitrary good for country n is $\pi_{ni} = T_i(c_i d_{ni})^{-\theta} / \sum_{k=1}^{N} T_k(c_k d_{nk})^{-\theta}$.[14] With a continuum of goods, π_{ni} is also the fraction of goods country n purchases from country i. Country n's average expenditure per good does not vary by source country, so that the fraction of country n's expenditure on goods from country i is also

(A.5)
$$\frac{X_{ni}}{X_n} = \frac{T_i(c_i d_{ni})^{-\theta}}{\sum_{k=1}^{N} T_k(c_k d_{nk})^{-\theta}},$$

where X_n is total expenditure in country n. Holding input prices constant, technology growth in country i increases its exports to country n through

---

14. The distribution of prices country i presents to country n is $G_{ni}(p) = \Pr[P_{ni} \le p] = 1 - F_i(c_i d_{ni}/p) = 1 - \exp(-T_i(c_i d_{ni})^{-\theta}p^{\theta})$. Country n buys from the lowest cost producer of each good, so that its realized price distribution is $G_n(p) = \Pr[P_n \le p] = 1 - \Pi_{i=1}^{N}[1 - G_{ni}(p)] = 1 - \exp(-p^{\theta}\sum_{i=1}^{N}T_i(c_i d_{ni})^{-\theta})$. The probability is $\pi_{ni} = \Pr[P_{ni}(j) \le \min\{P_{ns}(j); s \ne i\}] = \int_0^{\infty} \Pi_{s \ne i}[1 - G_{ns}(p)]dG_{ni}(p)$. See Eaton and Kortum (2002) for the full derivation of the price index.

entry into industries in which it was previously uncompetitive. Looking across import destinations for an industry in which it already exports, country i also becomes the lowest cost producer for more distant countries it could not previously serve due to the markup of transportation costs. Condition (A.5) also shows how trading costs d lead to deviations in the law of one price.

Defining Q_i to be the total sales of exporter i, Eaton and Kortum (2002) show how bilateral exports can be expressed as

$$(A.6) \qquad X_{ni} = \frac{(d_{ni} / p_n)^{-\theta} X_n}{\sum_{k=1}^{N} (d_{ki} / p_k)^{-\theta} X_k} Q_i,$$

where p_i is the price level of a country i. This equation shows how the trade connects with the aggregate size of the importer (X_n), the exporter (Q_i), and the price-adjusted distances between them (d_{ni}/p_n). The allocation of trade has an intuitive feel. The share of total exports of country i (Q_i) that go to country n is determined by how country n's size, bilateral distance, and prices compare to the other countries in the world, with the latter being summarized in the denominator through the summation of countries.

Rearranging this for the purposes of estimation, we have

$$\log(X_{ni}) = \log(Q_i) - \theta\log(d_{ni}/p_n) + \log(X_n) - \log\left(\sum_{k=1}^{N} (d_{ki}/p_k)^{-\theta} X_k\right)$$

or

$$\log(X_{ni}/X_n) = \log(Q_i) - \theta\log(d_{ni}/p_n) - \log\left(\sum_{k=1}^{N} (d_{ki}/p_k)^{-\theta} X_k\right).$$

The last term is a worldwide constant term that would be captured by intercepts or fixed effects in estimation.

Reflecting on this model, there are parts of it that are not well suited to thinking about a digital labor market. For example, the model assumes balanced trade across goods and that all goods are represented, but we are examining only a small slice of economic activity and there is no trade balance. On the other hand, the choice to contract on these platforms may be closer to the perfect competition and distance assumptions than other settings. This provides some context and grounding for applying the gravity equation in our empirical work.

Table 3A.1 Top employer-worker routes on Upwork

	Contract volume				Wage bill ($ millions)		
Rank (1)	Worker country (2)	Employer country (3)	Contracts (4)	Rank (5)	Worker country (6)	Employer country (7)	Wage bill (8)
1	Philippines	United States	358,671	1	United States	United States	221.7
2	India	United States	317,731	2	India	United States	211.6
3	United States	United States	235,225	3	Philippines	United States	193.0
4	Bangladesh	United States	218,882	4	Ukraine	United States	67.4
5	Pakistan	United States	140,552	5	Pakistan	United States	58.4
6	Philippines	Australia	71,119	6	Russia	United States	50.1
7	India	Australia	59,339	7	Bangladesh	United States	39.7
8	India	United Kingdom	47,279	8	Philippines	Australia	39.3
9	Philippines	United Kingdom	40,178	9	India	Australia	32.1
10	Philippines	Canada	36,838	10	China	United States	23.4
11	India	Canada	36,500	11	Canada	United States	21.2
12	Bangladesh	United Kingdom	32,957	12	India	United Kingdom	21.1
13	Bangladesh	Australia	30,667	13	India	United States	18.5
14	Ukraine	United States	30,612	14	United States	United Arab Emirates	17.2
15	India	United Arab Emirates	28,515	15	India	United Arab Emirates	16.9
16	Canada	United States	25,264	16	Poland	United States	16.5
17	Bangladesh	Canada	24,688	17	Philippines	Canada	14.7
18	India	India	23,294	18	United Kingdom	United States	14.2
19	Philippines	United Arab Emirates	23,200	19	Philippines	United Kingdom	11.2
20	Pakistan	United Kingdom	22,919	20	Belarus	United States	9.8
21	United Kingdom	United States	22,265	21	Romania	United States	9.8
22	Pakistan	Australia	20,804	22	United States	Australia	8.2
23	Philippines	Philippines	20,250	23	Argentina	United States	8.1
24	China	United States	20,055	24	Vietnam	United States	7.7
25	United States	Australia	19,750	25	United States	Canada	7.6
26	Russia	United States	19,305	26	Russia	United Kingdom	7.3
27	United States	Canada	19,270	27	Ukraine	United Kingdom	7.2
28	United States	United Kingdom	18,360	28	Indonesia	United States	7.1
29	Pakistan	Canada	17,200	29	Brazil	United States	6.6
30	Kenya	United States	16,461	30	Ukraine	Canada	6.6

Notes: See figures 3.3A and 3.3B.

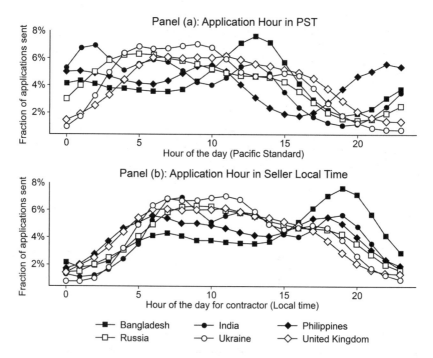

Fig. 3A.1   Hours of work on Upwork platform

Notes: Taken from Horton (2016a). Panel A describes application timing from the perspective of Pacific Standard Time on the West Coast of the United States. Panel B maps from the perspective of the contractor. Many countries have workers who adjust their work schedules to that of the United States.

References

Agrawal, Ajay, John Horton, Nicola Lacetera, and Elizabeth Lyons. 2015. "Digitization and the Contract Labor Market: A Research Agenda." In *Economic Analysis of the Digital Economy*, edited by Avi Goldfarb, Shane Greenstein, and Catherine Tucker, 219–50. Chicago: University of Chicago Press.

Agrawal, Ajay, Devesh Kapur, John McHale, and Alexander Oettl. 2011. "Brain Drain or Brain Bank? The Impact of Skilled Emigration on Poor-Country Innovation." *Journal of Urban Economics* 69 (1): 43–55.

Agrawal, Ajay, Nicola Lacetera, and Elizabeth Lyons. 2014. "Does Information Help or Hinder Job Applicants from Less Developed Countries in Online Markets?" NBER Working Paper no. 18720, Cambridge, MA.

Blinder, Alan, and Alan Krueger. 2013. "Alternative Measures of Offshorability: A Survey Approach." *Journal of Labor Economics* 31 (S1): S97–128.

Boudreau, Kevin, and Karim Lakhani. 2014. "Using the Crowd as an Innovation Partner." *Harvard Business Review.* https://hbr.org/2013/04/using-the-crowd-as -an-innovation-partner.

Clemens, Michael. 2011. "Economics and Emigration: Trillion-Dollar Bills on the Sidewalk?" *Journal of Economic Perspectives* 25 (3): 83–106.

Costinot, Arnaud, David Donaldson, and Ivana Komunjer. 2012. "What Goods Do Countries Trade? New Ricardian Predictions." *Review of Economic Studies* 79 (2): 581–608.

Cullen, Zoe, and Bobak Pakzad-Hurson. 2016. "Equal Pay for Equal Work? Evidence from the Renegotiations of Short-Term Work Contracts Online." Working Paper, Harvard Business School, Harvard University.

Eaton, Jonathan, and Samuel Kortum. 2002. "Technology, Geography, and Trade." *Econometrica* 70 (5): 1741–79.

Freeman, Richard. 2013. "One Ring to Rule Them All? Globalization of Knowledge and Knowledge Creation." NBER Working Paper no. 19301, Cambridge, MA.

Ghani, Ejaz, William Kerr, and Christopher Stanton. 2014. "Diasporas and Outsourcing: Evidence from oDesk and India." *Management Science* 60 (7): 1677–97.

Grossman, Gene, and Esteban Rossi-Hansberg. 2008. "Trading Tasks: A Simple Theory of Offshoring." *American Economic Review* 98 (5): 1978–97.

Helpman, Elhanan. 2014. "Foreign Trade and Investment: Firm-Level Perspectives." *Economica* 81:1–14.

Helpman, Elhanan, Marc Melitz, and Stephen Yeaple. 2004. "Export versus FDI with Heterogeneous Firms." *American Economic Review* 94:300–316.

Horton, John. 2016a. "Buyer Uncertainty about Seller Capacity: Causes, Consequences, and Partial Solution." Working Paper, Stern School of Business, New York University.

———. 2016b. "Price Floors and Employer Preferences: Evidence from a Minimum Wage Experiment." Working Paper, Stern School of Business, New York University.

———. 2017. "The Effects of Algorithmic Labor Market Recommendations: Evidence from a Field Experiment." *Journal of Labor Economics* 35 (2): 345–85.

Horton, John, and Ramesh Johari. 2016. "At What Quality and What Price? Eliciting Buyer Preferences as a Market Design Problem." Working Paper, New York University and Stanford University.

Horton, John, and Prasanna Tambe. 2015. "Labor Economists Get Their Microscope: Big Data and Labor Market Analysis." *Big Data* 3 (3): 130–37.

Huston, Larry, and Nabil Sakkab. 2006. "Connect and Develop: Inside Procter & Gamble's New Model for Innovation." *Harvard Business Review*. https://hbr.org/2006/03/connect-and-develop-inside-procter-gambles-new-model-for-innovation.

Kerr, Sari Pekkala, William Kerr, Çaglar Özden, and Christopher Parsons. 2016. "Global Talent Flows." *Journal of Economic Perspectives* 30 (4): 83–106.

———. 2017. "High-Skilled Migration and Agglomeration." Working Paper, Harvard Business School, Harvard University.

Kerr, William. 2007. "The Ethnic Composition of US Inventors." HBS Working Paper no. 08-006, Harvard Business School, Harvard University.

———. 2008. "Ethnic Scientific Communities and International Technology Diffusion." *Review of Economics and Statistics* 90 (3): 518–37.

———. 2016. "Heterogeneous Technology Diffusion and Ricardian Trade Patterns." Working Paper, Harvard University.

Kerr, William, and William Lincoln. 2010. "The Supply Side of Innovation: H-1B Visa Reforms and US Ethnic Invention." *Journal of Labor Economics* 28 (3): 473–508.

Lakhani, Karim, Hila Lifshitz-Assaf, and Michael Tushman. 2013. "Open Innovation and Organizational Boundaries: Task Decomposition, Knowledge Distribution and the Locus of Innovation." In *Handbook of Economic Organization: Integrating Economic and Organization Theory*, edited by Anna Grandori, 355–82. Northampton, MA: Edward Elgar Publishing.

Lazear, Edward, Kathryn Shaw, and Christopher Stanton. 2016. "Who Gets Hired? The Importance of Finding an Open Slot." NBER Working Paper no. 22202, Cambridge, MA.

Lyons, Elizabeth. 2016. "Team Production in International Labor Markets: Experimental Evidence from the Field." Working Paper, School of Global Policy and Strategy, University of California, San Diego.

Melitz, Jacques, and Farid Toubal. 2014. "Native Language, Spoken Language, Translation and Trade." *Journal of International Economics* 93 (2): 351–63.

Melitz, Marc. 2003. "The Impact of Trade on Intra-Industry Reallocations and Aggregate Industry Productivity." *Econometrica* 71:1695–725.

Mill, Roy. 2013. "Hiring and Learning in Online Global Labor Markets." NET Institute Working Paper no. 11-17. Available at SSRN: https://ssrn.com /abstract=1957962 or http://dx.doi.org/10.2139/ssrn.1957962.

Pallais, Amanda. 2014. "Inefficient Hiring in Entry-Level Labor Markets." *American Economic Review* 104 (11): 3565–99.

Ratha, Dilip, and William Shaw. 2007. "South-South Migration and Remittances." World Bank Working Paper no. 102.

Rauch, James, and Vitor Trindade. 2002. "Ethnic Chinese Networks in International Trade." *Review of Economics and Statistics* 84 (1): 116–30.

Santos Silva, J. M. C., and Silvana Tenreyro. 2006. "Log of Gravity." *Review of Economics and Statistics* 88 (4): 641–58.

Saxenian, AnnaLee. 2006. *The New Argonauts.* Cambridge, MA: Harvard University Press.

Saxenian, AnnaLee, with Yasuyuki Motoyama and Xiaohong Quan. 2002. *Local and Global Networks of Immigrant Professionals in Silicon Valley.* San Francisco: Public Policy Institute of California. https://pdfs.semanticscholar.org/5def /a4e27027360d03502c8928d3daaac4f01247.pdf.

Stanton, Christopher, and Catherine Thomas. 2016a. "Information Frictions and Observable Experience: The New Employer Price Premium in an Online Market." Working Paper, Harvard Business School. http://www.hbs.edu/faculty /Publication%20Files/InfoFrictExper_StantonThomas_Chicago_172205 _c68a4756-1c8e-4c3a-9f09-cd2428842e0d.pdf.

———. 2016b. "Landing the First Job: The Value of Intermediaries in Online Hiring." *Review of Economic Studies* 83 (2): 810–54.

Tervio, Marko. 2009. "Superstars and Mediocrities: Market Failure in the Discovery of Talent." *Review of Economic Studies* 76 (2): 829–50.

Xu, Guo. 2016. "How Does Collective Reputation Affect Hiring? Selection and Sorting in an Online Labour Market." Working Paper.

4

Understanding the Economic Impact of the H-1B Program on the United States

John Bound, Gaurav Khanna, and Nicolas Morales

An increasingly high proportion of the scientists and engineers in the United States were born abroad. At a very general level, the issues that come up in the discussion of high-skilled immigration mirror the discussion of low-skilled immigration. The most basic economic arguments suggest that both high-skilled and low-skilled immigrants (a) impart benefits to employers, to owners of other inputs used in production such as capital, and to consumers; and (b) potentially, impose some costs on workers who are close substitutes (Borjas 1999). Evidence suggests, however, that the magnitude of these costs may be substantially mitigated if US high-skilled workers have good alternatives to working in sectors most affected by immigrants (Peri, Shih, and Sparber 2013; Peri and Sparber 2011). Additionally, unlike low-skilled immigrants, high-skilled immigrants contribute to the generation of knowledge and productivity through patenting and innovation, both of which serve to shift out the production possibility frontier in the United States and may also slow the erosion of the US comparative advantage in high tech (Freeman 2006; Krugman 1979).

In this chapter, we study the impact that the recruitment of foreign com-

John Bound is professor of economics and research professor at the Population Studies Center at the University of Michigan and a research associate of the National Bureau of Economic Research. Gaurav Khanna is assistant professor of public policy economics at the University of California, San Diego, School of Global Policy and Strategy. Nicolas Morales is a PhD candidate in economics at the University of Michigan.

We would like to acknowledge the Alfred P. Sloan Foundation for generous research support. We thank Breno Braga, Gordon Hanson, Minjoon Lee, Rishi Sharma, Sebastian Sotelo, Sarah Turner, and seminar participants at the NBER Global Talent SI Conference, University of California, San Diego, University of California, Davis, and the University of Michigan for insightful comments and NE Barr for editorial assistance. For acknowledgments, sources of research support, and disclosure of the authors' material financial relationships, if any, please see http://www.nber.org/chapters/c13842.ack.

puter scientists on H-1B visas had on the US economy during the Internet boom of the 1990s. An H-1B is a nonimmigrant visa allowing US companies to temporarily employ foreign workers in specialized occupations. The number issued annually is capped by the federal government. During the 1990s, we observe a substantial increase in the number of H-1B visas awarded to high-skilled workers, with those in computer-related occupations becoming the largest share of all H-1B visa holders (US General Accounting Office 2000). Given these circumstances, it is of considerable interest to investigate how the influx of H-1B visa holders during this period might have affected labor market outcomes for US computer scientists and other US workers, and overall productivity in the economy.

We focus on the period 1994 to 2001 for a number of reasons. During the latter half of the 1990s, the US economy experienced a productivity growth attributable, at least in part, to the information technology (IT) boom, facilitated by the influx of foreign talent (Jorgenson, Ho, and Samuels 2016). At the same time, the recruitment of H-1B labor by US firms was at or close to the H-1B cap during this period, enabling us to treat foreign supply as determined by the cap. Finally, more recent growth of the IT sector in India and changes in the law authorizing the H-1B have complicated the picture since 2001.[1] Nonetheless, in the appendix we show that our model does a reasonable job of predicting employment and wages all the way until 2015.

In earlier work evaluating the impact of immigration on computer science (CS) domestic workers, we constructed a dynamic model that characterizes the labor supply and demand for CS workers during this period (Bound et al. 2015). We built into the model the possibility that labor demand shocks, such as the one created by the Internet boom, could be accommodated by three sources of CS workers: recent college graduates with CS degrees, US residents in different occupations who switch to CS jobs, and high-skilled foreigners. Furthermore, our model assumed firms faced a trade-off when deciding to employ immigrants: foreigners were potentially either more productive or less costly than US workers, but incurred extra recruitment/ hiring costs.

The approach we took in that analysis was distinctly partial equilibrium in nature—that is, we focused on the market for computer scientists and ignored any wider impacts that high-skilled immigration might have on the US economy (Nathan 2013). While we believe that approach could be used to understand the impact that the availability of high-skilled foreign labor might have had for this market, it precludes any analysis of the overall welfare impact of the H-1B program in particular, or of high-skilled immigration more generally.

The implications of the model regarding the impact of immigration on the employment and wages of native workers depended on the elasticity of

---

1. See Khanna and Morales (2015) for a long-run extension of this work that also models the Indian IT sector.

labor demand for computer scientists. As long as the demand curve sloped downward, the increased availability of foreign computer scientists would put downward pressure on the wages for computer scientists in the United States. However, in the case of computer scientists, other factors may affect this relationship. First, even in a closed economy, the contribution of computer scientists to innovation reduces the negative effects foreign computer scientists might have on the labor market opportunities for native high-skilled workers. In addition, in an increasingly global world, US restrictions on the hiring of foreign high-skilled workers are likely to result in greater foreign outsourcing work by US employers. Indeed, if computer scientists are a sufficient spur to innovation, or if domestic employers can readily offshore CS work, any negative effects that an increase in the number of foreign CS workers might have on the domestic high-skilled workforce would be offset by increases in the domestic demand for computer scientists.

In Bound et al. (2015), we used data on wages, domestic and foreign employment, and undergraduate degree completions by major during the late 1990s and early in the twenty-first century to calibrate the parameters of our model to reproduce the stylized facts of the CS market during the analytic period (1994 to 2001). Next, we used the calibrated model to simulate counterfactuals on how the economy would have behaved if firms had been restricted in the number of foreign CS workers they could hire to the 1994 level. Conditional on our assumptions about the elasticity of the demand curve for computer scientists, our simulation suggests that had US firms faced this restriction, CS wages and the number of Americans working in computer science and the enrollment levels in US CS programs would have been higher, but the total number of CS workers in the US would have been lower.

The predictions of our model did not depend on the specific choice we made for noncalibrated parameters, with one important exception: crowd-out in the market for computer scientists depended crucially on the elasticity of demand for their services. Ideally, we would have been able to use exogenous supply shifts to identify the slope of the demand curve for computer scientists, as we use exogenous shifts in demand to identify supply curves. In other contexts, researchers have treated the increase in foreign-born workers in the US economy as exogenous. However, in the current context, immigration law in the United States implies that most of the foreign-born and trained individuals who migrate to the United States to work as computer scientists do so because they are sponsored by US-based firms. Thus, it seems implausible to treat the number of foreign-born computer scientists in the United States as an exogenous increase in supply. In the end, without credible sources of identifying information, we resorted to parametrically varying the elasticity of the demand for computer scientists.

In the current analysis, we take a different track. We interpret the arguments about the potential productivity effects of high-skilled immigrants in terms of models of endogenous technical change. Within the context of a simple general-equilibrium model of the US economy, we link productivity increases in the US economy during the 1990s to increases in the utilization of computer scientists in the economy. This allows us to derive the demand curve for computer scientists.

Within the context of our model, it is possible to understand the effect that the availability of high-skilled foreign workers has on the earnings of both high- and low-skilled workers, the goods available in the economy, and profits in the high-tech sector of the economy. However, our conclusions are dependent both on our modeling choices and on values of our calibrated parameters. For this reason, we do extensive sensitivity analyses to determine which of our conclusions are robust.

A key feature of high-skilled immigrants is that they contribute to innovation. While this point is well understood, we know of no earlier work that has tried to quantify the magnitude of this effect within the context of an explicit model of the US economy. The magnitude of this effect is important because it speaks to the magnitude of any first-order gains to US residents of high-skilled immigration, and because it has a direct influence on the slope of the labor demand curve for close substitutes for high-skilled immigrants.

Our model is limited in a number of important respects. While we allow for endogenous technical change, we incorporate trade in a very stylized manner and do not allow explicitly for outsourcing.[2] As such, we think our model captures relatively short-run effects of H-1B immigration. Although in this sense our model is different from models incorporated in recent work by, for example, Grossman and Rossi-Hansberg (2008) or di Giovanni, Levchenko, and Ortega (2015), we believe that it captures important elements of the current debate about the H-1B program.

We review this literature in detail and describe the market for CS workers in section 4.1. Section 4.2 presents the model we build to characterize the market for CS workers when firms can recruit foreigners. In section 4.3, we describe how we calibrate the parameters of the model and in section 4.4 we run counterfactual simulations where firms have restrictions on the number of foreigners they can hire. Section 4.5 talks about welfare changes under this counterfactual scenario. We conclude with section 4.6, which presents a discussion based on the results of the analysis.

4.1   The Market for Computer Scientists in the 1990s

4.1.1   The Information Technology Boom of the Late 1990s

The mid-1990s marks the beginning of the use of the Internet for commercial purposes in the United States, and a concomitant jump in the

---

2. Available evidence suggests that outsourcing options were somewhat limited during the 1990s (Liu and Trefler 2008), though it is not clear that this is still true.

Table 4.1   **Immigration and the computer science workforce**

Year	1970 (%)	1980 (%)	1990 (%)	2000 (%)	2010 (%)
Computer scientists as a fraction of workers with a BA/MA	1.68	1.83	3.30	5.66	5.28
Computer scientists as a fraction of STEM college graduates	16.86	23.60	35.99	53.31	54.90
Immigrants as a fraction of BA/MAs	2.10	5.43	6.86	8.41	12.77
Immigrants as a fraction of computer scientists	2.37	7.09	11.06	18.59	27.82
Immigrants as a fraction of other STEM workers	3.63	9.72	10.71	12.69	18.21

Source: US Census (years 1970 to 2000); ACS (2010).

Note: Sample restricted to employed workers with a bachelor's or a master's degree. Definition of computer scientists and STEM workers determined by occupational coding (for details, see the "Details of the Data Used" section of the appendix). Immigrant defined as one born abroad and migrated to the United States after the age of eighteen.

number of Internet users. One indicator of a contemporaneous increase in demand for IT workers is the rise of research and development (R&D) expenditures among firms providing computer programming services and computer-related equipment. Specifically, the share of total private R&D expenditures for firms in these sectors increased from 19.5 percent to 22.1 percent between 1991 and 1998.[3] The entry and then extraordinary appreciation of tech firms like Yahoo!, Amazon, and eBay provide a further testament to the boom in the IT sector prior to 2001.

These changes had a dramatic effect on the labor market for computer scientists. According to the census, the number of employed individuals working either as computer scientists or computer software developers increased by 161 percent between the years 1990 and 2000. In comparison, during the same period, the number of employed workers with at least a bachelor's degree increased by 27 percent and the number of workers in other science, technology, engineering, and math (STEM) occupations increased by 14 percent.[4] Table 4.1 shows that computer scientists as a share of the college-educated workforce and the college-educated STEM workforce was rising before 1990, but increased dramatically during the 1990s. Indeed, by 2000 more than half of all STEM workers were computer scientists. In figure 4.1, panel A, we use Current Population Survey (CPS) data to show a similar pattern, additionally showing that the growth of CS employment started in the second half of the decade—a period corresponding to the dissemination of the Internet.

The Internet innovation affected educational choices as well as employment decisions. We show in figure 4.1, panel B, that the CS share of both all

3. Bound et al. (2015) calculation using Compustat data.
4. Here and elsewhere, our tabulations restrict the analysis to workers with at least a bachelor's degree and use the IPUMS-suggested occupational cross walk. Other STEM occupations are defined as engineers, mathematicians, and computer scientists. For more details see the "Details of the Data Used" section of the appendix.

A. Fraction of Computer Scientists in US Workforce

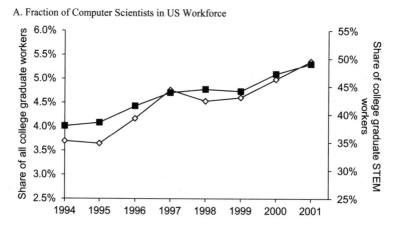

—◇—Share of all college graduates —■—Share of college graduate STEM workers

B. Computer Science Fraction of Bachelor Degrees

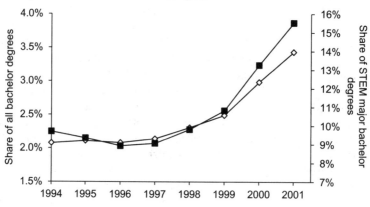

—◇—Share of all bachelor degrees —■—Share of STEM major bachelor degrees

Fig. 4.1   High-skilled immigration and the IT boom
Source: Panels A, C, and D, March Current Population Survey. Panel B, Integrated Postsecondary Education Data System (IPEDS). Panel E, author's calculations updating Lowell (2000).

bachelor's degrees and STEM major degrees increased dramatically during this period, in both cases rising from about 2 percent of all bachelor's degrees granted in 1994 to almost 3.5 percent in 2001.

The behavioral response would be different if the boom was only a temporary response to the Y2K bug. The employment and educational evidence, however, suggests that many expected this boom, as a response to technological innovations, to be permanent. Indeed, in 1997, the Bureau of Labor Statistics (BLS) projected a steady increase in CS employment after the turn of the century. More specifically, the BLS predicted that between

C. Earnings of Computer Scientists Relative to Other groups

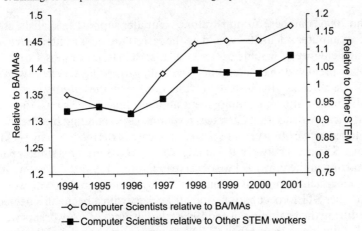

○— Computer Scientists relative to BA/MAs
■— Computer Scientists relative to Other STEM workers

D. Immigrants as Fraction of Workers by Occupation

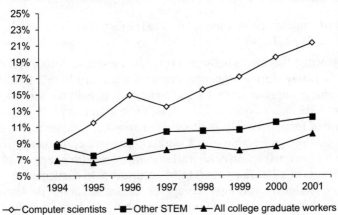

—◇— Computer scientists —■— Other STEM —▲— All college graduate workers

E. H-1 Visas

—△— H-1 Visas Granted —■— Estimated H-1 Population —●— H-1B Visa Cap

Fig. 4.1 (cont.)

1996 and 2006 "database administrators, computer support specialists, and all other computer scientists" would be the fastest growing occupation and "computer engineers" would be the second fastest in terms of jobs. Furthermore, they predicted that "computer and data processing services" would grow by 108 percent—the fastest growing industry in the country.[5]

In addition to affecting employment and enrollment decisions, there is also empirical evidence that CS wages responded to expanding Internet use. From the census we observe an 18 percent increase in the median real weekly wages of CS workers between 1990 and 2000. The CPS presents similar patterns: starting in the year 1994 we observe in figure 4.1, panel C, that wages of computer scientists increased considerably when compared to both workers with other STEM occupations and all workers with a bachelor's degree. In fact, during the beginning of the 1990s, the earnings of CS workers were systematically lower than other STEM occupations; the wage differential tends to disappear after 1998.

4.1.2   The Contribution of Immigration to the Growth of the High-Tech Workforce

Employment adjustments in the market for computer scientists occurred disproportionately among foreigners during the Internet boom. Evidence for this claim is found in table 4.1 and figure 4.1, panel D, where we use census and CPS data to compare the share of foreign computer scientists to the share of foreign workers in other occupations.[6] In the second half of the 1990s, the foreign fraction of CS workers increased considerably more than both the foreign fraction of all workers with a bachelor's degree and the foreign fraction of all workers in a STEM occupation. In particular, in 1994 the share of foreigners working in computer science was about the same as the share working in other STEM occupations, but later in the decade, during the boom in Internet use, the share of foreigners among all CS workers rose steeply, comprising about 30 percent of the increase in all CS workers during this period.

The growth in the representation of the foreigners among the US CS workforce was fueled by two supply-side developments in this period. First, the foreign pool of men and women with college educations in science and engineering fields increased dramatically (Freeman 2009). In India, an important source of CS workers in the United States, the number of first degrees conferred in science and engineering rose from 176,000 in 1990 to 455,000 in 2000. Second, the Immigration Act of 1990 established the H-1B visa program for temporary workers with at least a bachelor's degree work-

---

5. Source: BLS Employment Projections http://www.bls.gov/news.release/history/ecopro _082498.txt.

6. Here and elsewhere, we define foreigners as those who immigrated to the United States after the age of eighteen. We believe that this definition is a reasonable proxy for workers who arrived in the United States on nonimmigrant visas.

ing in "specialty occupations" including engineering, mathematics, physical sciences, and business among others.

Firms wanting to hire foreigners on H-1B visas must first file a Labor Condition Application (LCA) in which they attest that the firm will pay the visa holder the greater of the actual compensation paid to other employees in the same job or the prevailing compensation for that occupation, and the firm will provide working conditions for the visa holder that do not adversely affect the working conditions of the other employees. At that point, prospective H-1B nonimmigrants must demonstrate to the US Citizenship and Immigration Services Bureau (USCIS) in the Department of Homeland Security (DHS) that they have the requisite education and work experience for the posted positions. The USCIS may approve the petition for the H-1B holder for a period of up to three years, with the possibility of a three-year extension. Thus foreign workers can stay a maximum of six years on an H-1B visa, though firms can sponsor these workers for a permanent resident visa. Because H-1B visas are approved solely for the applying firm, H-1B foreign workers are effectively tied to their sponsoring company.

Since 1990, when the visa was initiated, the number of H-1B visas issued annually has been capped. The initial cap of 65,000 visas per year was not reached until the mid-1990s, when demand began to exceed the cap. However, the allocation tended to fill each year on a first-come, first-served basis, resulting in frequent denials or delays on H-1Bs because the annual cap had been reached. After lobbying by the industry, Congress raised the cap first to 115,000 for FY1999 and then to 195,000 for FY2000–2003, after which the cap reverted to 65,000. Figure 4.1, panel E, shows the growth in the number of H-1 visas (the H-1 was the precursor to the H-1B) issued 1976–2008, estimates of the stock of H-1 visas in the economy each year, and the changes in the H-1B visa cap.[7]

Through the decade of the 1990s, foreign workers with H-1B visas became an important source of labor for the technology sector. The National Survey of College Graduates shows that 55 percent of foreigners working in CS fields in 2003 arrived in the United States on an H-1B or a student-type visa (F-1, J-1). Furthermore, institutional information indicates a significant increase in the number of visas awarded to workers in computer-related occupations during the 1990s. A 1992 US General Accounting Office report shows that "computers, programming, and related occupations" corresponded to 11 percent of the total number of H-1 visas in 1989, while a

---

7. The Immigration and Nationality Act of 1952 established the precursor to the H-1B visa, the H-1. The H-1 nonimmigrant visa was targeted at aliens of "distinguished merit and ability" who were filling positions that were temporary. Nonimmigrants on H-1 visas had to maintain a foreign residence. The Immigration Act of 1990 established the main features of H-1B visa as it is known today, replacing "distinguished merit and ability" with the "specialty occupation" definition. It also dropped the foreign residence requirement and added a dual-intent provision, allowing workers to potentially transfer from an H-1B visa to immigrant status.

report from the US Immigration and Naturalization Service (2000) finds that computer-related occupations accounted for close to two-thirds of the H-1B visas awarded in 1999. More specifically, the US Department of Commerce (2000) estimated that during the late 1990s, 28 percent of all US programmer jobs went to H-1B visa holders.

While H-1B visa holders represent an important source of computer scientists, they do not represent all foreigners in the country working as computer scientists. A significant number of such foreigners are permanent immigrants, some of whom may have come either as children or as students. Other foreigners enter the country to work as computer scientists in the United States on L-1B visas, which permit companies with offices both in the United States and overseas to move skilled employees from overseas to the United States. While we know of no data showing the fraction of computer scientists working in the United States on L-1B visas, substantially fewer L-1(A&B) visas are issued than are H-1Bs.[8]

4.1.3   The Impact of Immigrants on the High-Tech Workforce in the United States

Critics of the H-1B program (Matloff 2003) argue that firms are using cheap foreign labor to undercut and replace skilled US workers, although even the fiercest critics do not claim that employers are technically evading the law (Kirkegaard 2005). Rather, they argue that firms skirt the requirement to pay H-1B visa holders prevailing wages by hiring overqualified foreigners into positions with low stated qualifications and concomitant low "prevailing wages." These critics claim that the excess supply of highly qualified foreigners willing to take the jobs in the United States, plus the lack of portability of the H-1B visa, limits the capacity of H-1B workers to negotiate fair market wages.

One way to get a handle on the extent to which H-1B visa holders are being underpaid relative to their US counterparts is to compare foreigners on H-1B visas to those with green cards—an immigrant authorization allowing the holder to live and work in the United States permanently, with no restrictions on occupation. Using difference-in-difference propensity score matching and data from the 2003 New Immigrant Survey, Mukhopadhyay and Oxborrow (2012) find that green card holders earn 25.4 percent more than observably comparable temporary foreign workers. Using log earnings regressions and data from an Internet survey, Mithas and Lucas (2010) find that IT professionals with green cards earn roughly 5 percent more than observationally equivalent H-1B visa holders. Comparisons between green card and H-1B holders are far from perfect. Since many green card holders begin as H-1B visa holders who are eventually sponsored by their employers for permanent residence status, it is reason-

---

8. See Yeaple (chapter 2, this volume) for a discussion on L-1 and H-1B visas.

able to assume that green card holders are positively selected on job skills. Given this consideration, it is somewhat surprising that the observed green card premium is not larger than this 5 percent.

Perhaps the most compelling work concerning productivity differences between H-1B visa holders and their US resident counterparts comes from a recent paper by Doran, Gelber, and Isen (2015), who analyze H-1B lotteries used in FY2006 and FY2007 to identify the productivity effects on firms of hiring an additional H-1B worker. During these two years, firms that submitted an LCA during the day the H-1B quota was hit would enter a lottery to determine whether they were permitted to hire the additional H-1B worker. Doran, Gelber, and Isen (2015) find that winning the lottery had no effect on subsequent patenting or employment in the affected firm, consistent with the notion that a firm unable to hire a H-1B worker would end up hiring an alternative, equally productive worker.[9]

While there may be no incontrovertible estimate of the productivity (conditional on earnings) advantage of foreign high-skilled labor, simple economic reasons suggest this advantage must exist. US employers face both pecuniary and nonpecuniary costs associated with hiring foreigners. A small GAO survey (US General Accounting Office 2011) estimated the legal and administrative costs associated with each H-1B hire to range from $2,300 to $7,500. Assuming that these workers earn $60,000 per year in total compensation, which would seem to be conservative, this amounts to no more than 2 percent of compensation spread over six years. It seems reasonable to assume that employers must expect some cost or productivity advantage when hiring foreigners, however modest. If not, why would they incur the associated effort and expense?

Whatever the perceived cost or productivity advantages, H-1B critics argue that US employers' use of foreign labor in high-skill jobs either "crowds out" native workers from these jobs or puts downward pressure on their wages. Although, as far as we know, critics of the H-1B program have not yet estimated the magnitude of either of these effects, recent work by economists has started to fill this void. Kerr and Lincoln (2010) and Hunt and Gauthier-Loiselle (2010) provide original empirical evidence on the link between variation in immigrant flows and innovation measured by patenting, finding evidence that the net impact of immigration is positive rather than simply substituting for native employment. Kerr and Lincoln (2010) also show that variation in immigrant flows at the local level related to changes in H-1B flows do not appear to adversely affect native employment and have a small, statistically insignificant, effect on their wages. More recently, Peri, Shih, and Sparber (2014) found positive effects of high-skilled

9. Doran, Gelber, and Isen (2015) point estimates suggest that replacing a US resident with a H-1B holder might raise patenting at small firms by 0.26 percent (95 percent CI −0.42 0.47 percent), implying that the H-1Bs visa holders are no more than 4.7 percent more productive than are US resident workers.

immigrant workers on the employment and wages of college-educated domestic workers.

A potential issue with the analyses of Kerr and Lincoln (2010) and Peri, Shih, and Sparber (2014) is that the observed, reduced-form outcomes may capture concurrent changes in area-specific demand for computer scientists. To circumvent the problem, each paper constructed a variable that is the total number of individuals working on H-1B visas nationally interacted with local-area dependency.[10] However, given the nature of the H-1B visa, the location of immigrants depends, in large part, on the location of employers hiring them. If, because of local agglomeration effects, the IT boom was concentrated in areas of the country that were already IT intensive (such as Silicon Valley), then the measure of local dependency would be endogenous, an issue that Kerr and Lincoln (2010) and Peri, Shih, and Sparber (2014) understand.

Ghosh, Mayda, and Ortega (2014) take a different approach. They match all LCAs with firm-level data on publicly traded US companies, comparing changes in labor productivity, firm size, and profits between 2001 and 2006 for firms that were highly dependent on H-1B labor with firms that were not. They argue that the H-1B-dependent firms would feel more effects than their counterparts from the dramatic drop in the H-1B cap from 195,000 to 65,000 in 2004. And, indeed, they find that, over this period, labor productivity, firm size, and profits all declined more for the H-1B-dependent firms, which they attribute to the loss of the H-1B labor. The concern here is that the firms more dependent in H-1B labor in 2001 would have been systematically different from those less dependent in ways correlated with the change in performance between 2001 and 2006.

In another paper, Peri, Shih, and Sparber (2015) use data on the number of LCAs filed by firms in local (metro) areas during 2007 and 2008 as a measure of potential demand for H-1B workers, and the number of H-1B applications filed by foreigners as their measure of H-1Bs hired. In 2007 and 2008, the number of H-1B applications exceeded the annual quotas, and lotteries were used in awarding visas. The large gap between these two measures represents the unmet demand for skilled foreign workers. Cross-metro-area variation in this variable is due to at least two sources: (a) cross-metro-area demand for foreign high-skilled labor, and (b) truly random fluctuations in the fraction of LCAs picked in the lotteries. While this second source of variation should be truly random, Peri, Shih, and Sparber (2015) find

10. Kerr and Lincoln (2010) and Peri, Shih, and Sparber (2014) hope that the variation in this variable is driven largely by changes in the cap on new H-1B visas that occurred over the last twenty years. That said, it is unclear to which the extent the variation they use is being driven by variation in the visa cap. Because of the dot-com bubble bust in 2000 and 2001, the variation in the H-1B cap is only loosely related to the actual number of H-1Bs issued. What is more, the cap will have different effects across areas, and one can worry about the exogeneity of this variation. In addition, it is hard to imagine that the cap was exogenous to the demand for IT workers.

too little of such variation to reliably identify the net effects of high-skilled labor immigration.

Previous researchers studying the impact of H-1B workers on the US economy have focused on identifying exogenous variation in the number of H-1B workers, typically finding that H-1B workers tend to raise productivity and act as complements to, rather than crowding out, college-educated native workers. However, as these researchers have acknowledged, it is easy to question the validity of the instruments used in these analyses. Rather than using a natural experiment to identify effects, we derive effects from a calibrated model. The model allows us to connect endogenous productivity advances in the IT sector during the 1990s to changes in the demand for CS labor. While the validity of the conclusions that Kerr and Lincoln (2010), Peri, Shih, and Sparber (2014, 2015), and Ghosh, Mayda, and Ortega (2014) depend on the validity of the natural experiments they use to identify effects, our conclusions depend on our model accurately reflecting key features of the US economy. As such, the credibility of our results hinges on the plausibility of our assumptions and/or the robustness of our conclusions to variations in the specific modeling choices we made.

4.2   A Model of the Product and Labor Markets

Our model consists of two major sections. The first is the product market where goods are produced by firms and sold to consumers. The second is the labor market for college graduates, where US workers decide whether to work as computer scientists or in other occupations. Our product market has two sectors: the IT sector and the "other" sector. The IT sector is monopolistically competitive, wherein firms produce different varieties of the same IT good. Firms in the IT sector are heterogeneous in terms of their level of productivity, which is exogenously drawn. Importantly, we include the possibility of endogenous technological change, whereby CS workers' innovation causes the production function to be increasing returns to scale at the aggregate level. All other goods in the economy are produced in the residual "other" sector, which is a perfectly competitive sector with homogeneous firms.

Every period a firm chooses its inputs to maximize profits. Since firms in the IT sector are monopolistically competitive, they have some market power when making these choices. Firms use intermediate inputs from the other sector and labor to produce their output. The labor inputs consist of three types of workers: computer scientists, college-educated non–computer scientists, and non-college-educated workers. In our model, all foreign immigrants are hired as computer scientists. The IT-sector firms are also able to export their products to foreign markets, whereas the US economy imports only non-IT goods. Consumers, on the other hand, choose how much of each good to consume in order to maximize their utility subject to their labor income. Like firms, they make these choices every period, and have no savings.

Building on this setup, we include the labor supply decisions of college graduates. Since human capital investments and career choices have long-term payoffs, US workers in our model are allowed to choose their fields of study and occupations based on the information they have today and their expected payoffs in the future. They are then allowed to switch occupations, by paying a switching cost, when a change occurs in the current or expected payoffs associated with any occupation. Given the labor supply decisions of US workers, the labor supply of immigrants, and the labor demand from firms in each sector, the market clears to determine the equilibrium wages for each type of worker. Equilibrium prices are determined in the product market, where the demand for the two types of goods from consumers meets the supply of these goods from firms.

4.2.1   Product Market

Household Problem

There are X number of consumers in the economy who supply one unit of labor each. Each consumer has the same preferences over the two goods: C_d produced by the IT sector and Y_d, the good produced by the residual sector in the economy. We assume that preferences can be represented by the constant elasticity of substitution (CES) utility function in equation (1).

$$(1) \qquad U(C_d, Y_d) = \left[\gamma C_d^{(\sigma-1)/\sigma} + (1-\gamma) Y_d^{(\sigma-1)/\sigma} \right]^{\sigma/(\sigma-1)}.$$

Y_d is assumed to be homogeneous, whereas the IT good C_d is composed of a continuum of varieties (indexed by v) in the framework introduced by Dixit and Stiglitz (1977):[11]

$$(2) \qquad C_d = \left(\int_{v \in \Omega} c_{di}^{(\varepsilon-1)/\varepsilon} \, dv \right)^{\varepsilon/(\varepsilon-1)},$$

where Ω is the set of varieties and ε is the elasticity of substitution between the varieties of IT goods. In our analysis, we set the consumption bundle to be the numeraire.[12] In appendix section "Consumer Demand for Goods," we solve for the demand for each good.

Consumers are also workers, and while they have identical consumption preferences, they do not all receive the same labor income as they work in different occupations earning different wages. Furthermore, workers can either be native workers (denoted by a subscript n) or foreign workers (denoted by a subscript F)

---

11. This setting with one composite and one homogeneous good follows recent papers such as Melitz and Ottaviano (2008), Demidova (2008), and Pfluger and Russek (2013).

12. This means that the ideal price index is normalized to 1: $\{\gamma + (1-\gamma)[(P_c/P_Y)[\gamma/(1-\gamma)]^\sigma]\}^{\sigma/(\sigma-1)}/\{P_c + P_Y[(P_c/P_Y)[\gamma/(1-\gamma)]^\sigma]\} = 1$.

We outline the details of the labor supply decisions in section 4.2.3, where we discuss how workers choose their field of college majors and occupations over time. The decision of whether to attend college or not is made outside this model. This means that the supply of non–college graduates $\bar{H}$ is exogenous, and so is the total supply of native college graduates $(\overline{L_n + G})$. Those who do get a college degree can choose whether to work as a computer scientists L_n, or in some other occupation that requires a college degree G.

High-skilled immigrants who come in on H-1B visas can do so only if they meet the skill requirements of the visa and only if firms recruit them. As we have mentioned before, during the 1990s immigrants coming in as H-1Bs were increasingly being recruited as computer scientists. For simplicity, we will assume that all recruited H-1Bs are computer scientists L_F.

The size of the labor force in the economy is $X = \bar{H} + \overline{L_n + G} + L_F$ and total income m can be written as the sum of the labor income for the different types of workers plus profits earned by firms in the IT sector (Π) as in equation (3):

$$(3) \qquad m = w(L_n + L_F) + sG + r\bar{H} + \Pi,$$

where w is the wage paid to computer scientists, s the wage earned by non-CS college graduates, and r is the wage paid to non–college graduates.

We assume that foreign computer scientists are willing to come and work in the United States at any available wage and are marginally more productive than native computer scientists. Each year the number of immigrants in the economy is capped at a given level $\bar{L}_F$ and because of this small productivity premium the cap always gets exhausted. Native computer scientists face a residual demand curve after all available foreigners have been hired.

One way to think about this assumption in our model is that any extra productivity is almost entirely offset by the recruitment costs of hiring foreigners. Also, due to H-1B restrictions, immigrants get paid the same wage as native computer scientists. In what remains of subsection 4.2.1 we will refer to foreign and native computer scientists as a single group, since from a firm's point of view they are indifferent between hiring the two at the going wage.[13]

Production in the IT Sector

The IT sector produces an aggregate IT good C. There are N monopolistically competitive heterogeneous firms that produce a different variety of this good as shown in equation (2). Following the framework introduced by Hopenhayn (1992) and Melitz (2003), each of these firms will have a different level of productivity. We assume each firm j has a Cobb-Douglas technology in the labor aggregate and intermediate inputs from the other sector as in equation (4):

---

13. In the data, we see that H-1Bs are almost entirely hired by larger firms. While this is an interesting and suggestive feature of the data, we leave it for future researchers to explore.

(4)
$$c_j = \phi_j L_c^\beta y_{cj}^{\psi_1} x_{cj}^{1-\psi_1},$$

where y_{cj} is the amount of intermediate goods from sector Y and x_{cj} is the labor aggregate. Firm technology, $A(\ell_j) = \phi_j L_c^\beta$, has an endogenous component L_c^β and an exogenous component ϕ_j, which is a productivity draw that varies across firms. The term L_c^β captures a technological spillover in the IT sector that depends on the total number of computer scientists employed. Since computer scientists are innovators, we assume that their innovations create spillovers that increase the productivity of all firms in the sector, and this is captured by the β term.

The firm employs all three types of labor available in the economy. We assume that production technology has a nested CES structure.

(5)
$$x_j = \left[\alpha^c h_j^{(\tau-1)/\tau} + \left(1 - \alpha^c\right) q_j^{(\tau-1)/\tau} \right]^{\tau/(\tau-1)},$$

where h_j is the number of non–college graduates and q_j is the labor aggregate for college graduates. Here τ is the elasticity of substitution between college graduates and non–college graduates. Due to the nested nature of the CES function, we know that q_j is

(6)
$$q_j = \left[(\delta + \Delta) \ell_j^{(\lambda-1)/\lambda} + (1 - \delta - \Delta) g_j^{(\lambda-1)/\lambda} \right]^{\lambda/(\lambda-1)},$$

where ℓ_j is the number of CS workers and g_j the non-CS college graduates employed by firm j. Here λ is the elasticity of substitution between the CS workers and non-CS college graduates.

In equation (4) it is clear that the IT-sector firms have two drivers of technological change. The exogenous component of technology ϕ_j, has been modeled similar to the setup in the trade and the industrial organization literature (Chaney 2008; Hopenhayn 1992; Melitz 2003). The endogenous component of technology, captured by β, depends on the total number of computer scientists hired by the IT sector. These computer scientists innovate and create new technologies, increasing overall firm productivity. Here, we modify the setup used in the literature on economic growth (Acemoglu 1998; Arrow 1962; Grossman and Helpman 1991; Romer 1990).[14]

In the IT sector, the number of potential entrepreneurs is assumed to be fixed and their productivities have a known distribution $\Psi(\phi_j)$ with a positive support over $(0, \infty)$ and an associated density function $\psi(\phi)$. There is a productivity cutoff $\phi = \phi^*$ that captures the productivity level of the firm that breaks even. Therefore, the marginal producing firm earns no profits $(\pi(\phi^*) = 0)$. Since profits are an increasing function of the productivity level, the equilibrium ϕ^* determines which firms produce $(\phi_j > \phi^*)$ and which

---

14. Since we do not model economic growth, there are some clear departures from this literature. While many papers assume that the *rate of change* of technology depends on the quantity of a type of labor, we assume the *level* of technology depends on labor. Furthermore, a lot of this literature models a separate R&D sector that sells patents for these technologies—whereas in our model technology is assumed to be nonexcludable.

ones do not ($\phi_j < \phi^*$). The conditional distribution of $\psi(\phi)$ on $[\phi^*,\infty)$ can therefore be written as

$$\mu(\phi) = \begin{cases} \dfrac{\psi(\phi)}{1 - \Psi\left(\phi^*\right)}, & \text{if } \phi \geq \phi^* \\ \\ 0, & \text{otherwise} \end{cases}.$$

The productivity distribution $\Psi(\phi_j)$ of entrepreneurs is assumed to be a Pareto distribution, with parameters k and ϕ_{min} such that $\Psi(\phi_j) = 1 - (\phi_{min}/\phi_j)^k$.

The intuition behind this modeling choice is that whenever economic conditions change, the firms that get pushed into/out of production are the marginal firms (those with ϕ_j closer to ϕ^*), while the larger more productive firms produce regardless. We expect such behavior in the IT sector when we allow more immigrants into the economy. As immigration allows firms to pay lower wages, the marginal firms are the ones that enter into production and large firms capture most of the increase in profits. For a given mass of potential producers, N_e, the total number of firms that produce can be written as in equation (7):[15]

$$(7) \qquad\qquad N = \left(1 - \Psi(\phi^*)\right) N_e.$$

Such a model follows an approach to market entry closer to Chaney (2008) rather than the original Melitz (2003) model where the potential pool of entrants is not fixed.[16]

The firm's problem therefore boils down to maximizing profits by choosing the amount of labor inputs. If they choose to produce, they pay an upfront fixed cost of production f, which is in terms of the cost of the non-IT good P_Y (equation [8]). Each firm is a monopolist for their own variety and faces a demand curve as in equation (A.2).

$$(8) \qquad \max_{\ell_j, g_j, h_j, y_{cj}} \pi_j = \phi_j P_c C^{1/\varepsilon} c_j^{(\varepsilon-1)/\varepsilon} - w\ell_j - sg_j - rh_j - P_Y y_{cj} - P_Y f.$$

The first-order conditions from this exercise determine the labor demand from the IT sector for each type of labor. Total labor hired by this sector is denoted by the subscript c, and aggregate employment of each type of worker can be expressed as L_c, G_c, and H_c.

15. While our model of firm entry does not have dynamic implications, Waugh (chapter 6, this volume) provides a more extensive treatment of the potential effects of skilled immigration on firm entry and exit dynamics.

16. In the original Melitz setting there are a number of potential entrants who have to pay an additional fixed cost f_e to get a productivity draw, and once they know their productivity they produce if $\phi_j > \phi^*$. New entrants in this model can be both high and low productivity and end up driving expected net profits to zero. Di Giovanni, Levchenko, and Ortega (2015) think of the case with a fixed pool of potential producers as the short run, where the number of varieties available only changes through the entry and exit of marginal firms, having small effects on aggregate welfare.

Production in the Non-IT Sector

The non-IT sector produces good Y and is assumed to be perfectly competitive. We assume the representative firm in this sector has a Cobb-Douglas constant returns-to-scale technology over intermediate inputs from the other sector and the labor aggregate.

$$(9) \qquad\qquad Y = C_y^{\psi_2} X_y^{1-\psi_2},$$

where again C_y represents intermediate inputs from the IT sector and X_y the labor aggregate. This sector also employs the three types of labor denoted by subscript Y. Therefore, X_y can be written as

$$(10) \qquad\qquad X_y = \left[\alpha^y H_y^{(\tau-1)/\tau} + \left(1 - \alpha^y\right) Q_y^{(\tau-1)/\tau} \right]^{\tau/(\tau-1)}.$$

Again, by the nested CES assumption, Q_y can be represented by

$$(11) \qquad\qquad Q_y = \left[\delta L_y^{(\lambda-1)/\lambda} + (1-\delta) G_y^{(\lambda-1)/\lambda} \right]^{\lambda/(\lambda-1)}.$$

This sector is less intensive in computer scientists than the IT sector. To capture this, we model the intensity of CS workers to be higher in the IT sector (the incremental share is captured by Δ in equation [6]), and allow the computer scientists in the IT sector to have an additional impact on the technology in the firm (captured by β). Both sectors have the same elasticity of substitution between college and non–college graduates (τ) and between computer scientists and non-CS college graduates (λ).

The representative firm in the non-IT sector has to therefore solve the following maximization problem:

$$(12) \qquad\qquad \max_{L_y, G_y, H_y, C_y} \Pi_y = P_y C_y^{\psi_2} X_y^{1-\psi_2} - w L_y - s G_y - r H_y - P_c C_y.$$

The first-order conditions determine the demand for the intermediate inputs and the different types of labor in this sector. Together with the demand for labor from the IT sector, we can then derive the aggregate labor demand for each worker. Section 4.2.3 describes the supply of the different types of workers, and section 4.2.4 describes the equilibrium, where we also detail how the labor demand curve shifts over time given the technological boom in the 1990s.

4.2.2 Trade with the Rest of the World

The US economy trades both IT goods and the other goods with the rest of the world (W). Information technology firms export final goods to consumers in other countries, whereas US consumers import the other goods from the rest of the world.[17]

---

17. While we do not explicitly model outsourcing decisions, we do allow for the fact that imported goods in the other sector can be used as intermediate goods in production for the IT sector.

We assume consumers in the rest of the world (W) have the same utility function as US consumers:

$$(13) \qquad U_W\left(C_W,Y_W\right) = \left[\gamma_W C_W^{(\sigma-1)/\sigma} + \left(1-\gamma_W\right)Y_W^{(\sigma-1)/\sigma}\right]^{\sigma/(\sigma-1)}.$$

Since the United States is the only producer of IT goods, foreign consumption is equivalent to US exports of IT goods. Imports into the United States from the rest of the world are represented by Y_{IM}. For convenience we assume trade is balanced, implying that the value of imports must equal the value of exports:

$$(14) \qquad P_c C_W = P_y Y_{IM}.$$

Here we assume that the United States is the only producer of IT. Even though Freeman (2006) stresses how high-skilled immigration may help the United States maintain its comparative advantage in IT, we may expect that immigration policy affects IT production elsewhere in the world, especially via the diffusion of knowledge. Khanna and Morales (2015) draw up a general-equilibrium model of both the United States and India—the other major producer of IT—to study how the H-1B program affects production, human capital accumulation, and labor market welfare for agents in both countries. The possibility of migrating to the United States induces students and workers in other countries to accumulate CS-specific human capital, and return migrants help facilitate the diffusion of technology. Over time, in the latter half of the first decade of the twenty-first century, India becomes the major exporter of IT, eroding the US's comparative advantage. Khanna and Morales (2015) can be thought of as a long-run extension of our current work, with consistent implications for the period of study here (the 1990s).

4.2.3   Labor Supply of US Computer Scientists

The firms' decision problem determines not only the product market equilibrium but also the demand curves for the different types of labor. To describe the workers' decisions, we develop a dynamic model of labor supply that captures the choices made in deciding a field of study in college and occupational choices later in life. The model builds on previous work by Freeman (1975, 1976) and Ryoo and Rosen (2004), and closely follows the setup of Bound et al. (2015). While Bound et al. (2015) was a partial-equilibrium model that studied the decisions made between CS and STEM occupations for a given labor demand elasticity, we extend it to a general-equilibrium framework that includes all types of labor and rigorously models the firm's decision to derive the labor demand curve that the workers face as well.

While we model the decisions to choose a field of study for US workers who attend college, we do not explicitly model the decision to attend college in the first place. This is because we assume that changes in wages for CS-related occupations do not greatly affect the college-going decision for students. The supply of workers who have only a high school degree $\bar{H}$ is therefore assumed to be the same whether or not there were changes in the number of foreign computer scientists in the labor market. Therefore, the total supply of US workers with a college degree $\overline{(L_n + G)}$ is also assumed to be fixed. However, we do model the decisions of these college-educated workers as they make choices between majoring in CS degrees or other degrees and then their occupation choices in each year of their lives until retirement.

In our model, there are three potential sources of CS workers. First, there are those who earn CS bachelor's degrees from US institutions and join the workforce only after they finish college. Second, there are college-educated US residents working in other occupations who can switch into computer science, but must pay costs to switch occupations. Third, there are foreigners who are being recruited on temporary work visas.

Given that most foreign workers that come on H-1Bs are computer scientists, we model computer science as the only profession that they get hired into. There are therefore two sources of non-CS college-educated workers— those who graduate with any degree that is not computer science and those that switch from CS work to non-CS work by paying the switching cost.

We model US college graduates as maximizing their lifetime utility by making two types of decisions. When they are twenty years old they choose their field of study in college, which influences their initial occupation at graduation. From ages twenty-two to sixty-five, they choose between working as a computer scientist or in another occupation. All individuals have rational, forward-looking behavior and make studying and working decisions based on the information available in each period.

The labor demand curve derived from the firms' decision problem discussed in the previous sections shifts out yearly due to productivity shocks. These shifts help identify the labor supply parameters and trace out the labor supply curve.

Field of Study Decision

In our model students choose their field of study when they are undergraduate juniors. Equation (15) captures this decision. At age twenty, a student i draws idiosyncratic taste shocks for studying computer science or another field: η_i^{cs} and η_i^o, respectively. This student has expectations about the prospects of starting a career in each occupation after graduation (age twenty-two), which have values V_{22}^{cs} and V_{22}^o, respectively. Given this information, an individual chooses between pursuing computer science or a different choice of major at the undergraduate level.[18]

---

18. We are assuming that students decide their major after the end of their second year in school. Bound et al. (2015) experiment with a four-year time horizon and doing so made little qualitative difference.

Worker utility is a linear function of their tastes and their career prospects in each sector and they discount their future with an annual discount factor ρ. Additionally, there is an attractiveness parameter θ_o for studying in a field that is not computer science that all students experience. This parameter may be negative if, on average, students prefer studying computer science

$$(15) \qquad \max\left\{\rho^2 \mathbb{E}_t V_{22}^{cs} + \eta_i^{cs}, \rho^2 \mathbb{E}_t V_{22}^{o} + \theta_o + \eta_i^{o}\right\}.$$

We assume that the individual taste parameters η_i^{cs} and η_i^{o} are independently and identically distributed and for $d = \{cs, o\}$, can be defined as $\eta_i^{d} = \sigma_0 v_i^{d}$, where σ_0 is a scale parameter and v_i^{d} is distributed as a standard Type I Extreme Value distribution. This assumption allows the decisions of agents to be formulated in aggregate probabilities, and is therefore commonly used in dynamic discrete choice models (Rust 1987; Kline 2008). We describe the probability of enrollment in degrees in the "Labor Supply Derivations" section in the appendix.

One crucial parameter for how studying choices are sensitive to different career prospects is the standard deviation of taste shocks. Small values of σ_0 imply that small changes in career prospects can produce big variations in the number of students graduating with a CS degree.

Occupational Choice

The field of study decisions determine if an individual enters the labor market at age twenty-two, either as a computer scientist or in a different occupation. However, individuals can choose to switch occupations between the ages of twenty-two and sixty-five. At the start of each period, individuals use the information at hand and choose their occupation in order to maximize the expected present value of their lifetime utility.

Switching occupations, however, is costly for the worker, and these costs vary with age. This is because workers have occupation-specific human capital that cannot easily be transferred across occupations (Kambourov and Manovskii 2009). The occupational switching costs are modeled as a quadratic function of a worker's age, allowing for the fact that it becomes increasingly harder to switch occupations as workers get older.[19]

Like in the college-major decision, we assume that workers have linear utility from wages, taste shocks, and career prospects.[20] The value functions of worker i at age a between twenty-two and sixty-four at time t if she starts the period as a computer scientist or other occupation are therefore going to be

$$(16) \quad V_{t,a}^{cs} = \max\left\{w_t + \rho \mathbb{E}_t V_{t+1,a+1}^{cs} + \varepsilon_{it}^{cs}, \; s_t - \zeta(a) + \rho \mathbb{E}_t V_{t+1,a+1}^{o} + \varepsilon_{it}^{o} + \theta_1\right\},$$

19. While our model has no general human capital accumulation and wages do not vary with the age of a worker, the implications of the model would still hold if individuals expect similar wage-growth profiles in each occupation.
20. Wages must be totally consumed in that same year and workers cannot save or borrow.

(17) $\quad V_{t,a}^o = \max\left\{w_t - \zeta(a) + \rho\mathbb{E}_t V_{t+1,a+1}^{cs} + \varepsilon_{it}^{cs}, s_t + \rho\mathbb{E}_t V_{t+1,a+1}^o + \varepsilon_{it}^o + \theta_1\right\},$

where $\zeta(a) = \zeta_0 + \zeta_1 a + \zeta_2 a^2$ is the monetary cost of switching occupations at age a, and θ_1 is the taste attractiveness parameter for not working as a computer scientist experienced by all workers. Finally, all workers retire at age sixty-five and their retirement benefits do not depend on their career choices. Therefore, at age sixty-five workers face the same decision problem without consideration for the future.

As in the college-major decision problem, we will assume that taste shocks are independently and identically distributed and for $d = \{cs, o\}$ can be defined as $\varepsilon_{it}^d = \sigma_1 v_{it}^d$ where σ_1 is a scale parameter and v_t^d is distributed as a standard Type I Extreme Value distribution.

The standard deviation of the taste shocks, the sector-attractiveness parameter, and the cost of switching occupations will affect the sensitivity of occupational switching to changes in relative career prospects. Since individuals are forward looking, the working decisions depend upon the equilibrium distribution of their career prospects. We describe the probabilities of employment, occupational switching, and the expected value of future prospects in the "Labor Supply Derivations" section in the appendix.

Labor Supply of Foreign Computer Scientists

We model high-skilled foreign workers as only being hired as computer scientists, since during the 1990s a majority of H-1Bs were hired into this occupation. By 2001, more than 21 percent of all computer scientists were born abroad and immigrated after the age of eighteen (March CPS). We assume that high-skilled foreigners have a perfectly elastic labor supply curve to the United States, since the wage that a computer scientist could obtain in countries like India or China, for instance, is substantially lower than it is in the United States (Clemens 2013). This wage premium creates a large queue of foreigners ready to take jobs in the United States. There is, however, an institutionally imposed cap on the total number of H-1Bs that restricts the number of foreign computer scientists each year.

Institutional requirements also force firms to pay foreigners the prevailing US wage. We assume that the additional costs of recruiting foreigners offset the productivity advantage that foreigners may have over their US counterparts. During the 1990s, a large fraction of the CS workers coming from abroad were on H-1B visas. Given that this was a period when the H-1B cap was usually binding, and given our assumption that foreign and domestic CS workers are effectively identical, we treat the quantity of foreign CS workers coming to the United States as exogenous.

4.2.4   Equilibrium

Equilibrium in each period can be defined as a set of prices and wages $(P_{ct}, P_{Yt}, w_t, s_t, r_t)$, quantities of output and labor $(C_t^*, Y_t^*, C_{dt}^*, C_{yt}^*, C_{Wt}^*,$

Y_{dt}^*, Y_{ct}^*, Y_{IMt}^*, L_{nt}^*, K_{Ft}^*, G_t^*, H_t^*), number of firms (N_t), and the productivity cutoff (ϕ_t^*) such that[21]

- Consumers in the United States and the rest of the world maximize utility by choosing C_t and Y_t taking prices as given, and choose their college major and occupations taking wages as given.
- Firms in both sectors maximize profits taking wages and aggregate prices as given.
- In the IT sector, the firm with productivity ϕ_t^* gets zero profits. All firms with $\phi_{jt} > \phi_t^*$ produce, while those with $\phi_{jt} < \phi_t^*$ do not.
- Output and labor markets clear. The equations for the market-clearing conditions are in the "Market-Clearing Conditions" section of the appendix.

Native college graduates face the decision of whether to work as computer scientists or in some other occupation that requires a college degree. This decision is no longer static, but has an intertemporal dimension that requires the definition of the dynamic equilibrium in the labor market for college graduates. As in Bound et al. (2015), this equilibrium is characterized by the system of equations ([15]–[17]) and a stochastic process Z_t. In the "Labor Supply Derivations" section of the appendix we characterize further equations, including future expectations, and the dynamic supply of colleges and workers.

A unique equilibrium is pinned down each period by an aggregate labor demand curve for US computer scientists relative to other college graduates that comes from the product market model.

Even though this labor demand curve from the two sectors has no closed-form solution, we will express it as in equation (18), a setup that will prove to be useful for the calculations in the following sections.

$$(18) \qquad \frac{L_{nt}}{G_t} = Z_t + \Upsilon\left(\frac{w_t}{s_t}\right),$$

where $\Upsilon(w_t/s_t)$ is a baseline-relative demand curve that depends on the relative wage; Z_t is a shifter that can be thought of as a combination of the productivity shocks from the IT boom that shifts out the relative demand for computer scientists every year and the cap of foreign computer scientists $\bar{L}_F$ that shifts in the relative demand curve every period; and Z_t is assumed to follow a random walk process with high persistence such that

$$(19) \qquad Z_t = 0.999 Z_{t-1} + 0.001 \bar{Z} + \xi_t,$$

where $\bar{Z}$ is the steady-state value of Z_t and ξ_t is an i.i.d. shock.[22]

The equilibrium in the labor market can be expressed by a mapping from

---

21. Note that we have introduced a t subscript to each of the variables to denote that there is a different equilibrium for each time period.

22. We assume workers consider both the technological progress from the IT boom as well as the increase in immigrants to be a series of highly persistent shocks.

the state variables: $s = \left\{ R_t, L_{n,t-1}^{22}, \ldots, L_{n,t-1}^{64}, G_{t-1}^{22}, \ldots, G_{t-1}^{64}, Z_{t-1} \right\}$ and exogenous productivity shock ξ_t to the values of L_{nt}, w_t, G_t, s_t, and $\mathbf{V}_t$, the vector of career prospects at different occupations for different ages, that satisfies the system of equations for labor supply as well as each period's relative demand curve.

4.3   Calibration

We calibrate the parameters of our model in order to determine how welfare changes due to immigration. We have a total of twenty-five parameters: σ, ε, γ, γ_W, ψ_1, ψ_2, β, α_c, α_y, τ, λ, δ, Δ, k, $\phi_{\min}$, N_e, and f from the product market, and σ_0, σ_1, θ_0, θ_1, ζ_0, ζ_1, ζ_2, and ρ from the US college graduates labor market. We focus on the period 1994–2001 that corresponds to the IT boom and when the H-1B cap was mostly binding.

In order to calibrate the different parts of the model, we follow a sequential approach. First, we calibrate the parameters in the product market assuming total labor supply of L_t, G_t, and H_t are fixed (i.e., ignoring the choice of native workers between L_t and G_t). What makes this possible in our model is the fact that adjustment costs imply that the stock of the different types of labor are fixed in the very short run. This approach is akin to the approaches taken by Freeman (1975, 1976) and Ryoo and Rosen (2004) in their modeling of adjustments on the labor market for scientists.

In the next step we use the calibrated parameters to derive the aggregate labor demand curve for computer scientists relative to other college graduates for every year. As a third step, we use the predicted shifts in labor demand to calibrate the parameters of the labor supply curve of different types of college graduates. Finally, we use the calibrated labor supply curve, labor demand curve, and product-demand parameters to calculate welfare under the economy where immigration is encouraged via the H-1B program and the counterfactual scenario where immigration is restricted.

4.3.1   Product Market Calibration

We calibrate the parameters of the product market to match different features of the data as explained in the following subsections. The details of the data we use, including sources and definitions of the different sectors and occupations, can be found in the "Details of the Data Used" section of the appendix.

The model is calibrated separately for each year between 1994 and 2001. While some parameters are assumed to be constant over time, others change in order to capture structural changes in the economy. Particularly, the production-function parameters (α_{ct}, α_{yt}, δ_t, Δ_t, ψ_{1t}, and ψ_{2t}) will be recalibrated every year to capture the technological change that affects the two sectors during this period. This can be thought of as describing the skill-biased technological change over this period, since the share of labor cost

Table 4.2   **Calibrated parameters from the product market**

Time-invariant parameters

σ	1.00	k	2.62
ε	3.20	N_e	0.25
τ	1.70	f	1.07–1.24
β	0.23	ϕ_{min}	1

Time-varying parameters

		1994	1995	1996	1997	1998	1999	2000	2001
γ		0.042	0.046	0.050	0.052	0.054	0.055	0.055	0.054
γ_W		0.014	0.015	0.015	0.016	0.014	0.015	0.016	0.013
ψ_1		0.522	0.524	0.525	0.524	0.523	0.521	0.517	0.513
ψ_2		0.055	0.054	0.054	0.053	0.053	0.052	0.052	0.051
α_c		0.438	0.432	0.427	0.419	0.410	0.401	0.395	0.390
α_y		0.502	0.494	0.486	0.479	0.473	0.468	0.465	0.463
	$\lambda = 1$	0.053	0.055	0.059	0.063	0.067	0.069	0.073	0.072
δ	$\lambda = 2$	0.224	0.227	0.233	0.240	0.248	0.253	0.262	0.260
	$\lambda = 4$	0.395	0.398	0.401	0.405	0.414	0.420	0.430	0.428
	$\lambda = 1$	0.217	0.215	0.215	0.218	0.225	0.237	0.249	0.270
Δ	$\lambda = 2$	0.174	0.168	0.153	0.147	0.146	0.157	0.158	0.175
	$\lambda = 4$	0.073	0.066	0.048	0.039	0.036	0.046	0.042	0.057

Notes: σ: elasticity of substitution between C and Y; ε: elasticity of substitution across IT varieties; τ: the elasticity of substitution between college graduates and non–college graduates; β: the technological spillover of computer scientists in IT; f: fixed cost of production; N_e: mass of potential producers; k and ϕ_{min}: distribution and scale parameters from the Pareto distribution; γ: distributional parameter of domestic CES utility; γ_W: distributional parameter of foreign CES utility; ψ_1, ψ_2: production-function parameters for intermediate inputs in IT and the other sector, respectively; α_c, α_y: distributional parameter for non–college graduates in the IT and other sector production function; δ: distributional parameter for computer scientists in both sectors; Δ: distributional parameter for computer scientists in IT; λ: elasticity of substitution between CS and non-CS college graduates.

that these sectors spend in computer scientists is increasing over time. The utility parameters γ_t and γ_{Wt} are also allowed to shift over time to capture changes in local and foreign consumer preferences toward the IT sector. A summary of all calibrated parameters in the product market can be found in table 4.2.

Domestic Utility Function Parameters

The three parameters in the consumer utility function are σ, ε, and γ_t; σ is the elasticity of substitution between the composite IT good C and the good Y. We calibrate this parameter using the ratio of first-order conditions of goods Y and C from the consumer's utility maximization problem: $[\gamma/(1-\gamma)](C/Y)^{-1/\sigma} = P_c/P_Y$.

This relationship can be reformulated as

$$(20) \qquad \log\left(\frac{C}{Y}\right) = -\sigma\log\left(\frac{1-\gamma}{\gamma}\right) - \sigma\log\left(\frac{P_c}{P_Y}\right).$$

We estimate σ using a regression of the relative quantity index on the relative price index. We use data from the Bureau of Economic Analysis (BEA) industry-specific price and quantity indices.[23] The BEA data allows us to distinguish prices and quantities in the IT sector, and all the other sectors in the economy. The coefficient of this regression is statistically indistinguishable from $\sigma = 1$. Given the plausibly exogenous technological change during the period that drives down prices, we use this estimate as our main specification and proceed using a Cobb-Douglas utility specification. We also run a series of robustness checks running the results for different values of σ that are summarized in the "Sensitivity Analysis" section of the appendix.

The elasticity across IT varieties, ε, is calibrated using the markup condition that comes from the IT firms' profit-maximization condition (equation [21]). We follow an approach similar to Gaubert (2015) and match average value added to cost ratios for the IT sector. The data for this is again taken from the BEA's annual industry accounts that report value added, as well as costs like compensation to employees and taxes. For a marginal cost $MC(c_i)$, the price markup can be used to determine the value of ε:

$$(21) \qquad p_i = \frac{\varepsilon}{\varepsilon - 1} MC(c_i).$$

We calibrate $\varepsilon = 3.26$. Bernard et al. (2003) calculate a value of 3.8 for all US plants, whereas Broda and Weinstein (2006) find a value of 2.2 for varieties of "automatic data processing machines and units." Since our estimates lie within this region, we believe them to be reasonable. We show that our results are robust to other reasonable values of this parameter in the "Sensitivity Analysis" section of the appendix.

We calibrate the distribution parameter γ_t to match the share of expenditures in the IT good (using equation [22]). Again we use data from the BEA on industry-specific gross domestic product (GDP) of IT as a share of total GDP.[24]

$$(22) \qquad \frac{P_c C}{m} = \frac{P_c}{P_c + [((1-\gamma)/\gamma)P_c]^\sigma}.$$

---

23. The BEA price indices methodology can be found here: http://www.bea.gov/national/pdf /chapter4.pdf and http://www.bls.gov/opub/hom/pdf/homch17.pdf. The specific methodology for personal computers and peripheral equipment are detailed at http://www.bls.gov/cpi/cpi faccomp.htm, where they discuss adjusting for quality as well. While they do adjust for quality differences, we may still underestimate quality changes in IT (Gordon 1990), which would affect our estimate of β. We do a rigorous sensitivity analysis for different values of β.

24. For all time-varying parameters that are matched to shares observed in the data we run a regression of the raw share on a linear and quadratic time trend to recover the time invariant parameters. We then predict the share using those coefficients and calibrate the parameters to match the predicted shares.

We calibrate γ_t conditional on the equilibrium prices, the share of consumption of the IT good γ and the calibrated value of σ. For the Cobb-Douglas specification we just use the share of IT-industry GDP to total domestic GDP. As already discussed, γ_t is time varying in order to capture potential changes in consumer preferences over time for the IT good relative to the rest of the goods in the economy. Table 4.2 shows how γ_t steadily rises from 0.042 at the start of the period to 0.052 by the year 2001.

Foreign Utility Function

Consumers from the rest of the world are assumed to have the same utility function as consumers in the United States. While we assume the elasticity of substitution σ is the same for both countries ($\sigma = 1$), the distribution parameter γ_{tW} is selected to match the share of consumption of the rest of the world for US IT products. We use the share of exports in IT to US GDP and the relative size of the US economy to the rest of the world to pin down this parameter. Again, we allow this parameter to change over time to capture potential changes in preferences for consumers abroad.

Production-Function Parameters

The elasticity of substitution between high school and college graduates (τ) and between computer scientists and other college graduates (λ) are assumed to be time invariant and equal across sectors. To calibrate τ we follow several influential papers that provide estimates for this parameter such as Katz and Murphy (1992), Card and Lemieux (2001), and Goldin and Katz (2007) and set $\tau = 1.7$, which is an average of their estimates.[25] We present our results for a range of values of λ (1, 2, and 4) that correspond to aggregate relative labor demand elasticities of 1.02, 1.99, and 3.98. Ryoo and Rosen (2004) estimate aggregate relative demand elasticities that lie between 1.2 and 2.2 for engineers, which are included in the range of values we use.

To calibrate the value of β, the technological spillover from total CS in the IT sector, we look at the relationship between the price decline in IT and the increase in total CS working in the sector. We use the aggregate CS in IT equilibrium condition that gives us a relationship between prices of IT and total labor in CS as in equation (23):

$$(23) \quad \log P_c = \mho(w_t, s_t, r_t) - \frac{1}{\varepsilon}\log C_t - \psi_1 \frac{\varepsilon-1}{\varepsilon}\log P_y + \frac{(1-\beta(\varepsilon-1))}{\varepsilon}\log L_c.$$

We run the regression of $\log(P_c)$ on a linear and quadratic time trend, the log of quantity of IT good, the log price of the other good, and the log of

---

25. Katz and Murphy (1992) find 1.41, Card and Lemieux (2001) find estimates between 2 and 2.5, and Goldin and Katz (2007) find 1.64. Strictly speaking, these numbers refer to the elasticity of substitution between college- and non-college-educated labor in the US economy, while our parameter is sector specific. The aggregate elasticity involves both within- and between-sector components. However, our simulations suggest that setting $\tau = 1.7$ produces an aggregate elasticity indistinguishable from 1.7 to the first digit.

total computer scientists in IT. The time trend aims to capture fluctuations in the wages of the different types of workers over time. The calibrated value of β is 0.233. Effectively, this procedure attributes all of the total factor productivity (TFP) change to the increase in computer scientists working for the IT sector, while in reality there are several other factors that also affect technical progress in IT. As a result, our estimates will tend to overestimate the impact of computer scientists on technological change. Our estimate is quite close to the Peri, Shih, and Sparber (2014) estimates of changes in TFP attributable to the total number of STEM workers. In the "Sensitivity Analysis" section of the appendix, we explore the sensitivity of our results to our estimate of β.

The production-function parameters α_{ct}, α_{yt}, δ_t, Δ_t, ψ_{1t}, and ψ_{2t} are calibrated separately every year to reflect the skill-biased technological change the two sectors face during the period. This allows us to capture that, increasingly, firms in both sectors spend a higher share of their expenditures on college graduates.

The shares of expenditures on non–college graduates in both sectors are matched to the observed share of labor income for each year in the March CPS. Here we define the shares observed in the data as $\vartheta_{t,C,H}$ and $\vartheta_{t,Y,H}$, such that

$$(24) \qquad \vartheta_{t,C,H} = \frac{\alpha_{ct}\bar{H}_{ct}^{(\tau-1)/\tau}}{\alpha_{ct}\bar{H}_{ct}^{(\tau-1)/\tau} + (1-\alpha_{ct})\bar{Q}_{ct}^{(\tau-1)/\tau}},$$

where $\bar{H}_{ct}$ and $\bar{H}_{ct}$ are the quantities observed in the CPS for each sector. We analogously calibrate α_{yt} using the shares observed in the data ($\vartheta_{t,Y,H}$, $\bar{H}_{yt}$, and $\bar{Q}_{ct}$).

In both sectors we have the parameter δ_τ that is the distribution parameter associated with computer scientists. We calibrate this parameter to match the relative wage of CS to other college graduates (w_t/s_t). The IT sector has a higher share of CS than the other sector, so we calibrate the parameter Δ to match the share of total labor expenditure spent in CS by the IT sector in a manner similar to our approach for calibrating α_{yt} and α_{ct}.

In table 4.2 we can see how skill-biased technological change in the economy changes these parameters over time; δ_t steadily increases over this period as both sectors want to hire more computer scientists. The values of α_{yt} and α_{ct} steadily decrease for both sectors, showing that they spend more of their income on college graduates than on high school graduates. Parameters associated with the intermediate inputs from another sector (ψ_{1t}, ψ_{2t}) are calibrated using the share of intermediate inputs from other sectors relative to the GDP, which we obtain from the BLS input-output tables.

Entry into Production in the IT Sector

There are four parameters related to the entry decision and productivity distribution in the IT sector. The number of firms in the sector depend on f, the fixed cost of production, and N_e, the mass of potential producers. The Pareto distribution parameters k and ϕ_{min}, determine the productivity levels of these firms. All these parameters are assumed to be time invariant.

We calibrate f to match the average firm size in the IT sector observed in the data for the steady-state year 1994. In order to do this we use information on the number of firms and total employment in the IT sector from the US Census Bureau's Statistics of US Businesses (SUSB).[26] In 1994 we calibrate f to match the ratio of total employees and number of firms in the data for the IT sector. The calibrated values for f are 1.24, 1.14, and 1.07 (for λ values of 1, 2, or 4, respectively). For the rest of the years we allow the number of firms N_t to adjust endogenously, as the profits from production change over time.

The parameter N_e is calibrated using information on establishment entry and exit.[27] We look at the total number of establishments over 500 employees in 2001 and calibrate the ratio of $(N_t/N_e) = (N_{94}/N_{01})$. Given that N_t in 1994 is used to calibrate f, we get the rescaled $N_e = 0.25$.[28]

The Pareto distribution parameter k is set to match the standard deviation of logarithm of US domestic plant revenues. Following Demidova (2008), we use the simulation reported by Bernard et al. (2003) of 0.84. In our model the standard deviation of $Ln(p_i c_i)$ is $(\varepsilon - 1)/k$, so given our value of $\varepsilon = 3.2$ we get a value of $k = 2.62$. The scale parameter ϕ_{min} is related to the choice of units in which to measure productivity, so we follow the convention in the literature and normalize it to 1.

Total Quantity of Labor

To calibrate the product market parameters, we use the total quantities observed in the data for each occupation type $\bar{L}_t$, $\bar{G}_t$, and $\bar{H}_t$ as if they were exogenously given. We normalize the US working population from the March CPS in 1994 to 100, and then allow for the population in our model to grow at the same rate as the growth in the US population. The shares of each type of worker are set equal to those observed in the data each year, which allows us to know the total number of college- and non-college-graduate workers, as can be seen in table 4.3.

26. This information comes from the 1992 Statistics of US Businesses (SUSB), http://www .census.gov/econ/susb/. Since the information was only available for 1992 and 1997–2012, we use the figures for 1992 as a proxy for 1994.

27. We get information on entry and exit of establishments in the IT sector by year from the Business Dynamics Statistics (http://www.census.gov/ces/dataproducts/bds/). Entry and exit was only available for establishments, not firms when looking at specific industries.

28. Other papers such as Demidova (2008) and Melitz and Redding (2015) use the exit rate to calibrate parameters related to fixed cost of production and entry, but unlike us calibrate the slightly different Melitz (2003) model. The strategy we use is somewhat different as we have a fixed pool of potential entrants.

Table 4.3   Normalized population and growth as observed in the data

Year	X_t	L_{tF}	L_{tn}	G_t	H_t
1994	100.00	0.13	0.99	24.30	74.59
1995	101.18	0.16	1.02	24.85	75.16
1996	103.31	0.19	1.12	25.61	76.39
1997	105.25	0.24	1.20	26.26	77.55
1998	107.35	0.26	1.27	27.06	78.76
1999	109.12	0.31	1.30	27.85	79.67
2000	110.95	0.37	1.35	28.71	80.52
2001	111.77	0.40	1.37	29.51	80.49

Note: Total working population as shown in the CPS is normalized to 100 in 1994. For subsequent years we allow total population to grow at the same rate as the working population in the United States. The shares of each type of occupation are then used to calculate the total number of workers in each category.

4.3.2   Deriving the Labor Demand Curve

Once we calibrate the product market parameters we are able to derive a labor demand curve for computer scientists relative to other college graduates. Such a demand curve does not have a closed-form solution that comes directly from the model, so we derive it by first changing the relative values of $\bar{L}_t / \bar{G}_t$ that we feed into the model and then calculating the predicted value of w_t/s_t. We run this exercise only for the steady-state year, 1994, and calculate w_t/s_t for different values of $\bar{L}_t / \bar{G}_t$ that ranges between 0.04 and 0.07.[29] We then fit a second-order polynomial to get a closed-form solution of the relative labor demand curve.[30]

The elasticity of labor relative demand for computer scientists to other college graduates depends crucially on the parameter λ. We derive the labor demand for our three values of λ and get what we call the baseline labor demand curve as in equation (25), calculated using the calibrated model for the steady-state year 1994:[31]

$$(25) \qquad \frac{\widehat{L}_t}{G_t} = \hat{Y}\left(\frac{w_t}{s_t}, \lambda\right).$$

For the remaining years we allow the demand curve to shift for two reasons. First, to capture the innovation taking place in the economy. This exogenous technological change is captured by the time-varying parameters

29. Relative total computer scientists to other college graduates in the data is 0.0406 in 1994 and goes up to 0.0466 in 2001. We therefore capture more than the range of possible values in the data.

30. The second-order polynomial perfectly predicts the model with a $R^2 = 1$. We experiment with higher-order polynomials to fit the labor demand curve and our results do not change.

31. The elasticity of the derived labor demand curve is very close to the value of λ, more specifically 1.015, 1.99, and 3.98 for λ equal to 1, 2, and 4, respectively.

of the production functions. Second, the demand curve shifts to capture the relative changes in the stock of college graduates to non–college graduates, which is determined outside of the model.

We can calculate the labor demand shifter Λ_t as in equation (26). This shifter applies to the total demand of computer scientists relative to other college graduates, including both native and foreign computer scientists.

$$(26) \qquad \hat{\Lambda}_t = \frac{L_t}{G_t} - \hat{Y}\left(\frac{w_t}{s_t}\right).$$

As a last step, in order to use the variation in the demand curve to trace out the relative supply curve for *native* computer scientists only, we subtract the relative number of foreign computer scientists each year to derive to the total demand shifter Z_t as presented in equation (18). As a reminder, we treat the quantity of foreign CS workers coming to the United States as exogenous since the H-1B cap was binding throughout this period. Given that we assume foreign CS workers are willing to work at any wage and are slightly more productive than natives, they get hired first until they exhaust the H-1B cap, while native workers face a residual labor demand curve. The total shifter $Z_t = \hat{\Lambda}_t - \left(\bar{L}_{tF} / G_t\right)$ allows us to write the labor demand for native CS relative to other college graduates as in equation (27):

$$(27) \qquad \frac{L_{nt}}{G_t} = Z_t + \hat{Y}\left(\frac{w_t}{s_t}\right).$$

In the steady state, $\hat{\Lambda} = 0$ and $\bar{Z} = -\left(\bar{L}_{94,F}/\bar{G}_{94}\right).$

4.3.3   Calibrating Labor Supply

On the labor supply side of the model, we have eight parameters that need to be calibrated—$\{\sigma_0,\theta_0,\sigma_1,\theta_1,\zeta_0,\zeta_1,\zeta_2,\rho\}$. Of these, we pick the annual discount rate to be $\rho = 0.9$, and calibrate the other parameters to match the data. In our model we assume the total quantities of non–college graduates $\bar{H}_t$, native college graduates $\left(L_n + G\right)_t$, and foreign computer scientists $\bar{L}_{tF}$ are determined outside the model.

In the way we set up the model, changes in lagged degree attainment, employment, and wages are driven by the exogenous technology shocks that shift out the demand curve for the different types of labor over this decade. As the demand curve shifts, it traces out the labor supply curve for workers. The technological developments that drive these shifts in the labor demand are assumed to not affect the parameters of the workers' labor supply decisions.

We use data on relative wages, employment, lagged degree attainment, and age shares to calibrate the remaining seven parameters. The first three series compare computer scientists to non-CS college-graduate workers. For example, relative wages compare the wages for CS workers with wages for non-CS college graduates. To do this, we use the March CPS. Details of the sample used in the data and specific variable definitions can be found in the "Details of the Data Used" section of the appendix.[32]

We simultaneously match wages, employment, and the share of US CS workers that are young (between age twenty-two and forty) in 1994 and 2001.[33] We also match relative degrees in computer science for 1994, 1997, and 2001. The series we use from the data are as follows:[34]

1. $L_{n,t}/G_t$ = (US computer scientists)/(Non–CS college educated US workers) for $t = \{1994, 2001\}$.

2. w_t/s_t = (Median weekly wages for computer scientists)/(Median weekly wages for non–CS educated) for $t = \{1994, 2001\}$.

3. $q_{t+2}^{cs} / q_{t+2}^{o}$ = [US computer science college degrees awarded (lagged 2 years)]/[US non–CS college degrees awarded (lagged 2 years)] for $t = \{1994, 1997, 2001\}$.

4. $\text{age}_t^{22,40}$ = (US computer scientists with age between 22 and 40)/(US $\text{CS}^{22,40}$ + US $\text{CS}^{41,65}$) for $t = \{1994, 2001\}$.

To simultaneously find parameter values that solve the model under these data restrictions, we use a Nelder-Mead simplex method. While the system uses all the data at the same time, there is strong intuition behind the identification of each parameter. For example, the relative degree-attainment data should help identify the taste parameters for field of major decisions (σ_0 and θ_0) as well as the fixed cost of switching occupations (ζ_0), whereas the relative employment data should help pin down the occupation-specific tastes (σ_1 and θ_1). The age shares in CS employment help identify the occupation switching cost parameters that depend on age (ζ_1 and ζ_2).

Labor Supply Calibration Results

Figure 4.2 shows the data used and the model fit from this exercise. The figures report both the path of the variables of interest predicted by the model and the CPS data we use for these series. We match two extreme years (1994 and 2001) for employment and wages and three years (1994, 1997, and 2001) for lagged degree attainment, and the remaining years plotted are an out-of-sample test of our method. The years in between (1995 to 2000) include years where there were observed changes to immigration laws, and other potentially structural changes that may make it difficult for the data to fit perfectly.

---

32. We exclude imputed wages and multiply top-coded values by 1.4. Bollinger and Hirsch (2007) show that including imputations can lead to biased results, whereas the top-coding adjustment is standard in the literature (Lemieux 2006). We smooth the raw data over three-year moving averages as follows: $X_{t,\text{smooth}} = (1/3)(X_{t-1,\text{raw}} + X_{t,\text{raw}} + X_{t+1,\text{raw}})$.

33. Given that in our labor supply model we impose all cohorts are the same size, we normalize the number of computer scientists of a given age group dividing by the total number of college graduates in that age group before calculating the age shares.

34. We have an exactly identified system as we use nine data moments to recover ten parameters $\{\sigma_0, \theta_0, \sigma_1, \theta_1, \zeta_0, \zeta_1, \zeta_2\}$, and two implied values of technology in the years we match the wage/employment data $\{A_{94}, A_{01}\}$.

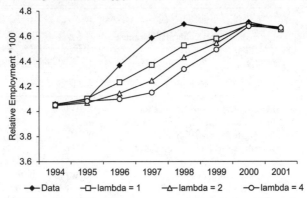

A. Matching Relative Labor Supply

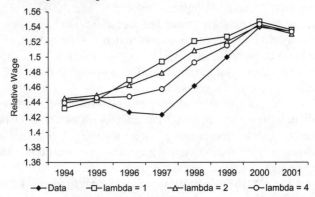

B. Matching Relative Wages

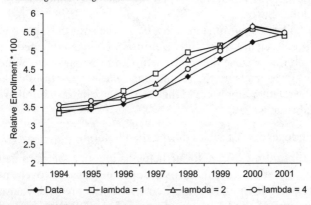

C. Matching Relative Degree Attainment

Fig. 4.2   Calibrating labor supply parameters

Notes: In the calibration exercise, the years 1994 and 2001 were used to match the data for employment and wages, whereas the years 1994, 1997, and 2001 were used to match the data on degree attainment (lagged two years). The years in between are an out-of-sample test. Wage and employment data come from the March CPS, whereas degree data is from IPEDS. See the "Details of the Data Used" section of the appendix for more details and the "Extended Out-of-Sample Tests (until 2015)" section of the appendix for a longer-run view of the out-of-sample tests in later years.

Table 4.4   Labor supply calibrated parameters

Parameter	Description	Calibrated value		
		$\lambda = 1$	$\lambda = 2$	$\lambda = 4$
σ_0	Std. dev. of study-area taste shocks	0.0141	0.0215	0.0217
σ_1	Std. dev. of occupation taste shocks	0.9420	0.8887	0.9282
θ_0	Mean taste for not studying CS	−0.1341	−0.1072	−0.1362
θ_1	Mean taste for not working in CS	2.1766	1.8627	1.9278
η_1	Sector-switching cost (constant)	0.3265	0.4059	0.4145
η_2	Sector-switching cost (linear)	0.0307	0.0529	0.0488
η_3	Sector-switching cost (quadratic)	−0.0001	−0.0007	−0.0006

The employment series in figure 4.2, panel A, and the wage series shown in panel B, fit well at the start and end of the period, but it misses some years in between, particularly because it can't match the dip in wages that occur after 1994 and the simultaneous spike in employment in that same period. Last, the lagged degree-attainment series can be seen in figure 4.2, panel C, and matches the data relatively well.

In figure 4A.1 in the appendix we extend this exercise to later years, and study how well our calibrated parameters match the data in the first decade of the twenty-first century. We do a good job of matching wages and employment in this out-of-sample exercise, but overpredict enrollment in computer science for the years after 2004.

Table 4.4 presents the values of the calibrated parameters for the different values of λ. On average, we can see that there is a mean taste for not working in CS occupations, which is consistent with the wage differential seen across CS and non-CS work.

These calibrated parameters allow us to trace out the labor supply curve for computer scientists relative to non-CS college-educated workers. In order to do this, we use the model setup and the parameters and vary the relative wage to measure the response in relative quantities of labor. This derives the relative supply curve that we then use in the labor market to find the equilibrium wage.[35]

4.3.4   Endogenous Variables during the IT Boom

The calibration exercise so far helps us identify the parameters in the model that govern the trends in the endogenous variables over time. We can study these trends to understand how our model predicts what is happening at the time of the IT boom and the influx of foreign computer scientists. Given the solution of the model in each period, we study how prices and wages, employment by occupation and sector, and quantities produced change over time.

35. Our estimated relative labor supply elasticities lie between 1.96 and 2.48.

While US workers were more likely to work in CS occupations over time, the fraction of foreigners in CS work was increasing at a yet faster rate. Also consistent with the trends seen in the data for this period, the wage for computer scientists increases faster than the wages in other occupations. This IT boom overall leads to an increase in consumption of the IT good and a fall in prices of the IT good, which benefits consumers.

Figure 4.3, panel A, shows how the ratio of US computer scientists to non-CS college graduates (L_{US}/G) evolves over this period according to our model for the different values of λ. During the time of the boom, this ratio increases from about 0.040 to 0.047 for $\lambda = 2$, as more and more US workers shifted into CS work. At the same time, there was an increasing share of foreigners in CS occupations—the ratio of foreign-to-US computer scientists ($L_{Foreign}/L_{US}$) more than doubled from about 0.13 in 1994 to about 0.29 in 2001.

Our model predicts that over this period IT-sector employment grew faster than employment in the other sector, and most of this was driven by hiring in CS occupations (figure 4.3, panel B). The ratio of employment in IT to non-IT sectors over time ($(L_C + G_C + H_C)/(L_Y + G_Y + H_Y)$) increases over this period, highlighting the importance of the IT boom in employing more workers. At the same time, with the influx of foreign computer scientists, the intensity of CS workers in the IT sector eventually increases. This can be seen in the series that plots the ratio of CS to non-CS workers in the IT sector $L_C/(G_C + H_C)$ in figure 4.3, panel B. The overall growth in the IT-sector employment, therefore, was skewed toward CS employment.

While employment for CS workers and the IT-sector workers as a whole was increasing over this period, we can also study how the relative wages for these types of workers change. Figure 4.3, panel C, plots the CS wage relative to the non-CS college-graduate wage (w/s) and relative to the non-college-graduate wage (w/r). Consistent with the data, the model predicts that wages for computer scientists increase at a faster rate than wages for the other types of workers.

The boom in the IT sector increased overall production and consumption for IT goods. Figure 4.3, panel D, shows how relative consumption (C/Y) increases and relative prices (P_c/P_y) fall over this period as the supply of IT goods from firms increases. The reduction in the price of IT goods will affect overall consumer utility as laid out by the model, and the following section will discuss how we calculate utility for the different types of workers and the owners of firms.

4.4   Counterfactuals

In order to isolate the impacts of high-skilled immigration on the various endogenous variables and on worker welfare, we conduct a counterfactual exercise. In the exercise we restrict the stock of immigrants to be constant

A. Ratio of Foreign to US Computer Scientists and US CS to US College Graduates

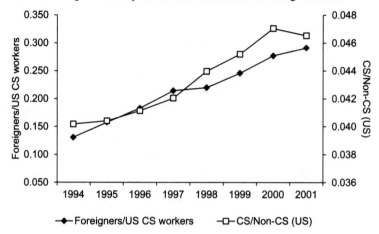

B. Computer Science Labor and Total Labor in IT

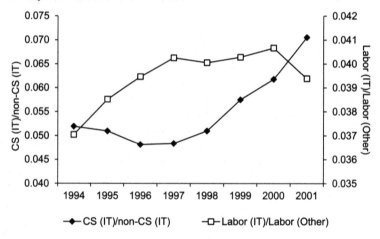

Fig. 4.3 Endogenous variables over time

Notes: Model predictions for ratio of endogenous variables over time:

1. Foreign CS workers to US CS workers ($L_{\text{Foreign}}/L_{\text{US}}$), and for US CS workers to all US college-graduate workers ($L_{\text{US}}/(L_{\text{US}} + G)$).

2. CS labor to non-CS labor in the IT sector ($L_c/(G_c + H_c)$) and the total labor in IT relative to total labor in the other sector (($L_c + G_c + H_c)/(L_y + G_y + H_y)$)).

3. CS wage relative to non-CS college-graduate wage (w/s) and the CS wage relative to non-college-graduate wage (w/r).

4. Relative prices for the IT good (P_c/P_y) and relative consumption (C/Y).

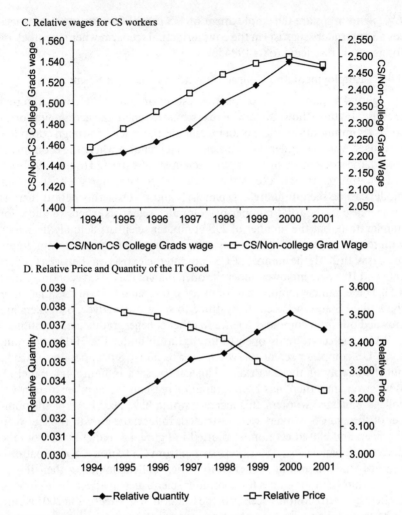

C. Relative wages for CS workers

D. Relative Price and Quantity of the IT Good

Fig. 4.3   (cont.)

at the 1994 level, and subject the economy to the same innovation shocks that were experienced during this period. Using the identified parameters, we can then trace out what happens to all the endogenous variables over this period in a situation where the stock of immigrants is fixed.

We use the notation "open" to refer to the real scenario under the H-1B regime, and "closed" to the counterfactual of restricted immigration. We can then define any endogenous variable, x_s, under the two scenarios $s = $ {open,closed}. For example, L_{open}^{US} is the number of US computer scientists in the "real" scenario under which high-skilled immigration is encouraged via the H-1B program, and all CS workers earn a wage w_{open}. In contrast,

L_{closed}^{US} and w_{closed} are the employment of US computer scientists and wages for all computer scientists in the counterfactual scenario where the stock of foreigners is restricted to its 1994 level.

4.4.1   Employment and College Degrees in Computer Science

Figure 4.4, panel A, describes the restriction under the counterfactual exercise. It shows how, under the real scenario where the economy is open to H-1B immigration, there is an increase in the stock of foreign computer scientists, whereas under the counterfactual scenario where the economy is closed, the stock of foreign computer scientists is restricted to the 1994 level.

How this restriction affects the stock of US computer scientists in our model can be seen in figure 4.4, panels B and C. Over this period there is an increase in the total number of computer scientists when we allow for immigration, but the number of US computer scientists actually decreases with respect to the closed economy every year as the number of immigrants increases. In 2001, the number of US computer scientists was between 6.1 percent and 10.8 percent lower under the open than in the closed economy (table 4.5). These numbers imply that for every 100 foreign CS workers that enter the United States, between thirty-three to sixty-one native CS workers are crowded out from computer science to other college-graduate occupations.

When the economy is open to immigration under the H-1B program, some US computer scientists switch over to non-CS occupations, shifting out the supply of these workers. This can be seen in figure 4.4, panel D. While over time there has been a rapid increase in the number of non-CS college-educated workers, this increase would have been lower if the number of foreign CS workers were restricted. In fact, the growth rate between the open and closed economies plotted in figure 4.4, panel D, mirrors the decrease in panel C as US workers switch from CS to non-CS occupations.

Since students in our model choose their college major in their junior year, a change in the wages for computer scientists will affect these choices. Under the open economy scenario, the fraction of CS degrees in 2001 would be between 1.3 and 2.6 percentage points lower than in the closed economy, as can be seen in figure 4.4, panel E.

4.4.2   Wages

Over the period of study, wages grew for CS workers, but this growth would have been higher if immigration was restricted (figure 4.5, panel B). An influx of foreign CS workers depresses the CS wage, and shifts some US workers into non-CS occupations. At the end of the decade, our model implies wages for CS workers would have been between 2.6 percent and 5.1 percent lower under the open economy (table 4.5).

With an increase in the foreign CS workforce, college-educated US CS workers shift into non-CS occupations, and this tends to lower the non-CS wage. At the same time, however, as the equilibrium amount of total

CS workers increases, so does the marginal product of non-CS college-educated workers. This increases the demand for non-CS workers, and tends to increase their wage, making the net effect positive (figure 4.5, panel C). Overall, table 4.5 shows an increase in the non-CS wage due to immigration of about 0.04 percent–0.28 percent in 2001. As expected, both the changes in CS wage and the non-CS wage for college graduates are sensitive to what value of λ we choose, but qualitatively our results do not change across specifications.

A. Foreign Computer Scientists

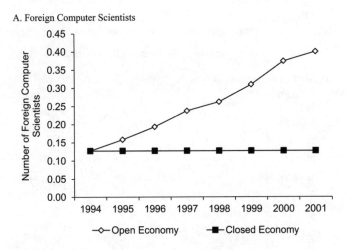

B. Total Computer Scientists

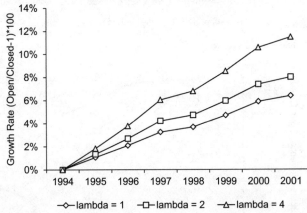

Fig. 4.4   Employment under the real and counterfactual scenarios
Note: The closed economy is where immigration is restricted to the 1994 levels, whereas in the open economy the stock of immigrants grows according to the data. Total size of the workforce is normalized to 100 in 1994.

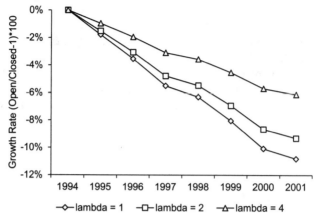

C. US Computer Scientists

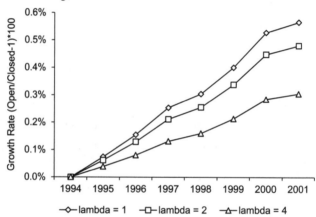

D. Non-CS College Educated Workers

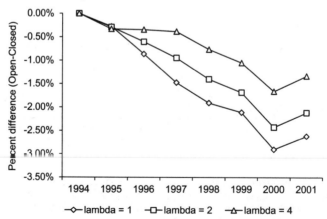

E. Fraction of CS Degrees

Fig. 4.4   (cont.)

Table 4.5   Percent changes when allowing immigration (2001)

	$\lambda = 1$	$\lambda = 2$	$\lambda = 4$
Relative price	−1.86	−1.85	−2.42
Relative quantity	1.89	1.89	2.48
Number of firms	0.50	0.51	0.56
Wage computer scientists	−5.13	−3.47	−2.57
Wage college graduates, non-CS	0.28	0.10	0.04
Wage non–college graduates	0.43	0.44	0.52
Total employment in CS	6.39	8.00	11.47
US computer scientists	−10.81	−9.32	−6.12
College graduates, non-CS	0.57	0.48	0.30

Notes: Percent changes are calculated using the endogenous variables from the closed and open economy. For each year we consider the situation of going from a closed to an open economy (allowing immigration), that is $[(X_{open} / X_{closed}) - 1] \times 100$. Results shown for different values of λ and only look at year 2001.

Since the labor supply of non–college graduates is assumed to be fixed and inelastic, only changes in the demand for non–college graduates determine the difference in their wages under the real and counterfactual scenarios. When the economy is open to immigration, the equilibrium number of total college graduates employed increases due to immigration. This raises the marginal product of non-college-graduate labor, and shifts out the demand for non-college-graduate workers, raising the overall wage for non–college graduates (figure 4.5, panel D). Under the open economy, wages for non–college graduates would have been between 0.43 percent and 0.52 percent higher by the end of this period (table 4.5).[36]

4.4.3   Prices, Output, and the Entry of Firms

While high-skilled immigration affected both employment and wages, it also affects overall output and prices of the different goods produced in the economy. These changes will affect overall consumer welfare, and also the profits accruing to firm owners.

Over the period of study, relative prices of IT goods were falling steadily, and some of this fall can be attributed to the increase in CS employment due to immigration. Figure 4.6, panel A, and table 4.5 show how under the open economy, prices would have been between 1.9 percent and 2.4 percent lower in 2001.

At the same time, the relative consumption of IT goods was increasing, and this increase would have been lower without the growth in the foreign workforce (figure 4.6, panel B). Immigration also raises the profits of firms who can now hire relatively cheaper labor, and this causes new firms to enter

---

36. Since the non-college-graduate workforce is a lot larger than the CS workforce, the relative shift in wages is a lot lower compared to the CS wage.

A. Wages of CS Relative to Non-CS College Wage

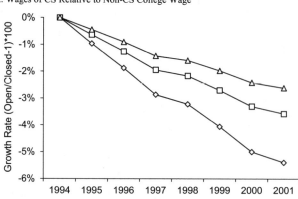

B. Wages for Computer Scientists

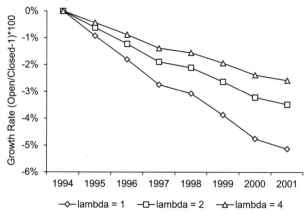

Fig. 4.5   Wages under the real and counterfactual scenarios

Notes: The closed economy is where immigration is restricted to the 1994 levels, whereas in the open economy, the stock of immigrants grows according to the data. All monetary values are in units of the numeraire (the consumption bundle).

the IT sector. Figure 4.6, panel C, shows how by allowing immigration, the number of IT firms would be higher. At the end of this period, there would be between 0.50 percent and 0.56 percent fewer IT firms if immigration was restricted (table 4.5).

4.5   Welfare

Using our estimated parameters and counterfactual exercises, we can measure the overall economic impacts on the different agents in the economy due to the increase in the number of foreign computer scientists. In order to

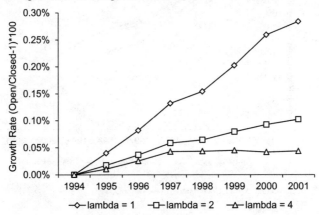

C. Wages for Non-CS College Educated Workers

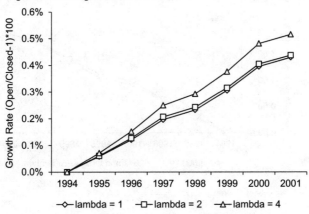

D. Wages for Non College Educated Workers

Fig. 4.5   (cont.)

compare losses and benefits and the distributional consequences of immigration, we look at the welfare of all types of workers and the owners of firms.

4.5.1   Calculating Welfare

Calculating Worker Welfare

Given the structure of our CES utility function, we can calculate consumer welfare as a function of the income of each type of agent. For a given income level m_i, the indirect utility of the agent is just the product of his income and the ideal price index. However, since the ideal price index is the numeraire, indirect utility is just the income of each type of worker: $V_i(m_i) = m_i$. We then compare the welfare of individuals under the two

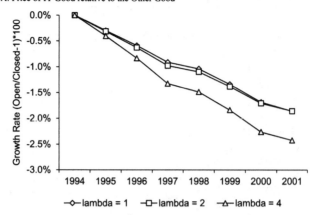

A. Price of IT Good relative to the Other Good

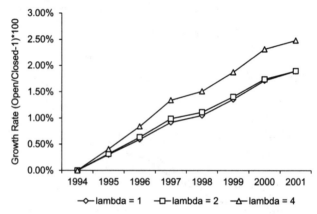

B. Consumption of IT Good relative to the Other Good

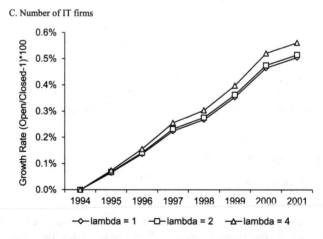

C. Number of IT firms

Fig. 4.6   Output and prices under the real and counterfactual scenarios

Notes: The closed economy is where immigration is restricted to the 1994 levels, whereas in the open economy, the stock of immigrants grows according to the data. Prices are in units of the numeraire (the consumption bundle).

scenarios: (a) the real scenario, where high-skilled immigration is encouraged under the H-1B program; and (b), the counterfactual scenario where the stock of immigrants is restricted to the 1994 level. For all welfare calculations we will only be focusing on welfare changes for those individuals who are US born, ignoring the changes in welfare for migrant computer scientists.

Workers are divided into four groups: those who are computer scientists and stay in CS occupations in the presence of immigration, those who are CS workers but switch to non-CS work because of immigration, those who were non-CS college graduates even before there was immigration, and those who are non–college graduates. We then proceed to calculate welfare changes in two different ways: percent utility changes and compensating variation.

Our model shows that when there is an influx of foreign computer scientists, the equilibrium wage for CS workers falls and pushes some native college-educated computer scientists into non-CS work. As the equilibrium number of hired computer scientists increases, the marginal product, and hence the demand for other types of workers, will also increase, tending to push up their wages. The wage for non-college-educated workers and non-CS college-educated workers unambiguously rises for all specifications of λ.

For those that stay in their occupation groups under both real and counterfactual scenarios, we can calculate the percent utility changes by just looking at the percent change in the wage for each group (e.g., the percent change in utility for the computer scientists that stay in CS occupations under the presence of immigration is just the percent change in w between the open and closed economy). For computer scientists that switch to non-CS occupations when we allow for immigration, we use information from both the utility change for the CS workers that stay and the change for those that were always non-CS college graduates.

By knowing the form of the indirect utility function, we can also calculate how much income we must compensate different types of workers who lose from immigration. This compensating variation (CV) depends on the indirect utility calculated at the original prices P_c and original income levels m_i, and compares it to a scenario with new prices and income ($P_c' m_c'$). A useful feature of the compensating variation is that we can scale up the results using total labor income in the US economy from the data to measure how much workers should be compensated (in USD) if immigration restrictions were imposed. Given that the ideal price index is our numeraire, we can write the compensating variation as $CV = m_i - m_i'$.

The number of computer scientists who stay in CS occupations even in the presence of immigration is L_{open}. Their overall change in income in the presence of increased immigration is therefore given by $(w_{\text{closed}} - w_{\text{open}})L_{\text{open}}$. When there is immigration, non-college-graduate workers benefit from the rise in wages that is caused by the increase in their marginal product. The increase in income for this group is therefore $r_{\text{open}} - r_{\text{closed}}\bar{H}$.

Similarly, the number of non-CS college-educated workers who were always in these other occupations is given by G_{closed}. Their overall change in income is given by $(s_{closed} - s_{open})G_{closed}$. Given that we find the wages for non-CS college-educated workers to be lower in the presence of immigration, there is a loss in income to these workers due to immigration.

Last, for the group of workers who switch from CS to non-CS work in the presence of immigration, we must take into account their switching costs and change in utility because of different tastes in each occupation. The marginal worker who switches experiences a different loss in utility than the inframarginal worker. The overall change in terms of income equivalent for this group of workers can be approximated by $(1/2)(L_{closed} - L_{open})$ $[(s_{closed} - s_{open}) + (w_{closed} - w_{open})]$.[37]

Calculating Profits

In our model, firms in the perfectly competitive residual sector earn no profits. In the monopolistically competitive IT sector, however, only the marginal firm earns 0 profits. In the current setup we follow Chaney (2008), where there is an underlying mass of firms that already know their entrepreneurial capabilities and choose whether to produce or not given their productivity. There is, therefore, free entry into the production decision that drives the profit for the marginal producing firm down to zero.

For the firms in the IT sector, the marginal producing firm has a productivity ϕ^*, and a profit $(\phi^*) = 0$. Using the notation highlighted in section 4.2.1, we know that the average profit for producing firms can be represented by

$$
(28) \quad \int_{\phi^*}^{\infty} \pi(\phi)\mu(\phi)d\phi = \int_{\phi^*}^{\infty} PC^{1/\varepsilon}c_j^{(\varepsilon-1)/\varepsilon}\mu(\phi)d\phi - w\int_{\phi^*}^{\infty} l_j\mu(\phi)d\phi
$$
$$
- s\int_{\phi^*}^{\infty} g_j\mu(\phi)d\phi - r\int_{\phi^*}^{\infty} h_j\mu(\phi)d\phi - f.
$$

The total profits are then the average profits times the number of firms $N = (1 - \Psi(\phi > \phi^*))N^e$, where N^e is the number of total potential producers in the sector.

We can also calculate profits for different types of firms using the features of this distribution. For example, we know that the cutoff productivity will change across the regimes where there is immigration and there is not. In the presence of immigration, firm profits will rise and allow newer firms to enter on the margin.[38] This then allows us to calculate the profits for the new entrants and the incumbent firms separately. Let ϕ_{open}^* and ϕ_{closed}^* be the cutoff values of productivity under each regime. The new firms that enter

37. The intuition for this expression is the following: a CS worker who switches experiences a change in welfare that equals the change in CS wage up to the relative wage that induces them to switch. From that point on, the additional change in welfare will equal the change in the wages of non-CS college graduates. We assume that for minor changes in wages the demand curve can be approximated linearly.

38. Alternatively, in the Melitz (2003) framework of the model, firms will enter at any point of the distribution.

when there is immigration will have a productivity $\phi_j \in [\phi^*_{open}, \phi^*_{closed}]$. Whereas the incumbents have a productivity $\phi_j \in [\phi^*_{closed}, \infty)$. These cutoffs, therefore, change the limits of integration and the conditional distribution functions.

The marginal distribution for the incumbents is determined by

$$\mu_{closed}(\phi) = \begin{cases} \dfrac{k\phi^{-(k+1)}}{1 - \Psi\left(\phi^*_{closed}\right)}, & \text{if } \phi \geq \phi^* \\[2ex] 0, & \text{otherwise} \end{cases}$$

with $\Psi(\phi^*_{closed}) = 1 - (1/\phi^*_{closed})^k$.

The total profits to incumbents is then these average profits times the number of incumbents: $N_{incumbent} = (1 - \Psi(\phi_{closed}))N^e$. The total profits for new entrants is simply the difference between the profits for incumbents and the total profits for all firms in the open economy scenario.

Such an exercise can also be done to derive the profits for the firm in any percentile. For example, the firm in the 90th percentile has a productivity $\phi_{90} = (1/0.1)^{1/k}$. Since the number of firms above the 90th percentile is simply $N_{90} = 0.1N_e$, we can derive the profits for these firms in the scenario with and without immigration.

4.5.2 Welfare Changes Due to Immigration

The changes to the welfare of workers in this economy depends on the changes in income and the prices due to immigration. Figure 4.7, panels A, C, and E, show how much workers, under a regime of restricted immigration, need to be compensated to maintain the same level of utility as they had in the open economy. These numbers have been translated into 1999 USD. Overall worker welfare is higher under immigration, and the amount of the compensating variation rises steadily between 1994 and 2001. The compensating variation for all workers in 2001 is between \$8.2 and \$10.9 billion, depending on the value of λ.

This overall increase in utility due to immigration, however, hides a lot of distributional changes. Figure 4.7, panels A, C, and E, split up the workers into four groups: (a) those who stay in CS occupations even after immigration, (b) those who switch from CS to non-CS, (c) college graduates who were always non-CS, and (d) non–college graduates. As these panels show, US computer scientists are negatively affected by immigration, while other workers gain. The positive effect for college graduates gets partly offset by the mobility of the college educated across occupations, where computer scientists switching to non-CS occupations depress the wage. The losses for computer scientists and the gains for non-CS college graduates get closer to zero when the ease of substitution between CS and non-CS college graduates gets higher. On the other hand, the compensating variation for non–college

A. Compensating Variation ($\lambda = 1$)

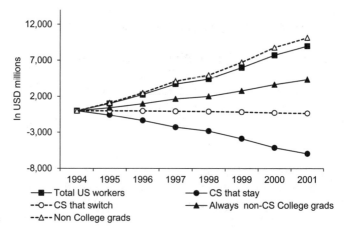

B. Change in Profits Due to Immigration ($\lambda = 1$)

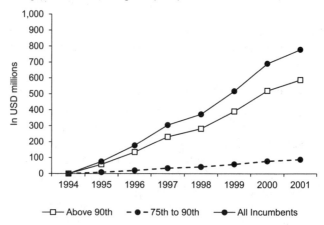

Fig. 4.7 Welfare changes due to immigration

Notes: The closed economy is where immigration is restricted to the 1994 levels, whereas in the open economy, the stock of immigrants grows according to the data. Compensating variation in this scenario is how much the workers must be compensated if immigration is restricted to the 1994 level. Compensating variation and profits are in millions of 1999 USD. The scaling up to USD was done using CPS data for the total amount of labor income across each year separately. Panels A, C, and E split up the workers into four groups—(a) those who stay in CS occupations even after immigration, (b) those who switch from CS to non-CS, (c) college graduates who were always non-CS, and (d) non–college graduates. Panels B, D, and F split up the firms into three different categories—(a) "all incumbents" are only the firms that still produce when immigration is restricted. Among these incumbents, the (b) "above 90th percentile" firms are those that have a productivity level that is above the 90th percentile in the productivity distribution, and similarly (c) "75th to 90th percentile" firms have a productivity level that lies between the 75th and 90th percentiles of the Pareto productivity distribution.

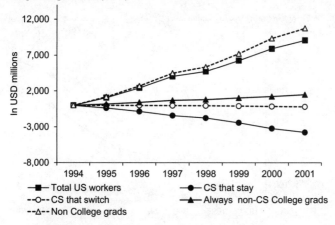

C. Compensating Variation ($\lambda = 2$)

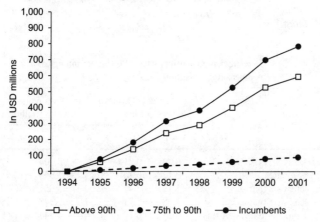

D. Change in Profits Due to Immigration ($\lambda = 2$)

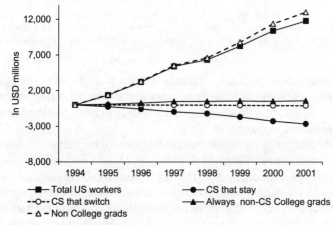

E. Compensating Variation ($\lambda = 4$)

Fig. 4.7 (cont.)

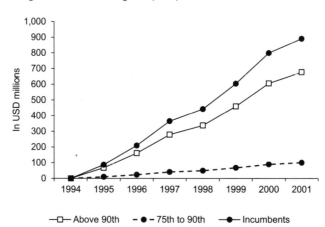

F. Change in Profits Due to Immigration ($\lambda = 4$)

Fig. 4.7   (cont.)

Table 4.6   **Percent change in utility when allowing for immigration and compensating variation**

	Percent change in utility			Compensating variation (million USD)		
	$\lambda = 1$	$\lambda = 2$	$\lambda = 4$	$\lambda = 1$	$\lambda = 2$	$\lambda = 4$
All US workers	0.20	0.21	0.27	8,204	8,290	10,904
All college graduates	−0.12	−0.16	−0.14	−1,955	−2,453	−2,110
Computer scientists that stay	−5.13	−3.47	−2.57	−5,951	−3,752	−2,631
Computer scientists that switch	−2.48	−1.71	−1.27	−348	−189	−85
Non-CS college graduates that stay	0.28	0.10	0.04	4,344	1,488	606
Non–college graduates	0.43	0.44	0.52	10,159	10,743	13,014

Note: We compare utility changes when going from a closed to an open economy, so percent changes are calculated for each year and subgroup as $[(V_{\text{open}}/V_{\text{closed}}) - 1] \times 100$, where V is indirect utility for that specific group. Compensating variation figures are expressed in million USD.

graduates increases when λ increases. Table 4.6 summarizes the utility percent changes from allowing immigration and compensating variation for 2001, corroborating the idea that there are significant distributional effects from increased immigration.

While workers as a whole benefit from more immigration, firms make higher profits, too. In figure 4.7, panels B, D, and F, the firms are split up into three different categories: (a) "all incumbents" are only the firms that still produce when immigration is restricted; among these incumbents, the (b) "above 90th percentile" firms are those that have a productivity level that is above the 90th percentile in the productivity distribution; and similarly, (c)

Table 4.7   **Percent change in profits when allowing for immigration (2001)**

	$\lambda = 1$		$\lambda = 2$		$\lambda = 4$	
	Share of profits	Percent change	Share of profits	Percent change	Share of profits	Percent change
All firms	—	0.61	—	0.62	—	0.70
All incumbent firms	100	0.61	100	0.62	100	0.70
90th–100th percentile	84.82	0.54	85.09	0.55	85.05	0.62
75th–90th percentile	9.64	0.71	9.59	0.73	9.60	0.82
< 75th	5.54	1.45	5.32	1.51	5.36	1.66

Notes: Columns titled "share of profits" show the share of profits among all incumbents by firm size for 2001 in the open economy. We compare profit changes when going from a closed to an open economy, so percent changes in aggregate profits for each year and subgroup are calculated as $[(\Pi_{open}/\Pi_{closed}) - 1] \times 100$. Percentiles are defined using the Pareto distribution we are assuming for productivities in the market. Rows 2–5 only consider incumbent firms (those that operate under the open and closed economy); row 1 shows the growth rate between open and closed taking into account the marginal firms that start producing in the open economy. Results shown for different values of λ and only look at year 2001.

"75th to 90th percentile" firms have a productivity level that lies between the 75th and 90th percentiles. Profits for all firms are increasing over this period, and most of the profits are captured by the firms in the top 10 percent of the productivity distribution. While we believe there is considerable heterogeneity in the profits firms receive as a result of the H-1B program, it is important to note that the distribution of profits in the model is determined by our assumption on the Pareto distribution of firm productivities. In 2001, the aggregate profits in the IT sector were between $0.78 and $0.89 billion (1999 USD), and between $0.59 and $0.68 billion went to the firms that had a productivity level above the 90th percentile. Table 4.7 summarizes the changes in profits for the different values of λ; overall profits increase between 0.61 percent and 0.70 percent in 2001 when allowing for immigration.

4.5.3   Alternative Modeling Specifications

We analyze how two particular features of the IT sector in our model affect our results. The first is our assumption of monopolistic competition and the existence of different varieties in IT products. This makes the IT sector smaller than the perfectly competitive optimal size. An increase in the number of immigrants, and therefore workers, will expand this sector and lead to welfare gains. At the same time, as more firms enter, the increase in varieties benefits consumers as well. The second nonstandard feature of our model is the presence of technological spillovers driven by innovation by computer scientists. An increase in the CS workforce due to immigration leads to more innovation and has an additional impact on overall production, lowering prices and increasing welfare for consumers.

In table 4.8 we compare the monopolistically competitive model with a traditional perfectly competitive setup, and also shut down the presence of technological spillovers to study how our results change. In moving from a perfectly competitive to a monopolistically competitive model, the welfare changes due to immigration are roughly similar. There is a slightly larger welfare gain due to immigration in the monopolistically competitive model both in the absence or the presence of technological spillovers. Shutting down the possibility of technological spillovers, however, has a larger impact on the gains from immigration. In the absence of spillovers, $\beta = 0$, the overall gains to worker utility is only between 0.02 percent and 0.03 percent, whereas the spillovers $\beta = 0.23$ increase these gains to about 0.21 percent. How the results change with other values of β is discussed in the "Sensitivity Analysis" section of the appendix. Therefore, while the monopolistic-competition assumption does not affect worker welfare much, the presence of technological spillovers does.

One advantage of the monopolistically competitive setup is that it allows us to get a measure of how firm profits are affected by immigration. The profit numbers should be interpreted with caution, however, since our framework implies that profits are simply a fixed proportion of total revenues. Nonetheless, given that IT firms spend a substantial amount of funds in lobbying Congress to raise the H-1B cap, it is reasonable to believe that firms stand to benefit from an influx of high-skilled immigrants.

Importantly, our model includes the labor supply decisions of college-educated US workers. This allows students and workers to move out of immigrant-intensive fields and occupations when there is an influx of high-skilled workers from abroad. The negative effects on CS workers are mitigated as US CS workers switch to non-CS jobs, and fewer students graduate with CS degrees. However, since CS workers are also innovators, the

Table 4.8   Percent change in utility—perfect competition versus monopolistic competition in the IT sector

	Perfectly competitive		Monopolistic competition	
	$\beta = 0$	$\beta = 0.23$	$\beta = 0$	$\beta = 0.23$
All US workers	0.02	0.20	0.03	0.21
All college graduates	−0.34	−0.16	−0.34	−0.16
Computer scientists that stay	−3.76	−3.58	−3.64	−3.47
Computer scientists that switch	−1.90	−1.76	−1.85	−1.71
Non-CS college graduates that stay	−0.08	0.10	−0.08	0.10
Non–college graduates	0.25	0.43	0.26	0.44

Note: We compare utility changes when going from a closed to an open economy, so percent changes are calculated for each year and subgroup as $[(V_{open}/V_{closed}) - 1] \times 100$, where V is indirect utility for that specific group. In the perfectly competitive cases, we assume that the IT sector is no longer under monopolistic competition. The $\beta = 0$ refers to the case where there is $\lambda = 0.23$.

Table 4.9   **Changes in profits and income for different labor supply specifications**

	Percent change in income/profits		Compensating variation/change in profits (million USD)	
	Baseline	Inelastic supply	Baseline	Inelastic supply
All US workers	0.21	0.46	8,290	17,798
All college graduates	−0.16	0.01	−2,453	225
Computer scientists that stay	−3.47	−7.51	−3,752	−8,467
Computer scientists that switch	−1.71	—	−189	—
Non-CS college graduates that stay	0.10	0.60	1,488	8,692
Non–college graduates	0.44	0.72	10,743	17,572
Profits	0.61	0.94	783	1,197

Note: The baseline case is when we apply our full labor supply model for college graduates. The inelastic case shows what happens when workers are not allowed to change occupations or degree-choice decisions. All specifications use a value of $\lambda = 2$, $\sigma = 1$, and $\beta = 0.23$. Dollar values for compensating variation and profits are in millions of 1999 USD. The scaling up to USD was done using CPS data for the total amount of labor income. Changes in income for different worker groups and profits are calculated as $[(X_{open}/X_{closed}) - 1] \times 100$.

economy as a whole no longer benefits as much from technological improvements when US workers leave CS occupations. In table 4.9, we compare our baseline model that allows for labor supply decisions to an inelastic supply model where US students and workers are no longer allowed to change their decisions in the face of high-skilled immigration. Immigration has even more negative impact on US CS workers when we restrict adjustments on the labor supply side. Since workers can no longer switch into non-CS occupations, the increase in labor supply from abroad depresses CS wages and hurts CS workers the most. On the other hand, welfare in the economy as a whole increases since there are more computer scientists and hence more innovators.

4.6 Discussion

Isolating the impacts of high-skilled immigration is challenging in the absence of credible instruments that exogenously vary the share of foreign workers. Nonetheless, given the rapidly increasing share of immigrants in the skilled labor force, it is an important issue to examine. We develop a general-equilibrium model of the US economy, calibrated using data from 1994 to 2001, to estimate how the increasing share of foreign high-skilled workers affects the welfare of different types of workers, firms, and consumers. We do so by examining the welfare of US natives under a counterfactual scenario where we restrict the fraction of immigrants to their 1994 levels.

While our conclusions depend on the specifics of our model, we believe them to be reasonable. As long as the supply curve of US workers is not infinitely elastic, and we believe that evidence indicates rather conclusively that it is not, the availability of high-skilled foreign immigrants will shift out the supply of high-skilled workers in the US economy. However, as long as the demand curve for high-skilled workers is downward sloping, the influx of foreign high-skilled workers will both crowd out and lower the wages of US high-skilled workers. As a result, output in the high-skill-intensive sector of the economy will rise, but will rise less than if the crowd-out effects were negligible. The fact that high-skilled workers contribute to innovation tends to mute such crowd-out effects, but our results suggest such effects are not nearly large enough to fully compensate for the crowd-out.

Overall, our results suggest that high-skilled foreign workers contribute to the well-being of the typical US consumer, mainly through the assumption that these workers contribute to innovation at the same rate as US high-skilled workers. Indeed, under our calibrations, accounting for foreign workers' effect on innovation, the gains to consumers are an order of magnitude larger than gains excluding this effect. At some level, this is hardly surprising. While simple models of the impact of immigration on native welfare suggests the immigrant surplus is second order (Borjas 1999), if the immigrants shift out the production possibility frontier, their effect will be first order.

In our model, immigration also raises profits in the IT sector. While the magnitude of these gains depends on the markup in the IT sector, as long as there is a markup, which we consider safe to assume, high-skilled immigrant labor raises IT sector profits. It is then no surprise that Bill Gates and other IT executives lobby in favor of increasing quotas for high-skilled immigrants.

Although our results suggest that the introduction and expansion of the H-1B program in the 1990s brought gains to both US consumers and IT-sector entrepreneurs, we also found indications of losses for US computer scientists and potential computer scientists. Recent work (Peri and Sparber 2009, 2011) has emphasized the importance of immigration affecting the occupational choice of US natives. Our results tend to support the importance of this view. Indeed, our estimates suggest that high-skilled immigration has had a significant effect on the choices made by US workers and students.

Researchers (e.g., Peri and Sparber 2011) have emphasized that high-skilled immigrants have the potential for opening up opportunities for US workers—someone who might otherwise have been an engineer or computer scientist now becomes a manager. We have no doubt that this is true and, in a primitive way, we have built this into our model. The influx of skilled immigrants induces some college graduates to leave computer science and raises the productivity of non-CS college graduates. Still, for many college graduates who entered or might have entered the CS field, their options have been curtailed.

Our model is far too simple to allow for policy evaluations of alternatives to our current system of high-skilled immigration. However, we note that our model (and simple economic reasoning) suggests that high-skilled immigration does tend to crowd out US workers to some extent. We suspect that allowing essentially unlimited immigration of high-skilled workers by, for instance, awarding green cards to all foreign students attending US colleges and universities would have dramatic effects on the US labor market. Not all of these would be positive.

In the end we want to emphasize the limitations of our work. While our focus is on how the influx of foreign workers affects the United States, we recognize that US policy on high-skilled immigration has profound effects on both labor-sending countries and other countries that produce in the IT sector. Also, our analysis is constrained to the 1990s, whereas in the long run, US immigration policy is likely to affect the position of the United States in the world economy. We leave exploration of these issues to future research.

Appendix

Additional Model Details

Consumer Demand for Goods

Given the consumer utility functions described in the "Household Problem" section, it is possible to write the price index P in the form of equation (A.1):

$$(A.1) \qquad P_c = \left(\int_{v \in \Omega} p_i^{1-\varepsilon} \, dv \right)^{1/1-\varepsilon}.$$

Consumers maximize utility in equation (1) subject to a budget constraint $m = P_c C_d + P_Y Y_d$, where m is total income. The utility-maximizing first-order condition for a given variety is therefore

$$(A.2) \qquad \left(\frac{c_{di}}{C_d} \right)^{-(1/\varepsilon)} = \frac{p_i}{P}.$$

We can then write the demand for aggregate goods as a function of prices, total income m and the parameters γ and σ.

$$(A.3) \qquad C_d = \frac{m}{P_c + P_Y \{[(1-\gamma)/\gamma](P_c/P_Y)\}^\sigma}$$

$$(A.4) \qquad Y_d = \frac{m\{[(1-\gamma)/\gamma](P_c/P_Y)\}^\sigma}{P_c + \{[(1-\gamma)/\gamma](P_c/P_Y)\}^\sigma}.$$

Labor Supply Derivations

In order to determine the labor supply of US-born workers, we use the setup described in section 4.2.3. First, we study the probability of students enrolling in CS degrees. Given the distributional assumptions and equation (15), it follows that the probability (q_t^{cs}) that a student graduates with a CS degree can be written in logistic form:

(A.5) $$q_t^{cs} = \left[1 + \exp\left(-\left(\rho^2 \mathbb{E}_{t-2}[V_{22}^{cs} - V_{22}^{o}] - \theta_o\right)/\sigma_0\right)\right]^{-1}.$$

This setup allows us to map the graduating probability described above to employment. Let $\left(L_t^a + G_t^a\right)$ be the number of college graduates with age a in time period t, then the number of graduates with a CS degree in year t is represented by $R_t = q_t^{cs}\left(L_t^{22} + G_t^{22}\right)$.

Next, we derive the occupational choice decisions based on the setup in the "Occupational Choice" section. Defining $q_{t,a}^{dD}$ as the probability that a worker at age a between twenty-two and sixty-four moves from occupation d to occupation D, it follows from the distributional assumptions that the probability of workers switching from computer science to other occupations, and vice versa, can be represented as

(A.6) $$q_{t,a}^{o,cs} = \left[1 + \exp\left(-\left(w_t - s_t - \zeta(a) - \theta_1 + \rho\mathbb{E}_t\left[V_{t+1,a+1}^{cs} - V_{t+1,a+1}^{o}\right]\right)/\sigma_1\right)\right]^{-1}$$

(A.7) $$q_{t,a}^{cs,o} = \left[1 + \exp\left(-\left(s_t - w_t - \zeta(a) + \theta_1 + \rho\mathbb{E}_t\left[V_{t+1,a+1}^{o} - V_{t+1,a+1}^{cs}\right]\right)/\sigma_1\right)\right]^{-1}.$$

Here we can see that the switching probabilities depend upon both the current wage differential and expected future career prospects in each occupation. The standard deviation of the taste shocks, the sector-attractiveness parameter, and the cost of switching occupations will affect the sensitivity of occupational switching to changes in relative career prospects.

Since individuals are forward looking, the working decisions depend upon the equilibrium distribution of their career prospects. Under the extreme value errors assumption, we can use the properties of the idiosyncratic taste shocks distribution to derive the expected values of career prospects (Rust 1987). The expected value functions for an individual at age a between twenty-two and sixty-four working as a computer scientist or in another occupation are respectively

(A.8) $$\mathbb{E}_t V_{t+1,a+1}^{cs} = \sigma_1\mathbb{E}_t[\varpi + ln\{\exp((w_{t+1} + \rho\mathbb{E}_{t+1}V_{t+2,a+2}^{cs})/\sigma_1)$$
$$+ \exp((s_{t+1} - \zeta(a) + \theta_1 + \rho\mathbb{E}_{t+1}V_{t+2,a+2}^{o})/\sigma_1)\}]$$

(A.9) $$\mathbb{E}_t V_{t+1,a+1}^{o} = \sigma_1\mathbb{E}_t[\varpi + ln\{\exp((s_{t+1} + \theta_1 + \rho\mathbb{E}_{t+1}V_{t+2,a+2}^{o})/\sigma_1)$$
$$+ \exp((w_{t+1} - \zeta(a) + \rho\mathbb{E}_{t+1}V_{t+2,a+2}^{cs})/\sigma_1)\}].$$

where gamma $\varpi = 0.577$ is the Euler's constant and the expectations are taken with respect to future taste shocks.

Given this setup we can use the occupational-switching probabilities to derive the aggregate employment in each sector. Since we allow workers at age twenty-two to also pay the switching costs and get their first job in an occupation that is different from their field of study, the number of computer scientists at age twenty-two is a function of the number of recent graduates with a CS degree and the occupational-switching probabilities:

(A.10) $$L_{nt}^{22} = (1 - q_{t,22}^{cs,o})R_t + q_{t,22}^{o,cs}[(L_{nt}^{22} + G_t^{22}) - R_t]$$

(A.11) $$G_t^{22} = (1 - q_{t,22}^{o,cs})[(L_{nt}^{22} + G_t^{22}) - R_t] + q_{t,22}^{cs,o}R_t$$

where R_t is the number of recent graduates with a CS degree, and $(L_{nt}^{22} + G_t^{22}) - R_t$ is the number of college graduates with any other degree. Similarly, the supply of computer scientists at age a from twenty-three to sixty-five is a function of past employment in each occupation and the switching probabilities:

(A.12) $$L_{nt}^a = \left(1 - q_{t,a}^{cs,o}\right)L_{n,t-1}^{a-1} + q_{t,a}^{o,cs}\left[G_{t-1}^{a-1}\right]$$

(A.13) $$G_t^a = \left(1 - q_{t,a}^{o,cs}\right)G_{t-1}^{a-1} + q_{t,a}^{cs,o}\left[L_{n,t-1}^{a-1}\right],$$

where L_{nt}^a is the exogenous number of workers in computer science at age a in time period t, and G_t^a is the number of workers at age a working in other occupations.

The aggregate domestic labor supply of computer scientists and other workers is the sum across all ages:

(A.14) $$L_{nt} = \sum_{a=22}^{a=65} L_{nt}^a$$

(A.15) $$G_t = \sum_{a=22}^{a=65} G_t^a.$$

Here we can see that the labor supply in each occupation depends on past employment, new college graduates, and on wages through the occupational-switching probabilities.

Market-Clearing Conditions

The following equations describe the market-clearing conditions for the labor and output markets. Total consumer expenditure equals labor income plus firm profits (equation [A.16]):

(A.16) $$P_{tc}C_{dt}^* + P_{yt}Y_{dt}^* = m = w_t(L_{nt}^* + L_{Ft}^*) + s_tG_t^* + r_tH_t^* + (\Pi_t + P_{yt}fN_t).$$

Total quantity produced in the IT sector equals domestic consumer demand, intermediate inputs in the other sector, and exports (equation [A.17]):

(A.17) $$N_t^{\varepsilon/(\varepsilon-1)}\left(\int_{\phi^*}^{\infty} c_{it}^{(\varepsilon-1)/\varepsilon}\mu(\phi)\,d\phi\right)^{\varepsilon/(\varepsilon-1)} = C_t^* = C_{dt}^* + C_{yt}^* + C_{Wt}^*.$$

Total quantity produced in the other sector, net of inputs, equals domestic consumer demand and intermediate inputs in the other sector (equation [A.18]):

(A.18) $$C_y^{*\psi_2}X_y^{*1-\psi_2} = Y_t^* = Y_{dt}^* + Y_{Ct}^* + fN_t^* - Y_{IMt}^*.$$

Trade in goods is balanced:

(A.19) $$P_{ct}^* C_{Wt}^* = P_{yt}^* Y_{IMt}^*.$$

Given that the supply of non–college graduates is inelastic $\bar{H}_t$, and the demand comes from both sectors, their labor market clears as in equation (A.20):

(A.20) $$\bar{H}_t = H_{ct}^* + H_{yt}^*.$$

Total labor supply for college graduates (CS and non-CS) is fixed, such that total demand for college graduates has to be equal to total supply in each period (equation [A.21]):

(A.21) $$\overline{L_{nt} + G_t} + \bar{L}_F = L_t^* + G_t^* = L_{ct}^* + L_{yt}^* + G_{ct}^* + G_{yt}^*.$$

Details of the Data Used

This study draws on a variety of data sets. Our descriptive statistics in table 4.1 rely on the IPUMS census from 1970 to 2000. We restrict the sample to employed workers. We use the IPUMS-suggested occupation crosswalk and define computer scientists as computer systems analysts, computer scientists, and computer software developers with at least a bachelor of arts (BA) degree. We define foreigners as either naturalized citizens or noncitizens who immigrated after the age of eighteen. For early census years, the year of immigration is only available in ranges. In order to construct a precise year of immigration value for workers in those samples, we choose to select a random value within the year range for each individual.

Data on earnings, domestic employment, and foreign employment used in the calibration procedure and in the descriptive figures come from the March CPS, obtained from the IPUMS and NBER websites. The sample consists of employed persons with at least a BA degree. A person is defined as foreign if he/she was born outside the United States and immigrated after the age of eighteen. Earnings are deflated to 1999 dollars, and top-coded values are multiplied by 1.4.

In our analysis we drop imputed earnings. In order to identify these imputed values, we use a methodology similar to Bollinger and Hirsch (2007). From the IPUMS database we use the qinclongj and qincwage variables, and from the NBER database we use the FL665 flag to identify imputations. The database also contains ten Census Bureau flags that identify a small fraction (less than 1 percent) of earnings as allocated. Over the period under study, around 26 percent of earnings were allocated. This fraction of imputations varies over time—between 19.14 percent (in 1994) and 29.47 percent (in 2003). These numbers are consistent with Bollinger and Hirsch (2007), who find that between 1998 and 2006, the nonresponse rate was about 20 percent. The small difference in our numbers arises both from using a different sample (restricted to those with a bachelor of arts or master of arts degree) and because nonresponse is not the only reason the CPS imputes earnings.

In order to define workers in computer science, we use the occupational codes in the CPS Outgoing Rotation Group (CPS-ORG) data set. The occupational coding in the CPS-ORG up to 2002 uses the 1990 census definition. We consider as computer scientists those under the occupational titles of: "055 electrical and electronic," "064 computer systems analysts and scientists," and "229 computer programmers."

College-degree-attainment data is based on Integrated Postsecondary Education Data System (IPEDS) Completions Survey. It consists of bachelor's degrees awarded by the National Science Foundation (NSF) population of institutions. We consider enrollment in computer science and electrical engineer as the number of degrees awarded in these fields lagged by two years. For 1994 and 1995, degree attainment in electrical engineering was not available by native and foreign students, but only shown together with all engineering degrees. We input the data for these two years by looking at the average growth in electrical engineering for 1996–2002.

In descriptive statistics, we compare the CS workforce to STEM workers. The STEM occupations are defined as engineers, computer systems analysts and computer scientists, computer software developers, operations and systems researchers and analysts, actuaries, statisticians, mathematicians and mathematical scientists, physicists and astronomers, chemists, atmospheric and space scientists, geologists, physical scientists n.e.c., agricultural and food scientists, biological scientists, foresters and conservation scientists, and medical scientists.

We use data on the prices, quantities, costs, and value added from the BEA, since this source allows us to look into data for specific industry groups. Data on firm entry and exit comes from the Business Dynamic Statistics (BDS), and the 1992 US Census Bureau's Statistics of US Businesses (SUSB). In these data sets we define the IT sector as the subsectors of "computer and electronic product manufacturing," "publishing industries, except Internet (includes software)," "data processing, Internet publishing, and other information services," and "computer systems design and related services" according to the NAICS 2002 classification. The non-IT sector is defined as all other sectors in the economy.

Extended Out-of-Sample Tests (until 2015)

In section 4.3.3 we describe how we calibrate our labor supply parameters for the period 1994–2001. We matched observed moments of relative wages, employment, and enrollment for three years, and performed an out-of-sample test for the years in between, as shown in figure 4.2. A natural question to ask is whether our calibrated parameters are able to predict movements in key data series for the years after 2001 as an additional out-of-sample test of our model.

In figure 4A.1, we perform such an out-of-sample analysis. To do this, we constructed the relative labor supply shocks Z_t from equation (27) using information on the relative wages, relative native employment, and relative foreign employment for the period 2002–2015 together with the relative labor demand curve for the base year 1994. In a second step, we fed those shocks into our labor supply model using the parameters calibrated for the

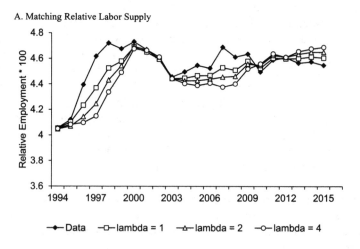

A. Matching Relative Labor Supply

—◆—Data   —□—lambda = 1   —△—lambda = 2   —○—lambda = 4

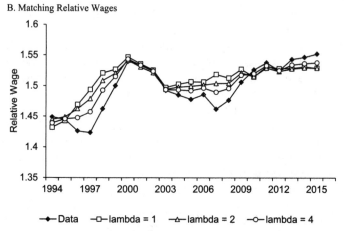

B. Matching Relative Wages

—◆—Data   —□—lambda = 1   —△—lambda = 2   —○—lambda = 4

Fig. 4A.1   Employment, wages, and enrollment (1994 to 2015)

Source: Wage and employment data come from the March CPS, whereas degree data is from IPEDS.

Notes: In the calibration exercise, the years 1994 and 2001 were used to match the data for employment and wages, whereas the years 1994, 1997, and 2001 were used to match the data on degree attainment (lagged two years). The years in between, and after 2001, are an out-of-sample test. See the "Details of the Data Used" section of the appendix for more details about the data.

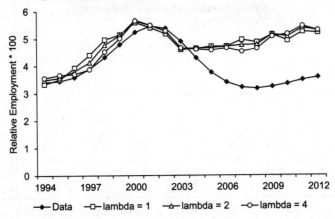

Fig. 4A.1   (cont.)

1994–2001 period to observe how relative wages, employment, and enrollment series are predicted by our model for the post-2001 period. As can
be seen in figure 4A.1, we consistently predict employment and wages for
the post-2001 years, but overestimate enrollment rates for the years 2005
onward.

Sensitivity Analysis

We check how sensitive our results are to variations in key parameters
and specifications of the model. So far we have presented all our results for
three different values of λ. Despite slight differences in the magnitudes of
changes in income and profits, the results are qualitatively similar across
different values of this parameter. For simplicity, we fix $\lambda = 2$ when doing
our sensitivity analysis on all the other parameters of the model.

First we look at how sensitive our results are to variations in the elasticity of substitution between the IT good and the non-IT good, represented
by the parameter σ. As we see in table 4A.1, the more elastic the relative
product-demand curve, the larger the income increase for all US workers is
when we allow for immigration. This is consistent with economic intuition,
since a higher value of σ implies that consumers are more willing to substitute consumption from non-IT to IT goods. When we allow for immigration, the larger number of computer scientists in the economy increases the
size of the IT sector and consumers shift into consuming more IT goods.
Profits for IT firms rise and workers that are complements to CS workers are
better off for higher values of σ. Furthermore, since IT production drives
technological change, as and when more resources are devoted to IT for
higher values of σ, the price of IT goods falls, increasing overall welfare.
Overall, our qualitative results are similar for different values of σ with the

Table 4A.1   Changes in profits and income for different elasticities of substitution between IT and non-IT good in consumer utility

	Percent change in income/profits			Compensating variation/change in profits (million USD)		
	$\sigma = 1$	$\sigma = 2$	$\sigma = 5$	$\sigma = 1$	$\sigma = 2$	$\sigma = 5$
All US workers	0.21	0.25	0.41	8,290	32,760	102,943
All college graduates	−0.16	−0.11	0.07	−2,453	7,060	34,637
Computer scientists that stay	−3.47	−3.65	−3.43	−3,752	−3,360	−1,471
Computer scientists that switch	−1.71	−1.78	−1.61	−189	−127	48
Non-CS college graduates that stay	0.10	0.16	0.34	1,488	10,547	36,061
Non–college graduates	0.44	0.48	0.63	10,743	25,700	68,305
Profits	0.62	1.66	7.70	783	2,106	9,160

Note: All specifications use a value of $\lambda = 2$ and $\beta = 0.23$. Dollar values for compensating variation and profits are in millions of 1999 USD. The scaling up to USD was done using CPS data for the total amount of labor income. Changes in income for different worker groups and profits are calculated as $[(X_{\text{open}}/X_{\text{closed}}) - 1] \times 100$.

only difference being that for high values of σ the population of all college graduates is better off due to immigration.

We also vary the technological change parameter and check how sensitive our results are to reasonable values of β. Our calibrated value of β is 0.233, and we redo our results for values of 0, 0.1, and 0.5. Table 4A.2 shows how the compensating variation and profits change as we vary β. Immigration is benefecial for higher values of β for all types of US workers and firms, since a larger CS workforce increases the gains from technology. Firms directly benefit from higher output, whereas consumers benefit from lower prices as the value of β rises. Overall, however, our qualitative results are similar across the different β levels. The only qualitative difference is that for the scenario where there is no technological progress ($\beta = 0$), the subpopulation of non-CS college graduates is worse off when there is immigration. This happens because without the spillover of aggregate computer scientists, the positive effect they had for being complements to computer science gets smaller and is offset by the lower wages caused by computer scientists switching occupations.

Last, we vary the elasticity of substitution between varieties of the IT good ε across a reasonable range. In section 4.5.3, we discuss results for the baseline case where the goods are perfect substitutes and all IT firms are similar. In table 4A.3, we see that as we lower the elasticity of substitution ε from a value of 3.2 to 2, the overall welfare gains from immigration are enhanced. While close substitutes in the labor market are worse off for smaller values of ε, complements are better off. The overall impacts, however, are similar both qualitatively and quantitatively.

In other results, we test to see whether using a Melitz-style (2003) model

Table 4A.2 **Changes in profits and income for different values of the technological spillover parameter**

	Percent change in income/profits				Compensating variation/change in profits (million USD)			
	$\beta = 0$	$\beta = 0.1$	$\beta = 0.233$	$\beta = 0.5$	$\beta = 0$	$\beta = 0.1$	$\beta = 0.233$	$\beta = 0.5$
All US workers	0.03	0.10	0.21	0.41	1,051	4,150	8,290	16,522
All college graduates	−0.34	−0.26	−0.16	0.05	−5,275	−4,066	−2,453	758
Computer scientists that stay	−3.64	−3.57	−3.47	−3.27	−3945	−3,862	−3,752	−3,530
Computer scientists that switch	−1.85	−1.79	−1.71	−1.54	−205	−198	−189	−171
Non-CS college graduates that stay	−0.08	0.00	0.10	0.31	−1,125	−6	1,488	4,458
Non–college graduates	0.26	0.33	0.44	0.64	6,326	8,216	10,743	15,764
Profits	0.43	0.51	0.62	0.82	554	653	783	1,047

Note: All specifications use a value of $\lambda = 2$ and $\sigma = 1$. Dollar values for compensating variation and profits are in millions of 1999 USD. The scaling up to USD was done using CPS data for the total amount of labor income. Changes in income for different worker groups and profits are calculated as $[(X_{open}/X_{closed}) - 1] \times 100$.

Table 4A.3 **Changes in profits and income for different values of the elasticity of substitution across varieties in consumer utility**

	Percent change in income/profits		Compensating variation/change in profits (million USD)	
	$\varepsilon = 0$	$\varepsilon = 3.2$	$\varepsilon = 0$	$\varepsilon = 3.2$
All US workers	0.26	0.21	10,272	8,290
All college graduates	−0.11	−0.16	−1,641	−2,453
Computer scientists that stay	−3.78	−3.47	−4,000	−3,752
Computer scientists that switch	−1.83	−1.71	−181	−189
Non-CS college graduates that stay	0.18	0.10	2,540	1,488
Non–college graduates	0.50	0.44	11,913	10,743
Profits	0.67	0.62	615	783

Note: All specifications use a value of $\lambda = 2$, $\sigma = 1$, and $\beta = 0.23$. Dollar values for compensating variation and profits are in millions of 1999 USD. The scaling up to USD was done using CPS data for the total amount of labor income. Changes in income for different worker groups and profits are calculated as $[(X_{open}/X_{closed}) - 1] \times 100$.

of entry significantly affects our conclusions and found out that it does not. In our baseline model, there is an underlying fixed number of potential entrepreneurs that always know their level of productivity ϕ_j, a setup closer to Chaney (2008). An alternative setup is one where firms do not initially know their level of productivity ϕ_j, but must pay a fixed sunk cost f_e to draw their level of productivity from the known distribution. Firms wish to pay this cost as long as their expected profits are positive. As more firms draw and produce, expected profits fall until they are zero. Once a firm draws their productivity ϕ_j, they may choose to pay another fixed cost f and produce if $\phi_j > \phi^*$. This setup is closer to the one described by Melitz (2003).[39]

We may expect these setups to have different implications for firm profits and overall welfare. In our baseline model, an increase in immigration tends to increase firm profits, and the marginal firms enter into producing goods. Since all firms already know their productivity level, the more productive firms always produce. The new entrants are therefore firms that have a productivity level in the immediate neighborhood of ϕ^*. The overall increase in productivity, therefore, is small since the new entrants are firms that have relatively low productivity. Furthermore, the increase in profits is almost entirely captured by the larger firms. In the alternative Melitz (2003) framework, entry may happen at any part of the productivity distribution. When the expected profits rise because of immigration, new entrants may potentially draw very high levels of productivity and enter at the extreme tails of the distribution. The overall increase in productivity is higher, which drives down the price of the IT good and increases consumer utility. Furthermore the new entrants capture all the increase in profits, whereas the profits for the incumbents do not change. Compared to the baseline model, we find that the change in welfare due to immigration is higher under the Melitz entry setup both because of higher aggregate profits and consumer utility. This is because the new firms that enter the industry are not just the firms with marginal productivity, but could also be firms with very high levels of productivity. These firms have higher profits and drive down the output prices more. Qualitatively, however, all our results stay the same across the two models.

References

Acemoglu, D. 1998. "Why Do New Technologies Complement Skills? Directed Technical Change and Wage Inequality." *Quarterly Journal of Economics* 113 (4): 1055–89.

Arrow, K. J. 1962. "The Economic Implications of Learning by Doing." *Review of Economic Studies* 29 (3): 155–73.

Bernard, A. B., J. Eaton, J. B. Jensen, and S. Kortum. 2003. "Plants and Productivity in International Trade." *American Economic Review* 93 (4): 1268–90.

Bollinger, C., and B. Hirsch. 2007. "How Well Are Earnings Measured in the Current Population Survey? Bias from Nonresponse and Proxy Respondents." For the North American Summer Meetings of the Econometric Society, Duke University,

39. To see a discussion about these two models in the context of immigration models, see di Giovanni, Levchenko, and Ortega (2015).

June 21–24. http://www2.gsu.edu/~ecobth/ES_Bollinger-Hirsch_Response_Bias
_Apr07.pdf.

Borjas, G. 1999. "The Economic Analysis of Immigration." In *Handbook of Labor Economics*, vol. 3A, edited by Orley Ashenfelter and David Card. Amsterdam: Elsevier.

Bound, J., B. Braga, J. Golden, and G. Khanna. 2015. "Recruitment of Foreigners in the Market for Computer Scientists in the US." *Journal of Labor Economics* 33 (S1, part 2): S187–223.

Broda, C., and D. Weinstein. 2006. "Globalization and the Gains from Variety." *Quarterly Journal of Economics* 121 (2): 541–85.

Card, D., and T. Lemieux. 2001. "Can Falling Supply Explain the Rising Return to College for Younger Men? A Cohort-Based Analysis." *Quarterly Journal of Economics* 116 (2): 705–46.

Chaney, T. 2008. "Distorted Gravity: The Intensive and Extensive Margins of International Trade." *American Economic Review* 98 (4): 1707–21.

Clemens, M. A. 2013. "Why Do Programmers Earn More in Houston Than Hyderabad? Evidence from Randomized Processing of US Visas." *American Economic Review, Papers & Proceedings* 103 (3): 198–202.

Demidova, S. 2008. "Productivity Improvements and Falling Trade Costs: Boon or Bane?" *International Economic Review* 49 (4): 1437–62.

di Giovanni, J., A. Levchenko, and F. Ortega. 2015. "A Global View of Cross-Border Migration." *Journal of the European Economic Association* 13 (1): 168–202.

Dixit, A. K., and J. E. Stiglitz. 1977. "Monopolistic Competition and Optimum Product Diversity." *American Economic Review* 67 (3): 297–308.

Doran, K., A. Gelber, and A. Isen. 2015. "The Effect of High-Skilled Immigration Policy on Firms: Evidence from H-1B Visa Lotteries." NBER Working Paper no. 20668, Cambridge, MA.

Freeman, R. B. 1975. "Supply and Salary Adjustments to the Changing Science Manpower Market: Physics, 1948–1973." *American Economic Review* 65 (1): 27–39.

———. 1976. "A Cobweb Model of the Supply and Starting Salary of New Engineers." *Industrial and Labor Relations Review* 29 (2): 236–48.

———. 2006. "Does Globalization of the Scientific/Engineering Workforce Threaten US Economic Leadership?" In *Innovation Policy and the Economy*, vol. 6, edited by Adam B. Jaffe, Josh Lerner, and Scott Stern. Cambridge, MA: MIT Press.

———. 2009. "What Does Global Expansion of Higher Education Mean for the US?" NBER Working Paper no. 14962, Cambridge, MA.

Gaubert, C. 2015. "Firm Sorting and Agglomeration." Working Paper, University of California, Berkeley.

Ghosh, A., A. M. Mayda, and F. Ortega. 2014. "The Impact of Skilled Foreign Workers on Firms: An Investigation of Publicly Traded US Firms." IZA Discussion Paper no. 8684, Institute for the Study of Labor.

Goldin, C., and L. F. Katz. 2007. "Long-Run Changes in the Wage Structure: Narrowing, Widening, Polarizing." *Brookings Papers on Economic Activity* 2 (2007): 135–65.

Gordon, R. 1990. *The Measurement of Durable Goods Prices*. National Bureau of Economic Research Monograph. Chicago: University of Chicago Press.

Grossman, G. M., and E. Helpman. 1991. "Quality Ladders in the Theory of Growth." *Review of Economic Studies* 58 (1): 43–61.

Grossman, G. M., and E. Rossi-Hansberg. 2008. "Trading Tasks: A Simple Theory of Offshoring." *American Economic Review* 98 (5): 1978–97.

Hopenhayn, H. A. 1992. "Entry, Exit, and Firm Dynamics in Long Run Equilibrium." *Econometrica* 60 (5): 1127–50.

Hunt, J., and M. Gauthier-Loiselle. 2010. "How Much Does Immigration Boost Innovation?" *American Economic Journal: Macroeconomics* 2 (2): 31–56.

Jorgenson, D. W., M. S. Ho, and J. D. Samuels. 2016. "Education, Participation and the Revival of US Economic Growth." NBER Working Paper no. 22453, Cambridge, MA.

Kambourov, G., and I. Manovskii. 2009. "Occupational Specificity of Human Capital." *International Economic Review* 50 (1): 63–115.

Katz, L. F., and K. M. Murphy. 1992. "Changes in Relative Wages, 1963–1987: Supply and Demand Factors." *Quarterly Journal of Economics* 107 (1): 35–78.

Kerr, W. R., and W. F. Lincoln. 2010. "The Supply Side of Innovation: H-1B Visa Reforms and US Ethnic Invention." *Journal of Labor Economics* 28 (3): 473–508.

Khanna, G., and N. Morales. 2015. "The IT Boom and Other Unintended Consequences of Chasing the American Dream." Working Paper no. 460, Center for Global Development.

Kirkegaard, J. 2005. "Outsourcing and Skill Imports: Foreign High-Skilled Workers on H-1B and L-1 Visas in the United States." Working Paper no. 05-15, Washington, DC, Peterson Institute for International Economics.

Kline, P. 2008. "Understanding Sectoral Labor Market Dynamics: An Equilibrium Analysis of the Oil and Gas Field Services Industry." Cowles Foundation Discussion Paper no. 1645, Cowles Foundation for Research in Economics, Yale University.

Krugman, P. 1979. "A Model of Innovation, Technology Transfer, and the World Distribution of Income." *Journal of Political Economy* 87 (2): 253–66.

Lemieux, T. 2006. "Increasing Residual Wage Inequality: Composition Effects, Noisy Data, or Rising Demand for Skill?" *American Economic Review* 96:461–98.

Liu, R., and D. Trefler. 2008. "Much Ado about Nothing: American Jobs and the Rise of Service Outsourcing to China and India." NBER Working Paper no. 14061, Cambridge, MA.

Lowell, B. Lindsay. 2000. "H-1B Temporary Workers: Estimating the Population." CCIS Working Paper no. 12, Center for Comparative Immigration Studies, University of California, San Diego. http://escholarship.org/uc/item/4ms039dc#page-1.

Matloff, N. 2003. "On the Need for Reform of the H-1B Non-Immigrant Work Visa in Computer-Related Occupations." *University of Michigan Journal of Law Reform* 36 (4): 815–914.

Melitz, M. 2003. "The Impact of Trade on Intra-Industry Reallocations and Aggregate Industry Productivity." *Econometrica* 71:1695–725.

Melitz, M., and G. Ottaviano. 2008. "Market Size, Trade, and Productivity." *Review of Economic Studies* 75:295–316.

Melitz, M., and S. Redding. 2015. "New Trade Models, New Welfare Implications." *American Economic Review* 105 (3): 1105–46.

Mithas, S., and H. C. Lucas. 2010. "Are Foreign IT Workers Cheaper? US Visa Policies and Compensation of Information Technology Professionals." *Management Science* 56 (5): 745–65.

Mukhopadhyay, S., and D. Oxborrow. 2012. "The Value of an Employment-Based Green Card." *Demography* 49:219–37.

Nathan, M. 2013. "The Wider Economic Impacts of High-Skilled Migrants: A Survey of the Literature." IZA Discussion Paper no. 7653, Institute for the Study of Labor.

Peri, G., K. Shih, and C. Sparber. 2013. "STEM Workers, H1B Visas and Productivity in US Cities." Working Paper, University of California, Davis, and Colgate University.

———. 2014. "Foreign STEM Workers and Native Wages and Employment in US Cities." NBER Working Paper no. 20093, Cambridge, MA.

————. 2015. "Foreign and Native Skilled Workers: What Can We Learn from H-1B Lotteries?" NBER Working Paper no. 21175, Cambridge, MA.

Peri, G., and C. Sparber. 2009. "Task Specialization, Immigration, and Wages." *American Economic Journal: Applied Economics* 1 (3): 135–69.

————. 2011. "Highly Educated Immigrants and Native Occupational Choice." *Industrial Relations* 50 (3): 385–411.

Pfluger, M., and S. Russek. 2013. *Firms in the International Economy—Firm Heterogeneity Meets International Business*. Cambridge, MA: MIT Press.

Romer, P. 1990. "Endogenous Technological Change." *Journal of Political Economy* 98 (5, part 2): S71–102.

Rust, J. 1987. "Optimal Replacement of GMC Bus Engines: An Empirical Model of Harold Zurcher." *Econometrica* 55 (5): 999–1033.

Ryoo, J., and S. Rosen. 2004. "The Engineering Labor Market." *Journal of Political Economy* 112 (S1): S110–40.

US Department of Commerce. 2000. "Digital Economy 2000." Technical report, Washington, DC, US Department of Commerce.

US General Accounting Office. 2000. "H-1B Foreign Workers: Better Controls Needed to Help Employers and Protect Workers." Technical Report GAO/HEHS 00-157, Washington, DC, US General Accounting Office.

————. 2011. "H-1B Visa Program: Reforms Are Needed to Minimize the Risks and Costs of Current Program." Technical Report GAO/HEHS 00-157, Washington, DC, US General Accounting Office.

US Immigration and Naturalization Service. 2000. "Characteristics of Specialty Occupation Workers (H 1B)." Technical report, Washington, DC, US Immigration and Naturalization Service.

High-Skilled Immigration, STEM Employment, and Nonroutine-Biased Technical Change

Nir Jaimovich and Henry E. Siu

5.1 Introduction

Immigration has constituted an important source of growth in high-skilled employment, innovation, and productivity in the United States during the past thirty-five years. In this chapter, we study the role of this immigration in accounting for changes in the occupational-skill distribution and wage inequality experienced during this time period.

There is a growing body of empirical work studying the labor market implications of high-skilled immigration. Most of this work focuses on the impact on employment outcomes for other high-skilled workers and, specifically, whether there is "crowding out" or displacement of the native born. Though methodological approaches differ across studies, a rough summary of the literature is that there is mixed or little evidence that such displacement exists.[1] However, as noted by Kerr (2013), much less is known about

Nir Jaimovich is professor of economics at the University of Zurich and a research associate of the National Bureau of Economic Research. Henry E. Siu is associate professor of economics at the University of British Columbia and a faculty research fellow of the National Bureau of Economic Research.

We thank David Green, Valerie Ramey, and participants at the Bank of Canada Labour Workshop and NBER Global Talent SI Conference for valuable comments and discussion. Siu thanks the Social Sciences and Humanities Research Council of Canada for support. For acknowledgments, sources of research support, and disclosure of the authors' material financial relationships, if any, please see http://www.nber.org/chapters/c13845.ack.

1. See Hunt and Gauthier-Loiselle (2010), Kerr and Lincoln (2010), and Peri, Shih, and Sparber (2015). Kerr (2013) provides a very useful overview of the literature on immigration, high-skilled labor markets, and innovation. In recent work, Doran, Gelber, and Isen (2016) find evidence of crowding out among high-skilled workers at the firm level. It should be noted that firm-level effects do not necessarily extend to the aggregate level that we are interested in here. See also Borjas and Doran (2015) and Bound et al. (2015) for analyses of mathematicians and computer scientists, respectively.

the long-run and general-equilibrium impacts of high-skilled immigration on the US labor market. The aim of this chapter is to contribute on this dimension and provide a quantitative theoretic framework in which such questions can be addressed.

The starting point of our analysis, as documented in section 5.2 and by Hanson and Slaughter (2016), is the fact that high-skilled immigrants represent a large and growing share of employment in *STEM occupations*— fields related to research, development, and innovation which are key to productivity growth and technological progress. As such, these high-skilled immigrants and foreign-born innovators contribute disproportionately to US growth. As we show in section 5.2, the likelihood of high-skilled immigrants working in a STEM occupation has increased over time, while this likelihood has remained essentially constant for the native born. This differential change is not due simply to differences in demographic change between native- and foreign-born workers; rather, relative to native-born, high-skilled workers, the foreign born have either experienced a much larger change in their propensity to work in STEM occupations conditional on (observable) demographic characteristics, or there has been an important change in unobservable characteristics of the foreign born, or both.

During the same time of increased high-skilled immigration, the economy has experienced technical change that is *nonroutine biased*, allowing technology to substitute for labor in performing "routine tasks" during the past thirty-five years.[2] Given this, we present in section 5.3 a unified framework of endogenous nonroutine-biased technical change (NBTC) with both native- and foreign-born workers. In the model, workers face an occupational choice between employment in production or innovation jobs. As such, NBTC is the outcome of purposeful activity, namely, the equilibrium allocation of workers to innovation. These elements of the model provide a framework to simultaneously assess the general-equilibrium implications of high-skilled immigration and changes in occupational sorting documented in section 5.2.

In section 5.4, we discuss the calibration and quantitative specification of the model. We then use the model to quantify the role of high-skilled immigration on nonroutine-biased technical change, its associated polarization of employment opportunities, and the evolution of wage inequality since 1980. We find that, contrary to expectation, high-skilled immigration has contributed to a narrowing of wage inequality.

---

2. While others have referred to this process as "routine-biased" technical change (see, e.g., Goos, Manning, and Salomons 2014, Autor, Dorn, and Hanson 2015), we depart from the literature and use the term nonroutine biased. This is in keeping with the use of terminology in the literature on skill-biased technical change (see, e.g., Violante 2008) in which recent technological progress has benefited skilled (versus unskilled) workers. As argued here and in the literature on *job polarization* (discussed below), recent technical change has benefited workers in nonroutine (versus routine) occupations.

Table 5.1   **High-skilled employment by occupational group**

	1. Total		2. NRC		3. STEM	
	1980	2010	1980	2010	1980	2010
Foreign born	1,368	7,061	951	4,948	172	1,063
Native born	16,283	34,973	11,933	25,256	1,238	2,653
Foreign-born share						
Employment	0.078	0.168	0.074	0.164	0.122	0.286
Employment growth (%)	23.3		23.1		38.6	

Source: Data from 1980 census and 2010 American Community Survey. See text for details.
Notes: Employment among twenty to sixty-four-year-olds with ≥ four years of college/bachelor's degree, in thousands.

5.2   Empirical Facts

5.2.1   Immigration and High-Skilled Employment

According to the US Census Bureau, the foreign-born share of the population has more than doubled between 1980 and 2010, from 6.2 percent to 12.9 percent (see Grieco et al. 2012). As a result, the foreign-born share of high-skilled employment has increased as well. In table 5.1, we present evidence of this using the 5 percent sample of the 1980 decennial census and the 1 percent sample of the 2010 American Community Survey (ACS), made available by IPUMS (see Ruggles et al. 2010). We restrict attention to the twenty- to sixty-four-year-old (or "working age") population. Given differences in the questionnaire, we define *high-skilled* workers as those with at least four years of college in the 1980 census, and those with at least a bachelor's degree in the 2010 ACS.[3]

Evidently, high-skilled, foreign-born employment increased by 5.7 million workers during this period. As a fraction of total high-skilled employment (*in levels*), the foreign-born share increased from 7.8 percent in 1980 to 16.8 percent in 2010, mirroring the proportional increase in the overall population. The bottom row of column (1), table 5.1 indicates that, of the total *growth* in high-skilled employment, approximately 23 percent is accounted for by the foreign born.

Among high-skilled workers, employment is concentrated within certain occupations. To illustrate this, we adopt the classification system used in the job-polarization literature that documents changes in the occupational-employment distribution since the 1980s (see, e.g., Acemoglu and Autor 2011; Cortes et al. 2015). We delineate occupations along two dimensions—

---

3. For highly related results to those presented in this subsection and the next, see Hanson and Slaughter (2016) who provide more detailed analysis disaggregated by educational attainment and occupation, analysis of wages and earnings, and discussion on the H-1B visa program and means of entry.

"cognitive" versus "manual" and "routine" versus "nonroutine"—based on the skill content of tasks performed on the job. The distinction between cognitive and manual jobs is based on the extent of mental versus physical activity. The distinction between routine and nonroutine occupations is based on the work of Autor, Levy, and Murnane (2003). If the tasks involved can be summarized as a set of specific activities accomplished by following well-defined instructions and procedures, the occupation is considered routine. If instead the job requires mental or physical flexibility, problem solving, or human-interaction skills, the occupation is nonroutine.

High-skilled employment is concentrated in *nonroutine cognitive* (NRC) occupations. Not surprisingly, these jobs occupy the upper tail of the occupational wage distribution (see, e.g., Goos and Manning 2007; Acemoglu and Autor 2011). This is true of both native- and foreign-born workers. The second set of columns of table 5.1 display these employment figures.[4] Among the foreign born, $951 \div 1,368 = 69.5$ percent of high-skilled individuals worked in a nonroutine cognitive occupation in 1980. This has held remarkably constant over time, at 70.1 percent in 2010. Similarly, approximately 72 percent of high-skilled, native-born workers work in NRC occupations in both 1980 and 2010.[5]

This occupational concentration, coupled with increasing immigration, implies that the foreign-born share of nonroutine cognitive employment has risen over time. This share increased from 7.4 percent in 1980 to 16.4 percent in 2010, closely mirroring the proportional increase observed in high-skilled employment and population. Of the total increase in nonroutine cognitive employment, approximately 23 percent is accounted for by the foreign born.

While the sorting of high-skilled workers into nonroutine cognitive occupations is similar between the native and foreign born, sorting into jobs *within* this broad occupational group differ in important ways. High-skilled, foreign-born workers tend to work in occupations with a quantitative emphasis, whereas the native born specialize in occupations emphasizing communication and interpersonal skills (see, e.g., Chiswick and Taengnoi 2007; Hunt and Gauthier-Loiselle 2010; Peri and Sparber 2011). This is evident in the native- and foreign-born representation in the subset of nonroutine cognitive occupations related to STEM fields: science, technology, engineering, and mathematics, displayed in the third set of columns of table 5.1.[6]

4. In our analysis, nonroutine cognitive jobs correspond to those under the categories of management, business and financial operations, and professional occupations in the 2010 Standard Occupational Classification. See Cortes et al. (2015) for a more detailed discussion, as well as how occupation codes are linked across the 1980 and 2010 classification systems.

5. Perhaps unsurprisingly, the approximately 30 percent of the high skilled not working in NRC jobs is concentrated in the young. For instance, the fraction of twenty- to twenty-four-year-old high-skilled workers employed in a nonroutine cognitive occupation is only 57 percent.

6. In particular, we define STEM jobs as those listed under computer and mathematical, architecture and engineering, and life and physical science occupations, a subset within the professional occupation category in the 2010 Standard Occupational Classification.

While the foreign born accounted for 7.4 percent of employment in non-routine cognitive jobs in 1980, they represented 12.2 percent of employment in STEM occupations. In 2010, high-skilled, foreign-born workers account for 28.6 percent of STEM employment, an increase of a factor of approximately 2.5. Of the total increase in STEM employment in the United States between 1980 and 2010, approximately 39 percent is accounted for by the foreign born (see also Kerr and Lincoln 2010).[7] Finally, as discussed in the literature, such occupations are closely related to innovation, research and development (R&D), and thus, technological progress; as such, high-skilled immigration has played an important role in the output of these occupations as indicated by statistics on patenting, high-tech start-ups, and other measures (see, e.g., Hunt and Gauthier-Loiselle [2010]; Hunt [2011]; Peri [2012]; Kerr [2013] and the references therein).

5.2.2   Nativity Differences in STEM Employment

In this subsection, we take a closer look at occupational sorting among high-skilled workers. Our interest is in the tendency to work in STEM occupations—how this differs between the native and foreign born, and how this difference has changed over time. Panel A of table 5.2 presents the fraction of high-skilled workers who are employed in a STEM occupation; panel B presents the fraction, conditional on being employed in a nonroutine cognitive occupation. The basic data are taken from table 5.1.

From the perspective of nativity, it is clear that the foreign born are more likely to work in STEM occupations than the native born. For instance, the fraction of high-skilled workers employed in STEM is 5.0 percentage points greater in 1980 (12.6 percent versus 7.6 percent); similarly, conditional on being a nonroutine cognitive worker, the likelihood of being a STEM worker is 7.7 pp greater. As a point of comparison, the tendency for high-skilled workers born in either India or China to work in STEM is approximately three times that of the native born.

Over time this difference has become more pronounced. Consider the tendency of the high skilled to work in STEM, conditional on either employment in any occupation, or in a nonroutine cognitive occupation. As the third column in table 5.2 makes clear, this tendency has remained essentially constant for the native born between 1980 and 2010. By contrast, the fraction of foreign-born workers in STEM has increased by 2.5 pp in panel A and 3.4 pp in panel B. As such, the foreign-born tendency toward STEM employment is now twice that of native-born workers.[8]

This differential change in tendency is not due simply to differences in

---

7. Interestingly, about 21 percent of the total increase in STEM employment in the United States is accounted for by the source countries of India and China alone.

8. See also Peri and Sparber (2011), who find that the occupational choice among native-born "job switchers" is affected by the foreign-born worker share. This is consistent with our findings on differential trends in sorting into STEM and Kerr, Kerr, and Lincoln (2013), who study the impact of skilled immigrants on the employment structures of US firms.

Table 5.2   **High-skilled employment in STEM occupations**

	1980	2010	Change	Unexplained
A. Per worker (%)				
Native born	7.6	7.6	+0.0	+0.4
Foreign born	12.6	15.1	+2.5	+5.3
India & China	23.6	30.6	+7.0	+13.7
B. Per NRC worker (%)				
Native born	10.4	10.5	+0.1	+1.1
Foreign born	18.1	21.5	+3.4	+7.2
India & China	30.5	38.0	+7.5	+13.0

Source: Data from 1980 census and 2010 American Community Survey. See text for details.
Notes: Employment among twenty- to sixty-four-year-olds with ≥ four years of college/bachelor's degree, in thousands.

observable demographic change between native- and foreign-born workers. To see this, let π_{it} be a dummy variable that takes on the value of 1 if individual i works in a STEM occupation and 0 otherwise (conditional on either employment or employment in a nonroutine cognitive job). We consider a simple linear probability model for working in STEM:

$$(1) \qquad \pi_{it} = X_{it}\beta + \varepsilon_{it},$$

for $t \in \{1980,2010\}$. Here, X_{it} denotes standard demographic characteristics of individual i that can be observed in the census and ACS: age, gender, marital status, and an indicator for whether the worker has greater than college education.[9] The fractions of STEM workers presented in the first two columns of table 5.2 are simply the sample averages:

$$(2) \qquad \frac{1}{N}\sum_{i}^{N} \pi_{it} = \overline{\pi}_{t}.$$

As such, the change in tendency reported in the third column of table 5.2, $\overline{\pi}_{2010} - \overline{\pi}_{1980}$, can be decomposed into a component that is "explained" by differences in observables, and an "unexplained" component owing to changes in coefficients, β, over time (see Oaxaca 1973; Blinder 1973). We perform this Oaxaca-Blinder decomposition separately for the native- and foreign-born samples.

The final column of table 5.2 presents the estimated unexplained component.[10] In all cases, the unexplained component is greater than the actual, observed change.[11] As a result, the changes observed in the data are *not* due

9. That is, we control for whether the worker has five or more years of college in the 1980 census and either a master's, professional, or doctoral degree in the 2010 ACS.

10. We implement this from a pooled regression over both time periods. Results in which coefficient estimates are obtained for either the 1980 or 2010 period are essentially unchanged.

11. This is due primarily to the fact that the explained component is dominated by the increasing female share of high-skilled employment. Since men are more likely to work in STEM jobs, this change implies that the contribution of the demographic change is negative.

to the explained component. In addition, as with the observed change in the third column, the native and foreign born differ in terms of the magnitude of the unexplained effect. For instance, in panel A the effect is an order of magnitude larger for the foreign born. Hence, relative to native-born, high-skilled workers, the foreign born have either experienced a much larger change in their propensity to work in STEM occupations or there has been an important change in unobservable characteristics of the foreign born, or both. For instance, conditional on having at least a college education, the quality of immigrants' education or their fields of study or college major may have changed (more than among the native born) over time. Unfortunately, this type of information is not available in the census. Perhaps more importantly, the type of visa with which immigrants first entered the United States may have changed since 1980. This is particularly relevant given the expansion of the H-1B visa program (see Hunt [2011] for further discussion).

To summarize, the tendency of the foreign born to work in STEM occupations has increased since 1980, while the tendency of high-skilled native born has not. Moreover, this relative increase is unexplained by observable demographic change.

5.2.3 Nonroutine-Biased Technical Change

As discussed above, STEM occupations are those involved with R&D, innovation, and technical change. We discuss in this subsection the fact that technical change since the 1980s has been *nonroutine biased* in nature. That is, in the past thirty years, advances in information and communication technology, robotics, and automation has allowed technology embodied in machinery, equipment, and software to substitute for labor in performing routine tasks. A growing body of literature documents the prevalence of nonroutine-biased technical change (NBTC) in the United States and other industrialized economies.[12]

This literature argues that NBTC resulted in a stark change in the occupational-skill distribution of employment. Industrialized economies have experienced *job polarization*: the labor market has become polarized, with employment share shifting away from middle-skill, routine occupations, toward both the high- and low-skill tails of the distribution. To illustrate this, figure 5.1 replicates a figure from Jaimovich and Siu (2012). Each bar represents the percent change in an occupational group's share of total employment. Over time, the share of employment in high-skill (nonroutine cognitive) and low-skill (nonroutine manual) jobs has been growing. This has been accompanied by a hollowing out of the middle-skill, routine occupations. In 1982, routine occupations accounted for approximately 56 per-

---

12. See, for instance, Autor, Levy, and Murnane (2003), Violante (2008), Firpo, Fortin, and Lemieux (2011), Acemoglu and Autor (2011), Goos, Manning, and Salomons (2014), Levy and Murnane (2014), and Jaimovich and Siu (2015).

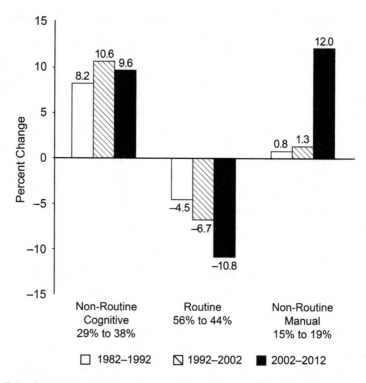

Fig. 5.1   Percent change in employment shares by occupation group
Source: Data from the Current Population Survey, BLS. See Jaimovich and Siu (2012) for details.

cent of total employment; in 2012, this share has fallen to 44 percent. Hence, according to this literature, NBTC has led to a polarization in employment away from routine, middle-skill occupations toward nonroutine cognitive and manual jobs.

5.3   Model

Motivated by the findings of section 5.2, we consider a simple model of endogenous NBTC. Nonroutine-biased technology is modeled as technology that is substitutable with routine labor in production. Advances in this technology are the outcome of employment devoted to innovation activities.

A key element to the model is occupational choice. There are two types of individuals in the economy: low skilled and high skilled. Given the data presented in section 5.2, high-skilled individuals work in nonroutine cognitive occupations. For the sake of exposition, we refer to their choice as either working as *innovators* (in STEM occupations) in the production of technology, or as *managers* (in other nonroutine cognitive jobs) in the production of goods. Low-skilled individuals choose to work in either *routine* or *service* occupations (both of which produce goods).

In section 5.4, we use this model to quantify the impact of high-skilled immigration, and the increasing tendency of immigrants to work in innovation, on the pace of NBTC and labor market outcomes.

5.3.1   Production

Industrial Structure

The model features three sectors of production. In the first sector, perfectly competitive, price-taking firms produce gross output (Y) using a Cobb-Douglas function in "managerial tasks" and "routine tasks." Managerial tasks are derived from labor input of managers, L_M. Routine tasks are derived from routine labor input, L_R, and *automation technology*, A. Specifically,

$$(3) \qquad Y = (zL_M)^\alpha [\lambda A^\rho + (1-\lambda)(zL_R)^\rho]^{(1-\alpha)/\rho}, \ \rho < 1.$$

Here, z represents labor-augmenting technology, which grows exogenously at the rate $g \geq 0$. By contrast, growth in the automation technology is endogenous to purposeful innovation activities as described below. The degree of substitutability between automation technology and routine labor is governed by ρ: as $\rho \to 1$, the two factors approach perfect substitutes.

The input of automation technology is composed of intermediate goods, x_i, with measure n, and a fixed factor $\bar{F}$ according to[13]

$$(4) \qquad A = \bar{F}^{1-\sigma} \int_0^n x_i^\sigma \, di, \ 0 < \sigma < 1.$$

We note that this specification of production is related to other work on nonroutine-biased technical change.[14]

The second sector produces intermediate goods, x. We consider a Romer-style (1990) model in which growth is driven by innovation that expands the variety of intermediate inputs. We assume that the innovator of a specific variety of input owns a permanent patent on the production of its associated intermediate good. Each unit of intermediate good is produced with η units of gross output.

In the third sector, perfectly competitive, price-taking firms produce output as a linear function of labor input into service occupations: L_S units of service labor input produce $w_S L_S$ units of output. Finally, to complete the description of production, we note that gross output is either consumed or used as an input in the production of x.

---

13. The fixed factor is included simply for technical reasons, namely, to ensure that production of Y is homogeneous of degree one in factor inputs L_M, L_R, $\bar{F}$, and x_i for all $i \in [0,n]$.

14. See, for example, Jung and Mercenier (2014) and Acemoglu and Restrepo (2015), as well as Caselli (2015), who studies the effects of experience-biased technical change.

Optimization

Normalizing the price of output to one, the first-order conditions for profit maximization in the first sector provide expressions for wage rates on managerial and routine labor, the rental rate on the fixed factor, and the price of intermediate inputs, respectively:

(5)
$$w_M = \alpha Y L_M^{-1}$$

(6)
$$w_R = (1-\alpha)Y\Omega(1-\lambda)z^\rho L_R^{\rho-1}$$

(7)
$$r = (1-\alpha)Y\Omega\lambda(1-\sigma)\bar{F}^{(1-\sigma)\rho-1}\left[\int_0^n x_i^\sigma\, di\right]^\rho$$

(8)
$$p_i = (1-\alpha)Y\Omega\lambda\bar{F}^{(1-\sigma)\rho}\left[\int_0^n x_i^\sigma\, di\right]^{\rho-1}\sigma x_i^{\sigma-1},$$

where $\Omega = [\lambda A^\rho + (1-\lambda)(zL_R)^\rho]^{-1}$.

In the intermediate goods sector, the per-period profit earned by the innovator of input variety i is $\pi_i = (p_i - \eta)x_i$. Substituting in equation (8), the first-order condition (FOC) is given by

(9)
$$x_i = \left(\frac{\sigma\Phi}{\eta}\right)^{1/(1-\sigma)},$$

where $\Phi = (1-\alpha)Y\Omega\lambda\bar{F}^{(1-\sigma)\rho}\left[\int_0^n x_i^\alpha di\right]^{\rho-1}\sigma$. In a symmetric equilibrium, denote $x_i \equiv x$ for all i. Substituting equation (9) into equation (8) and the definition of profit yields that the price is a constant markup over marginal cost:

(10)
$$p_i = \frac{\eta}{\sigma} \equiv p,$$

and that profits are given by

(11)
$$\pi_i = (1-\sigma)\Phi^{1/(1-\sigma)}\left(\frac{\sigma}{\eta}\right)^{\sigma/(1-\sigma)} \equiv \pi.$$

In the third sector, given the linearity of the production function, optimizing behavior implies that the productivity parameter in this sector, w_S, is equal to the service-occupation wage. We assume that w_S grows exogenously at the rate g.

Differential Effects of NBTC

Having characterized optimal demand for the various factors of production, we note the following. The marginal product of routine labor (MPL_R) is given by the right-hand side of equation (6). As such,

(12)
$$\text{sign}\left(\frac{\partial MPL_R}{\partial A}\right) = \text{sign}(1-\alpha-\rho).$$

Hence, an increase in automation technology shifts the "demand curve" for routine labor *down* whenever $\rho > 1 - \alpha$. This condition captures the effect of the substitution between automation technology and routine labor, and the degree of the diminishing returns to the "routine tasks" composite. To see this, consider the extreme case where production is linear in routine tasks, i.e. $\alpha = 0$: for every $\rho < 1$, an increase in A increases the marginal productivity of routine labor. More generally, when the composite exhibits diminishing returns (when $\alpha > 0$), there is a smaller set of ρ values for which this is true.

Moreover, given the Cobb-Douglas functional form of (3), managerial labor and routine tasks are complementary. Thus, we consider an economy where the effects of automation-technology growth are differential: all else equal, it decreases the marginal productivity of routine workers while increasing the marginal productivity of managers, when $\rho > 1 - \alpha$.

5.3.2   Households

The economy is populated by a representative household. The household is composed of a continuum of individuals, which we refer to as "workers." Each worker supplies one unit of labor inelastically. Within the household, *native-born* workers are of measure μ^{nat}, and *foreign-born* workers are of measure μ^{for}. There are two types of native-born workers: high skilled and low skilled; we let ϕ denote the share of high-skilled native born. For simplicity, given our interest in high-skilled immigration, we assume that all foreign born are high skilled.

Low-skilled workers can be employed in either a routine occupation or a service occupation. Low-skilled workers differ in their routine work ability, u, which is distributed $Y(u)$. By contrast, they are identical in their service-occupation ability, which we normalize to unity. Given the date t wage per unit of (effective) routine labor, w_{Rt}, a worker with ability u earns $u \times w_{Rt}$ employed in the routine occupation. Alternatively, workers earn w_{St} employed in the service occupation, regardless of u. Hence, it is optimal for the household to allocate all low-skilled workers with $u < u_t^*$ to employment in the service occupation, where

(13) $$u_t^* w_{Rt} = w_{St}.$$

All workers with $u \geq u_t^*$ are allocated to routine work. We denote $s_t^{lo} = Y(u_t^*)$ as the fraction of low-skilled (native-born) workers employed in the service occupation.[15]

---

15. Note that we have specified workers as supplying labor inelastically; workers do not face a labor-leisure trade-off, nor do they face the possibility of nonemployment. As such, job polarization—generated by our experiments in the following section—is a result of changes in occupational sorting among low-skilled workers. Any decline in routine employment is reflected as a rise in the number of workers allocated to the service occupation. An alternative would be to introduce an explicit possibility of nonemployment for low-skilled workers. See Cortes, Jaimovich, and Siu (2016) for a model of exogenous NBTC where workers choose between nonemployment, employment in service jobs, and employment in routine jobs.

High-skilled workers work either as managers or innovators. While they are identical in their ability as managers (which we normalize to unity), high-skilled workers differ in their innovation ability, a. This ability is distributed $\Gamma(a)$. For simplicity, we assume this is true of both the native and foreign born. A native-born worker with ability a develops $a \times f^{nat} \times n_t$ new ideas at date t, to which the innovator's household is bestowed a permanent patent. Here, $f^{nat} > 0$ is a productivity parameter, and n_t represents the externality of the aggregate stock of ideas on an individual's innovative activity, as in Romer (1990). Similarly, a foreign-born worker with ability a develops $a \times f^{for} \times n_t$ new ideas.

Alternatively, a high-skilled worker earns w_{Mt} employed as a manager, regardless of a. It is optimal for the household to allocate all native-born, high-skilled workers with $a < a_t^{nat*}$ as managers, where

$$(14) \qquad \zeta_t a_t^{nat*} f^{nat} n_t = \theta_t w_{Mt}.$$

Here, ζ_t represents the shadow value to the household of an additional idea, and θ_t the shadow value of an additional unit of income, both of which we derive below. Workers with $a \geq a_t^{nat*}$ are allocated to innovation. Similarly, the foreign-born cutoff, a_t^{for*}, is defined as the value that satisfies

$$(15) \qquad \zeta_t a_t^{for*} f^{for} n_t = \theta_t w_{Mt}.$$

We denote $s_t^{hi} = \Gamma\left(a_t^{nat*}\right)$ and $s_t^{for} = \Gamma\left(a_t^{for*}\right)$ as the fraction of high-skilled native- and foreign-born workers employed as managers, respectively.[16]

The household's date τ problem is to maximize

$$(16) \qquad \sum_{t=\tau} \beta^{t-\tau} \left[\int_0^{\phi\mu^{nat}} \log(C_{it})\, di + \int_{\phi\mu^{nat}}^{\mu^{nat}} \log\left(C_{jt}\right) dj + \int_{\mu^{nat}}^{\mu^{nat}+\mu^{for}} \log(C_{kt})\, dk \right],$$

subject to the budget constraint

$$(17) \qquad \int_0^{\phi\mu^{nat}} C_{it}\, di + \int_{\phi\mu^{nat}}^{\mu^{nat}} C_{jt}\, dj + \int_{\mu^{nat}}^{\mu^{nat}+\mu^{for}} C_{kt}\, dk + B_{t+1} \leq R_t B_t + r_t \bar{F} +$$

$$m_t \pi_t + w_{Mt}\left[\mu^{nat}\phi s_t^{hi} + \mu^{for} s_t^{for}\right] + \left[w_{St} s_t^{lo} + w_{Rt} \int_{u_t}^{\infty} u\, dY(u)\right]\mu^{nat}(1-\phi),$$

and the law of motion for the household's stock of patents

$$(18) \qquad m_{t+1} = m_t + n_t\left[\mu^{nat}\phi f^{nat} \int_{a_t^{nat*}}^{\infty} a\, d\Gamma(a) + \mu^{for} f^{for} \int_{a_t^{for*}}^{\infty} a\, d\Gamma(a)\right],$$

for all $t \geq \tau$. In equation (17), B_{t+1} denotes one-period bonds purchased at date t that pay a return of R_{t+1} at date $t + 1$.[17] Rental income on the house-

---

16. Given that $\Gamma'(a)$ is identical across nativity, $f^{nat} \neq f^{for}$ allows the model to generate differences in occupational sorting across high-skilled native- and foreign-born workers; this is made explicit via equation (29) below. An alternative would be to allow the distributions to differ by nativity.

17. In equilibrium, such bonds are in zero net supply and simply allow us to designate the household's discount factor in the derivations to follow.

hold's fixed factor is given by $r_t \bar{F}$. The second line of equation (17) denotes household labor income earned by workers in management, service, and routine employment.

At date t, the household's stock of ideas is m_t. With symmetry, each idea earns flow profit π_t. Patents do not expire or depreciate, so that equation (18) indicates that m_{t+1} is simply the stock today augmented by new ideas developed by high-skilled workers at date t.[18]

Let θ_t and ζ_t denote the Lagrange multipliers associated with the date t budget constraint (equation [17]) and law of motion (equation [18]), respectively. Given preferences, optimality involves allocating the same consumption level to all workers, regardless of nativity, skill, or occupation: $C_{it} = C_{jt} = C_{kt} = C_t$, $\forall i, j, k$. As such, our model is suited to the analysis of changes in wage and income inequality; it is not suited to analyzing consumption or welfare inequality.[19] Moreover, optimality implies $\theta_t = 1/C_t$. The FOC for bond holding is

$$(19) \qquad \theta_t = \beta \theta_{t+1} R_{t+1}.$$

The FOC for the household's stock of ideas is given by

$$(20) \qquad \zeta_t = \beta \zeta_{t+1} + \beta \theta_{t+1} \pi_{t+1}.$$

Iterating forward, this becomes

$$(21) \qquad \zeta_t = \beta \theta_{t+1} \pi_{t+1} + \beta^2 \theta_{t+2} \pi_{t+2} + \beta^3 \theta_{t+3} \pi_{t+3} + \dots$$

Dividing by θ_t and using equation (19) obtains

$$(22) \qquad \frac{\zeta_t}{\theta_t} = \frac{\pi_{t+1}}{R_{t+1}} + \frac{\pi_{t+2}}{R_{t+1} R_{t+2}} + \frac{\pi_{t+3}}{R_{t+1} R_{t+2} R_{t+3}} + \dots$$

As a result, the cutoff condition (equation [14]) can be rewritten as

$$(23) \qquad w_{Mt} = a_t^{nat*} f^{nat} n_t \sum_{i=1}^{\infty} \left[\frac{\pi_{t+i}}{\prod_{j=1}^{i} R_{t+j}} \right].$$

That is, occupational choice among high-skilled natives is such that, at a_t^{nat*}, the return to working as a manager (in terms of current wage income) is equated to the present value of future profit that worker would generate from innovation. Obviously, equation (15) can be rewritten in the analogous way, with $a_t^{for*} f^{for}$ replacing $a_t^{nat*} f^{nat}$ above.

18. For simplicity, we have assumed that patents do not depreciate. Instead, one could assume that patents depreciate at a constant rate δ. This would introduce an additional parameter to calibrate, but importantly, would not qualitatively change the nature of our analysis or results.

19. Addressing these latter issues would require the explicit modeling of heterogeneous agents and tracking the distribution of capital and savings as aggregate state variables. Doing so would muddle the analysis of occupational employment and wage outcomes that are of primary concern, and is therefore beyond the scope of this chapter.

5.3.3   Equilibrium and Balanced Growth

Equilibrium in this model is defined in the usual way. Optimization on the part of firms is summarized by the FOCs equation (5) through (9). Household optimization is summarized by equations (13) through (15), and equation (17) holding with equality.

Since bonds are in zero net supply, $B_t = 0$. Labor market clearing requires

(24) $$L_{St} = \mu^{\text{nat}}(1-\phi)s_t^{\text{lo}},$$

(25) $$L_{Rt} = \mu^{\text{nat}}(1-\phi)\int_{u_t^*}^{\infty} u\, dY(u),$$

(26) $$L_{Mt} = \mu^{\text{nat}}\phi s_t^{\text{hi}} + \mu^{\text{for}}s_t^{\text{for}}.$$

In the ideas market, $m_t = n_t$. Using equation (18), this implies that the growth rate of the aggregate stock of ideas is given by

(27) $$g_{t+1}^n = \frac{n_{t+1}-n_t}{n_t} = \mu^{\text{nat}}\phi f^{\text{nat}}\int_{a_t^{\text{nat}*}}^{\infty} a\, d\Gamma(a) + \mu^{\text{for}}f^{\text{for}}\int_{a_t^{\text{for}*}}^{\infty} a\, d\Gamma(a).$$

Finally, the household budget constraint can be used to derive the aggregate resource constraint:

(28) $$(\mu^{\text{nat}} + \mu^{\text{for}})C_t = Y_t + w_{St}L_{St} - \eta x_t n_t.$$

Equation (27) allows us to consider the determinants of the growth of ideas, that is, nonroutine-biased technical change. For instance, an increase in the productivity of innovation, either f^{nat} or f^{for}, has a direct effect of increasing g^n. In addition, such a change has an effect on occupational choice: the more productive is innovation, the lower is the threshold productivity ($a^{\text{nat}*}$ and $a^{\text{for}*}$) required to equate returns to managerial work and innovation in equations (14) and (15), all else equal. Hence, increases in f^{nat} and f^{for} have an equilibrium effect of inducing greater resources devoted to innovation that reinforce the direct effect.

In addition, increases in the high-skilled population, either $\mu^{\text{nat}}\phi$ or μ^{for}, increase NBTC. That is, our model displays a version of the "scale effect" on growth shared by Romer-style (1990) models; here, the scale effect is in terms of the measure of high-skilled workers (as opposed to total population per se).

Finally, note that changes in the composition of high-skilled workers affect g^n when $a^{\text{nat}*} \neq a^{\text{for}*}$. From equations (14) and (15), it is easy to see that

(29) $$\frac{a_t^{\text{nat}*}}{a_t^{\text{for}*}} = \frac{f^{\text{for}}}{f^{\text{nat}}}.$$

Suppose, for instance, that $f^{\text{for}} > f^{\text{nat}}$ so $a^{\text{nat}*} > a^{\text{for}*}$; given that the distribution, Γ, is identical across nativity, this implies that sorting into the innovation occupation is greater among the foreign born. In this case, a compositional shift toward more foreign-born workers that leaves the total measure of high-skilled workers unchanged has the effect of increasing the growth rate of ideas.

Given this discussion and the characterization of equilibrium, it is possible to consider balanced growth in our economy. In particular, the model admits a balanced growth path (BGP) in which labor allocations are constant ($u_t^* = u^*$, $a_t^{nat*} = a^{nat*}$, and $a_t^{for*} = a^{for*}$), and the stock of ideas (n_t), labor-augmenting technology (z_t), and the service-occupation wage (w_{St}) all grow at the same, constant rate ($g_{t+1}^n = g^n = g$). It is straightforward to show that along such a BGP the service flow (x_t) and profit (π_t) from each idea is constant; the gross real interest rate (R_t) is constant; and automation technology (A_t), wages (w_{St}, w_{Rt}, w_{Mt}), and consumption (C_t) grow at rate g.

5.4 Quantitative Results

5.4.1 Calibration and Parameter Specification

In this subsection, we discuss how to quantify the model economy to a BGP. This is meant to represent the US economy *prior* to the onset of job polarization. We view the past thirty-five years as a period of "unbalanced" growth, characterized by a declining share of employment in routine occupations due to NBTC; we defer discussion of unbalanced growth/NBTC to subsection 5.4.2.

There are fourteen parameters that need to be specified. To maintain comparability to the literature, we perform a standard calibration when possible. The initial BGP is calibrated to the United States in 1980.

First we normalize $\eta = 1$ and $\bar{F} = 1$. We then set the BGP growth rate of the technology variables (n, z, and w_S) to 2 percent per year. To accord with an annual risk-free rate of 4.6 percent, we set $\beta = 0.975$. We set the nativity and skill shares of the employed population to match those observed in the 1980 census. Normalizing $\mu^{nat} + \mu^{for} = 1$, we set $\mu^{for} = 0.0137$ to accord with the fraction of high-skilled, foreign-born workers in the economy. Of the native born, $\phi = 0.17$ specifies the split between high- and low-skilled workers.

To match the fat right tail of returns to innovation and entrepreneurial activity observed in US data, we specify the $\Gamma(a)$ distribution to be Pareto. This has the computational advantage of introducing only one calibration target, namely the shape parameter, which we denote κ.[20] Recall that we restrict the innovation ability distributions to be identical across the native and foreign born. As a result, nativity differences in sorting across innovation and managerial employment are reflected in the productivity parame-

---

20. The location parameter of the Pareto distribution is simply a normalization relative to f^{nat} and f^{for}, for the purposes of calibration.

ters f^{nat} and f^{for}. For the sake of consistency, we specify $Y(u)$ to also be Pareto, with corresponding shape parameter v.

Given this, we jointly calibrate the following six parameters: the production share parameters α and λ, the shape parameters v and κ, and the innovation productivity parameters f^{nat} and f^{for} as follows. In order to identify these we specify that along the BGP, the model matches the following six moments from the 1980 census data. First, we match three "quantity moments." Given the results of section 5.2, we calibrate the BGP values $s^{hi} = 0.896$ and $s^{for} = 0.819$ to match the fraction of nonroutine cognitive workers in managerial (i.e., non-STEM) occupations for the native and foreign born, respectively. We set s^{lo} 0.2 to match the fraction of low-skilled workers that work in service (i.e., nonroutine manual) occupations. The remaining three moments relate to prices: (a) a share of total labor income paid to low-skilled (routine and service) labor of 47 percent, (b) a median routine-to-service-occupation wage ratio of 1.75, and (c) a median managerial-to-routine-occupation wage ratio of 1.6.

This leaves the two elasticity parameters in production to be specified. Given the nature of our results, we set $\rho = 0.995$. That is, we set the elasticity of substitution between automation technology and routine labor as close to infinite as (computationally) possible; this allows the model to maximize the negative effect of increased innovation and NBTC on the demand for routine labor. Finally, we set $\sigma = 0.5$. In numerical experiments, we find that our results are extremely robust to the choice of this parameter.

5.4.2 Nature of the Experiments

As discussed above, the period since 1980 is not well characterized as displaying balanced growth. The phenomenon of job polarization has meant that employment allocations have not been constant: the share of employment in routine occupations has been falling, while the shares in nonroutine cognitive and service occupations have been rising. Moreover, inequality between high- and low-skilled wages has increased; more recently, routine- and service-occupation wages have converged (see Acemoglu and Autor 2011).

From the perspective of the model, the past thirty-five years has been a period of unbalanced growth. In particular, NBTC and the accumulation of automation technology has led to an inward shift in the demand for routine labor and an outward shift in the demand for high-skilled labor, all else equal. Moreover, rising educational attainment has meant a shift in the composition of labor supply toward high-skilled workers, and immigration policy has led to a rise in the foreign-born share of the high-skilled population.

As such, we conduct a series of quantitative experiments in the model to *isolate the role of immigration* for the evolution of the economy during this unbalanced growth period. In our experiments we assume the economy was on a BGP in 1980 and then hit by a number of shocks that we specify below.

After the arrival of the shocks, we track the perfect foresight transition path of the economy to a new BGP. We specify that the economy arrives at the new BGP in the year 2070, ninety years after the arrival period of the shock.[21]

Specifically, we assume that in 1980 the economy is hit with two shocks. First, we allow the fraction μ^{for} to increase at a constant rate; this growth is specified so that after thirty years of growth, the fraction of high-skilled, foreign-born workers matches that observed in 2010 in the US data. Given that the high skilled can select into innovation, this increase alone accelerates the growth of automation technology that substitutes for routine labor input.

But as reported in the bottom panel of table 5.2, the tendency of high-skilled, foreign-born workers to work in innovation occupations increased between 1980 and 2010. As discussed in section 5.2, this represents either a true "propensity" change or a change in the unobserved characteristics of foreign-born workers. Hence, we also allow for a one-time increase in the innovation productivity, f^{for}, that causes foreign-born workers to sort more heavily into innovation as opposed to managerial labor that replicates the changes observed in table 5.2.[22]

As discussed in subsection 5.3.3, these two changes (increasing μ^{for} and f^{for}) increase the number of innovators in the economy, and results in an endogenous rise in the growth rate of ideas. Our experiment causes g^n to rise, while leaving the growth rates of labor-augmenting productivity (z) and the service-occupation productivity (w_S) unchanged at their previous BGP value. The new BGP is attained in 2070 when the growth rates of z and w_S make a one-time increase from g to the endogenously determined value of g^n in that period. From 2070 onward, μ^{for} becomes constant.

5.4.3   Results

Figure 5.2 presents the foreign-born population share for the period 1980 to 2010. In all figures, the line with circles indicates the time series under the original BGP, while the line with squares represents the immigration

21. In principle, the results of the experiment depend on the "terminal date" at which the new BGP is attained, since agents in the model operate with perfect foresight. However, in experiments not reported here, we find that the results for the transition path are incredibly insensitive to the choice of this date. For instance, when we set the terminal date to 2010, the results for the period of interest—1980 to 2010—are surprisingly similar to the case reported here, with the terminal date set to 2070. We specify a ninety-year transition period in the baseline experiment in order to better understand the model's implications for the "very long run" (see section 5.4.4 for further discussion).

22. Note that other changes that cause greater equilibrium sorting of the foreign born into innovation in equilibrium are equivalent to increasing f^{for}. For instance, one could argue that the unobservable characteristics of the foreign born have changed over time due to the H-1B visa. This might be reflected as a rightward shift of the distribution, $\Gamma(a)$, of innovation ability of the foreign-born relative to natives. But given our specification of production in innovation, $a \times f \times b_f$, allowing for a change in the location parameter of the Pareto distribution for the foreign born is isomorphic to changing the productivity parameter, f^{for}.

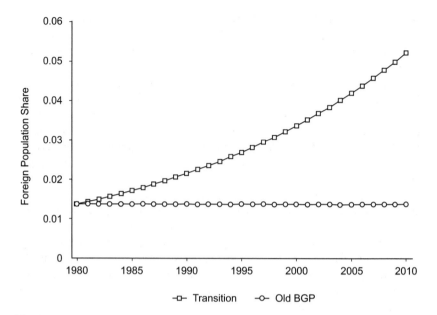

Fig. 5.2   High-skilled immigration experiment, overview

Note: The line with circles indicates the time series under the original balanced growth path; the line with squares represents the immigration experiment. See text for details.

experiment detailed in the previous subsection. By construction, the values for 1980 and 2010 along the experiment's transition path correspond with the values observed in the 1980 census and 2010 ACS data, representing a fourfold increase. Recall that the foreign-born population in the model represents only foreign-born, high-skilled employment.

In the upper-left panel of figure 5.3, we present the fraction of high-skilled workers who sort into innovation $(1 - s^{for})$ among the foreign born. By construction, this increases as observed in the US data due to the increase in foreign-born innovation productivity. The upper-right panel presents the same variable for the native born. In response to the increase in the number of foreign-born innovators, the fraction of native born who sort into innovation falls.

Though this effect on native-born innovation is quantitatively small, it is instructive to understand the force generating it. Native sorting into innovation falls, despite production of new ideas being linear in the number of innovators; that is, the fall occurs despite innovation productivity of the native born, f^{nat}, remaining unchanged in the experiment. Instead, the fall is due to the general-equilibrium effect on the real interest rate.

Specifically, the increase in high-skilled immigration endogenously increases economic growth. This is evidenced in the middle row of figure 5.3. During the first thirty years of transition, the growth rate of ideas and con-

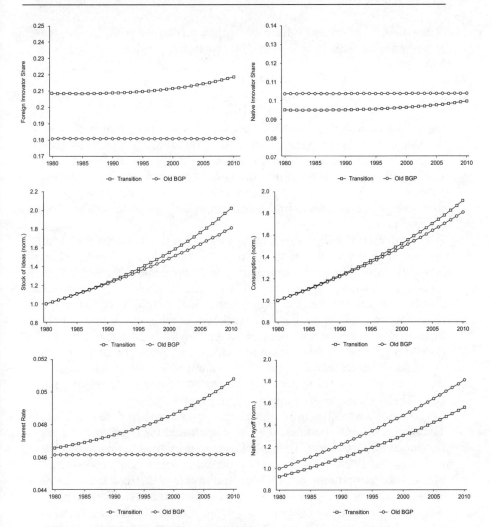

Fig. 5.3   High-skilled immigration experiment, all workers
Note: The lines with circles indicate the time series under the original balanced growth path; the lines with squares represent the immigration experiment. See text for details.

sumption are higher than under the original BGP (both variables are normalized to one in 1980). Because the representative household has concave preferences, it desires to smooth consumption intertemporally and transfer some of the additional future consumption growth forward in time. Obviously, this reallocation of consumption is not possible in equilibrium (of our closed economy model). This necessitates an increase in the real interest rate or return to saving, as displayed in the bottom-left panel of figure 5.3.

The increase in the interest rate, in turn, affects the equilibrium return to innovation. Recall that the payoff to innovation, displayed in the bottom-right panel, is the present value of the future profit stream accruing to the generated ideas. This is summarized by equation (23), which we reproduce here:

$$w_{Mt} = a_t^{\text{nat}*} f^{\text{nat}} n_t \sum_{i=1}^{\infty} \left[\frac{\pi_{t+i}}{\Pi_{j=1}^{i} R_{t+j}} \right].$$

Higher real interest rates mean that future profits are discounted more heavily. All else equal, sorting into innovation becomes more selective; the ability level at which high-skilled, native-born workers are indifferent between working in management and innovation must rise. Since the high-skilled, native-born workers did not experience a shock to their innovation productivity, less of them sort into innovation (though, as stated above, the effect is quantitatively small).

The upper and middle rows of figure 5.4 present the time series for managerial labor. As the population of high-skilled, foreign-born workers increases, so too does the number of foreign-born managers.[23] By 2010, this increase is quantitatively large. The number of native-born managers also increases due to the change in occupational sorting described above, though again, this is quantitatively small. As a result, total employment in the managerial occupation increases by approximately 20 percent over the thirty-year period, as displayed in the middle-left panel, due largely to the foreign-born increase. As a result of this immigration-induced increase in the supply of labor, the managerial wage rate falls relative to the original BGP. This is displayed in the middle-right panel.

The bottom row of figure 5.4 presents the time series for routine labor. Though the effect is quantitatively small, increased high-skilled immigration has the effect of *increasing* employment in routine occupations. That is, during the 1980 to 2010 transition period of our model's experiment, high-skilled immigration has *not* been responsible for a decrease in routine employment among the native born. And as indicated in the bottom-right panel, the increase in the high-skilled, foreign-born workforce has not led to a fall in the wage earned by routine workers. Because the quantitative effect is small, we plot this as a *log* deviation from the original BGP. Nonetheless, the result of the immigration experiment is to *increase* the marginal product of routine labor.

To understand this, note that an increase in high-skilled immigrants has two effects on the demand for routine labor. First, because of the increase in the number of innovators, there is an increase in the growth rate of ideas and an increase in the accumulation of automation technology. Because automation technology and routine labor are substitutes in production, this lowers routine labor demand, as derived in equation (12). However, high-

---

23. Note that foreign-born managerial labor actually falls slightly in the very first period, relative to the original BGP. This is due to the increased sorting into innovation.

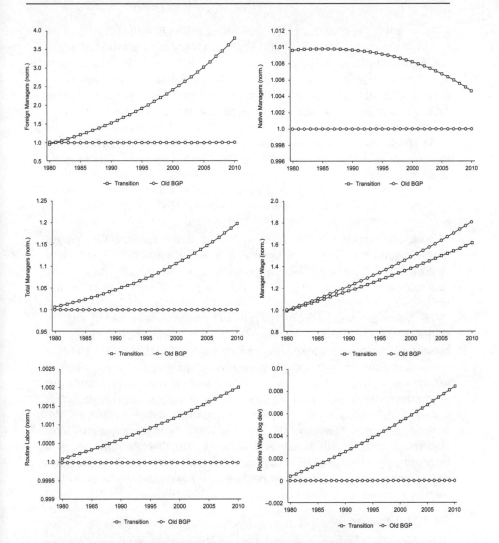

Fig. 5.4   High-skilled immigration experiment, managerial labor
Note: The lines with circles indicate the time series under the original balanced growth path; the lines with squares represent the immigration experiment. See text for details.

skilled immigrants also work as managers. Though the foreign born sort more intensively into innovation relative to the native born, the majority are employed in managerial occupations. Hence, the increase in immigration increases managerial labor. Because managerial labor and routine tasks—and, therefore, routine labor—are complements in production, this raises routine labor demand. This complementarity effect dominates the substitution effect, resulting in an equilibrium increase in employment *and* wages in routine occupations.

As a result, the model predicts that increased high-skilled immigration has led to a *narrowing* of inequality between low- and high-skilled workers. This is displayed in figure 5.5. The upper-left panel plots the ratio of wages between routine and managerial labor; this has been normalized so that its value in the original BGP is one. Evidently, increased immigration causes this ratio to rise, shrinking the wage gap between routine workers and managers.

As an alternative measure of inequality, the upper-right panel displays the ratio of labor income earned by native-born routine workers to managers, specifically,

$$(30) \qquad \frac{w_{Rt} \int_{u_t^*}^{\infty} u \, dY(u)(1-\phi)}{w_{Mt} \phi s_t^{hi}}.$$

This differs from the ratio of wages, w_{Rt}/w_{Mt}, in that it accounts for changes in routine and managerial employment among the native born via changes in occupational sorting.[24] While this statistic is conceptually different, it generates decreasing inequality that is quantitatively very similar to that observed in the wage gap.[25]

The lower-left panel displays the ratio of labor income earned by all low-skilled workers to native-born managers. That is, it adds the income earned by service-occupation workers to the numerator of equation (30). Relative to equation (30), this provides greater scope for worsened relative outcomes for the low skilled, as employment gains in routine occupations come out of employment in the service occupation. Nonetheless, the change in this statistic is quantitatively very similar to those discussed above. Finally, the bottom-right panel displays the share of total income accruing to low-skilled (native-born) labor. Between 1980 and 2010, this falls only modestly by about 2 pp; this is primarily a mechanical result of the fact that total low-skilled employment is constant while the experiment adds only high-skilled, foreign-born workers over time.

5.4.4   Further Analysis

In this section, we provide analytical results to illustrate that relative to the 1980 BGP, the increase in high-skilled immigration has a quantitatively small effect on nonroutine-biased technical change. As a result, early in the transition path to a new BGP, the substitution effect of increased automation technology on the demand for routine labor is small.

To see this, consider equation (27) describing the equilibrium growth rate

---

24. In addition, increases in routine employment are drawn from the lower end of the skill distribution, $Y(u)$ from workers who previously sorted into the service occupation.

25. In the first two periods of the experiment, the income ratio falls relative to the original BGP; this is due primarily to the larger increase manager employment relative to routine employment among the native born. However, as the transition progresses, this quickly reverses.

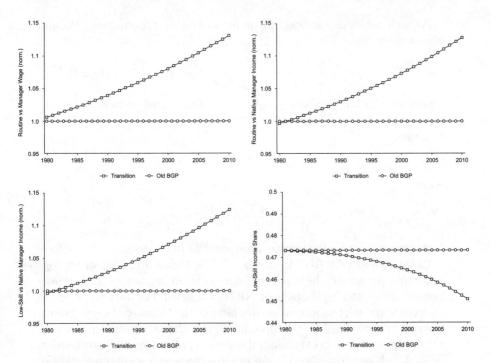

Fig. 5.5   High-skilled immigration experiment, gap between low-skilled and high-skilled workers

Note: The lines with circles indicate the time series under the original balanced growth path; the lines with squares represent the immigration experiment. See text for details

of ideas, where we have used the fact that $\Gamma(a)$ is a Pareto distribution with shape parameter κ:

$$g_{t+1}^n = \mu^{\text{nat}}\phi f^{\text{nat}}\overline{\kappa}(a_t^{\text{nat}*})^{1-\kappa} + \mu^{\text{for}} f^{\text{for}}\overline{\kappa}(a_t^{\text{for}*})^{1-\kappa},$$

where $\overline{\kappa} \equiv \kappa / (\kappa - 1)$. Taking a first-order, log-linear approximation to this equation obtains

$$(31) \quad \hat{g}^n = \frac{\mu^{\text{nat}}\phi f^{\text{nat}}\overline{\kappa}(a^{\text{nat}*})^{1-\kappa}}{\mu^{\text{nat}}\phi f^{\text{nat}}\overline{\kappa}(a^{\text{nat}*})^{1-\kappa} + \mu^{\text{for}} f^{\text{for}}\overline{\kappa}(a^{\text{for}*})^{1-\kappa}}[\hat{\mu}^{\text{nat}} + \hat{\phi} + \hat{f}^{\text{nat}} + (1-\kappa)\hat{a}^{\text{nat}*}]$$

$$+ \frac{\mu^{\text{for}} f^{\text{for}}\overline{\kappa}(a^{\text{for}*})^{1-\kappa}}{\mu^{\text{nat}}\phi f^{\text{nat}}\overline{\kappa}(a^{\text{nat}*})^{1-\kappa} + \mu^{\text{for}} f^{\text{for}}\overline{\kappa}(a^{\text{for}*})^{1-\kappa}}[\hat{\mu}^{\text{for}} + \hat{f}^{\text{for}} + (1-\kappa)\hat{a}^{\text{for}*}].$$

In our immigration experiment, we leave the measure of high-skilled, native-born workers and native productivity unchanged ($\hat{\mu}^{\text{nat}} = \hat{\phi} = \hat{f}^{\text{nat}} = 0$). Moreover, as displayed in figure 5.3, occupational choice among the native born hardly changes; this implies that the native cutoff ability hardly changes ($\hat{a}^{\text{nat}*} \approx 0$).

As such, we focus our attention on the second term in equation (31), and approximate it as

$$(32) \quad \hat{g}^n \approx \frac{\mu^{\text{for}} f^{\text{for}}(a^{\text{for}*})^{1-\kappa}}{\mu^{\text{nat}} \phi f^{\text{nat}}(a^{\text{nat}*})^{1-\kappa} + \mu^{\text{for}} f^{\text{for}}(a^{\text{for}*})^{1-\kappa}} [\hat{\mu}^{\text{for}} + \hat{f}^{\text{for}} + (1-\kappa)\hat{a}^{\text{for}*}].$$

Under the Pareto distribution, $(a^*)^{-\kappa}$ is the fraction of high-skilled workers who sort into innovation. Using this and equation (29), equation (32) becomes

$$(33) \quad \hat{g}^n \approx \varphi[\hat{\mu}^{\text{for}} + \hat{f}^{\text{for}} + (1-\kappa)\hat{a}^{\text{for}*}],$$

where

$$\varphi \equiv \frac{\mu^{\text{for}}(a^{\text{for}*})^{-\kappa}}{\mu^{\text{for}}(a^{\text{for}*})^{-\kappa} + \mu^{\text{nat}}\phi(a^{\text{nat}*})^{-\kappa}}.$$

Note that φ is simply the foreign-born share of innovators.

Calculated at 1980 BGP values, $\varphi = 0.122$. Hence, to a first-order, log-linear approximation, the impact of high-skilled immigration on the growth rate of ideas—that is, the pace of NBTC—is small. For instance, suppose we were to consider an immediate doubling of the measure of foreign-born workers in 1980 (i.e., $\hat{\mu}^{\text{for}} = 1$); this is large given that it took fifteen years for the model economy to experience the same-sized increase (as displayed in figure 5.2). Using equation (33), this would increase g^n from the original BGP value of 2 percent to 2.224 percent.[26] This illustrates how, during the 1980 to 2010 period under consideration, the substitution effect of automation-technology growth on routine labor demand is dominated by the direct complementarity effect of increased managerial labor supply, brought about by high-skilled immigration.

Note, however, that the relative importance of these substitution and complementarity effects depends on the time horizon under consideration. The strength of each grows at a different rate in our experiment. Consider the complementarity effect of managerial labor. In the long run, the growth rate of managers is bounded above by the (constant) growth rate of high-skilled immigration. By contrast, the substitution effect is governed by the stock of ideas. The growth rate of ideas, displayed in equation (27), depends on the *level* of high-skilled labor, given our Romer-style (1990) specification of technical change. Hence, the direct effect of immigration implies that the growth rate of ideas and automation technology is increasing over time, so that the relative strength of the two effects in the "very long run" is a quantitative question.

---

26. Of course, the accuracy of this log-linear approximation is compromised for such a large shock, $\hat{\mu}^{\text{for}}$. Note also that our experiment discussed in the previous two subsections also considered a positive shock, $\hat{f}^{\text{for}} > 0$; however, the equilibrium effect of this is to induce an offsetting fall, $\hat{a}^{\text{for}*} < 0$. All things considered, the nature of the result remains that the effect of immigration on NBTC is small.

This is illustrated in figure 5.6, where we plot the ninety-year transition path of the immigration experiment. Recall that the experiment involves growth of the high-skilled, foreign-born workforce at a constant rate (which generates increasing idea growth, g^n), leaving the growth rate of the other forms of technology (specifically, z and w_S) constant. In the ninetieth period, immigration stops and the growth rates of z and w_S make a one-time increase to the endogenous value of g^n so that the economy is forced to enter a new BGP.

As the top row of figure 5.6 makes clear, the stock of ideas exhibits much greater growth than the number of managers in the very long run. The substitution effect of automation technology on routine labor demand can eventually dominate the complementarity effect of increased managerial labor. The middle row displays routine employment and the routine wage. Both display about fifty-five periods of growth during the experiment. However, they begin to decline in about 2035, cross below the values implied by the original BGP in about 2050, and fall thereafter. The bottom row displays two measures of inequality between low- and high-skilled workers. Consider, for instance, the routine-to-manager wage ratio. If high-skilled immigration growth and NBTC were to continue as predicted by the model until 2070, this wage ratio would be approximately one-third of its value in the 1980 BGP.

Hence, the impact of high-skilled immigration on polarization and wage inequality are evident only in the very long run of this numerical exercise. There are many good reasons to question the predictions from this experiment for outcomes fifty to sixty years hence. This is because of the stark assumptions made in the analysis of the specific model experiment. For instance, the experiment assumes constant growth of the high-skilled, foreign-born population over ninety years at the substantial growth rates observed between 1980 and 2010. Future immigration policy is obviously uncertain. In addition, and perhaps more controvertible, it assumes that the *direction* of technical change via innovation remains nonroutine biased over the entire ninety-year period. That is, innovative activity augments automation technology leaving, for instance, the path of labor-augmenting technology unchanged. While this may be a reasonable representation of the job-polarization period of the past thirty years, it may not remain the case for the next sixty. Finally, the model assumes Romer-style (1990) scale effects on the growth of nonroutine-biased ideas. Augmenting the model to diminish or eliminate these scale effects would weaken the long-run substitution of automation technology for routine labor.

As such, we view the predictions of figure 5.6 as uncertain and clearly representing a quantitative theoretic upper bound of the effects of high-skilled immigration on increasing inequality. In terms of the 1980–2010 experience, the model indicates that high-skilled immigration has, in fact, reduced inequality.

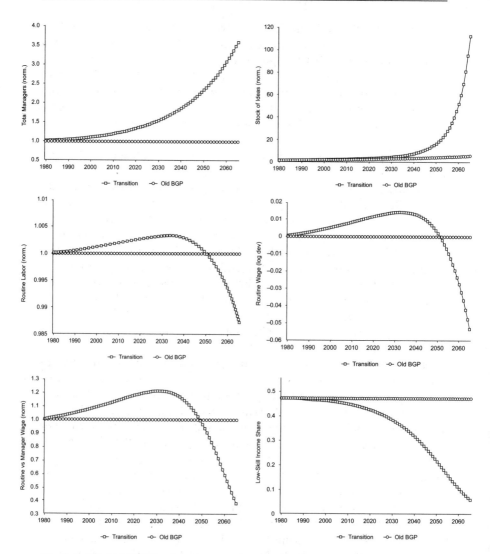

Fig. 5.6   High-skilled immigration experiment, extended

Note: The lines with circles indicate the time series under the original balanced growth path; the lines with squares represent the immigration experiment. See text for details.

5.5   Conclusion

In the last thirty to forty years, immigration has constituted an important source of growth in high-skilled employment, innovation, and productivity in the United States. At the same time, the United States has experienced technical change that is nonroutine biased, allowing technology to substitute for labor in performing routine tasks leading to job polarization and wage polarization in the labor market.

In this chapter, we study the role of high-skilled immigration in accounting for these changes in the occupational-skill distribution and wage inequality. We do so in a general-equilibrium model featuring endogenous nonroutine-biased technical change. We use this model to quantify the impact of high-skilled immigration and the increasing tendency of the foreign born to work in innovation, on the pace of technical change, the polarization of employment opportunities, and the evolution of wage inequality since 1980. We find that high-skilled immigration has led to a narrowing of inequality.

References

Acemoglu, Daron, and David Autor. 2011. "Skills, Tasks and Technologies: Implications for Employment and Earnings." In *Handbook of Labor Economics*, vol. 4B, edited by Orley Ashenfelter and David Card, 1043–171. Amsterdam: Elsevier.

Acemoglu, Daron, and Pascual Restrepo. 2015. "The Race between Man and Machine: Implications of Technology for Growth, Factor Shares and Employment." Working Paper, Massachusetts Institute of Technology.

Autor, David H., David Dorn, and Gordon H. Hanson. 2015. "Untangling Trade and Technology: Evidence from Local Labour Markets." *Economic Journal* 125:621–46.

Autor, David H., Frank Levy, and Richard J. Murnane. 2003. "The Skill Content of Recent Technological Change: An Empirical Exploration." *Quarterly Journal of Economics* 118 (4): 1279–333.

Blinder, Alan. 1973. "Wage Discrimination: Reduced Form and Structural Estimates." *Journal of Human Resources* 8:436–55.

Borjas, George, and Kirk Doran. 2015. "Cognitive Mobility: Labor Market Responses to Supply Shocks in the Space of Ideas." *Journal of Labor Economics* 33 (S1): S109–45.

Bound, John, Breno Braga, Joseph M. Golden, and Gaurav Khanna. 2015. "Recruitment of Foreigners in the Market for Computer Scientists in the United States." *Journal of Labor Economics* 33 (S1): S187–223.

Caselli, Francesco. 2015. "Experience-Biased Technical Change." CEPR Discussion Paper no. 10752, Centre for Economic Policy Research.

Chiswick, Barry, and Sarinda Taengnoi. 2007. "Occupational Choice of High-Skilled Immigrants in the United States." *International Migration* 45 (5): 3–34.

Cortes, Guido Matias, Nir Jaimovich, Christopher J. Nekarda, and Henry E. Siu. 2015. "The Micro and Macro of Disappearing Routine Jobs: A Flows Approach." Working Paper, University of British Columbia.

Cortes, Guido Matias, Nir Jaimovich, and Henry E. Siu. 2016. "Disappearing Routine Jobs: Who, How, and Why?" Working Paper, USC Marshall School of Business.

Doran, Kirk, Alexander Gelber, and Adam Isen. 2016. "The Effects of High-Skilled Immigration Policy on Firms: Evidence from Visa Lotteries." Working Paper, University of Notre Dame.

Firpo, Sergio, Nicole M. Fortin, and Thomas Lemieux. 2011. "Occupational Tasks and Changes in the Wage Structure." Working Paper, University of British Columbia.

Goos, Maarten, and Alan Manning. 2007. "Lousy and Lovely Jobs: The Rising Polarization of Work in Britain." *Review of Economics and Statistics* 89 (1): 118–33.

Goos, Maarten, Alan Manning, and Anna Salomons. 2014. "Explaining Job Polarization: Routine-Biased Technological Change and Offshoring." *American Economic Review* 104 (8): 2509–26.

Grieco, Elizabeth M., Edward Trevelyan, Luke Larsen, Yesenia D. Acosta, Christine Gambino, Patricia de la Cruz, Tom Gryn, and Nathan Walters. 2012. "The Size, Place of Birth, and Geographic Distribution of the Foreign-Born Population in the United States: 1960 to 2010." Population Division Working Paper no. 96, US Census Bureau.

Hanson, Gordon H., and Matthew J. Slaughter. 2016. "High-Skilled Immigration and the Rise of STEM Occupations in US Employment." NBER Working Paper no. 22623, Cambridge, MA.

Hunt, Jennifer. 2011. "Which Immigrants Are Most Innovative and Entrepreneurial? Distinctions by Entry Visa." *Journal of Labor Economics* 29 (3): 417–57.

Hunt, Jennifer, and Marjolaine Gauthier-Loiselle. 2010. "How Much Does Immigration Boost Innovation?" *American Economic Journal: Macroeconomics* 2 (2): 31–56.

Jaimovich, Nir, and Henry E. Siu. 2012. "Job Polarization and Jobless Recoveries." NBER Working Paper no. 18334, Cambridge, MA.

———. 2015. "Jobless Recoveries." *Third Way NEXT*. http://www.thirdway.org /report/jobless-recoveries.

Jung, Jaewon, and Jean Mercenier. 2014. "Routinization-Biased Technical Change and Globalization: Understanding Labor Market Polarization." *Economic Inquiry* 52 (4): 1446–65.

Kerr, Sari Pekkala, William R. Kerr, and William F. Lincoln. 2013. "Skilled Immigration and the Employment Structures of US Firms." NBER Working Paper no. 19658, Cambridge, MA.

Kerr, William. 2013. "US High-Skilled Immigration, Innovation, and Entrepreneurship: Empirical Approaches and Evidence." NBER Working Paper no. 19377, Cambridge, MA.

Kerr, William, and William Lincoln. 2010. "The Supply Side of Innovation: H-1B Visa Reforms and US Ethnic Invention." *Journal of Labor Economics* 38 (3): 473–508.

Levy, Frank, and Richard J. Murnane. 2014. "Dancing with Robots: Human Skills for Computerized Work." *Third Way NEXT*. content.thirdway.org/publications /714/Dancing-With-Robots.pdf.

Oaxaca, Ronald. 1973. "Male-Female Wage Differentials in Urban Labor Markets." *International Economic Review* 14:693–709.

Peri, Giovanni. 2012. "The Effect of Immigration on Productivity: Evidence from US States." *Review of Economics and Statistics* 94 (1): 348–58.

Peri, Giovanni, Kevin Shih, and Chad Sparber. 2015. "Stem Workers, H-1B Visas, and Productivity in US Cities." *Journal of Labor Economics* 33 (S1): S225–55.

Peri, Giovanni, and Chad Sparber. 2011. "Highly Educated Immigrants and Native Occupational Choice." *Industrial Relations* 50 (3): 385–411.

Romer, Paul M. 1990. "Endogenous Technological Change." *Journal of Political Economy* 98 (5): S71–102.

Ruggles, Steven, J. Trent Alexander, Katie Genadek, Ronald Goeken, Matthew B. Schroeder, and Matthew Sobek. 2010. Integrated Public Use Microdata Series: Version 5.0 [machine-readable database]. Minnesota Population Center, University of Minnesota.

Violante, Giovanni L. 2008. "Skill-Biased Technical Change." In *The New Palgrave Dictionary of Economics*, 2nd ed., edited by Steven N. Durlauf and Lawrence E. Blume. London: Palgrave Macmillan.

6

Firm Dynamics and Immigration
The Case of High-Skilled Immigration

Michael E. Waugh

6.1 Introduction

How does immigration affect relative wages, output, and welfare? How are the gains (or losses) from changes in immigration policy accrued over time? I show how the dynamics of the firm yields new insights into the short- and long-run responses of relative wages, output, and consumption to changes in immigration policy.

The theoretical starting point is a dynamic, heterogeneous firm model, as in Hopenhayn (1992), Hopenhayn and Rogerson (1993), and Melitz (2003). Firms are monopolistic competitors that differ in their productivity and firms must pay a per-period fixed cost of operation. There is free entry, and firms endogenously exit when the value of operating is less than that of exiting. I model labor demand by following the immigration literature: firms employ a constant elasticity of substitution composite of skilled and unskilled labor. The key departure that I entertain is the possibility that the skill intensity of production varies with a firm's productivity.

Nontrivial dynamics in relative wages arise from the interaction between firm productivity and skill. I analytically show how this interaction breaks the "industry standard" constant-elasticity relationship between wages and

Michael E. Waugh is associate professor of economics at the Stern School of Business, New York University, and a research associate of the National Bureau of Economic Research.

I benefited from the research assistance of Zhemin Yuan, discussions with Kim Ruhl, participants at the Taipei International Conference on Growth, Trade and Dynamics, NBER meeting on Global Talent, Columbia, NYU Macro Lunch, and the editors Gordon Hanson, William Kerr, and Sarah Turner. The code associated with this chapter is at https://github.com/mwaugh0328. For acknowledgments, sources of research support, and disclosure of the author's material financial relationships, if any, please see http://www.nber.org/chapters/c13843.ack.

skill supply (which is widely used in the immigration literature; see, e.g., Card [2009]; Borjas [2014]). In particular, the deviation from the constant-elasticity benchmark depends on the distribution of firms; thus, the change in relative wages with respect to a change in labor supply depends, in part, on the evolution of the distribution of firms. In contrast, if there is no inter-action between firm productivity and skill, then firm heterogeneity and firm dynamics play no role in shaping the aggregate skill premium and its response to immigration.

I quantitatively illustrate these issues by evaluating two types of policies: a "neoliberal" policy that expands the H-1B visa program and a "nationalistic policy" that eliminates it. The H-1B program is a large visa program for the temporary immigration of skilled labor to the United States. At current rates, the general quota allows up to 65,000 employment-based immigrants per year, with an additional 20,000 visas for those with advanced degrees from US universities. Business leaders (e.g., Mark Zuckerberg of Facebook and Bill Gates of Microsoft) argue that this cap is constraining and that an expansion of the H-1B visa program is vital for their firms (and others) to expand, grow, and innovate. However, some policymakers have expressed concerns that this program incentivizes firms to substitute into cheaper, immigrant labor at the cost of displacing domestic workers and/or lowering their wages.

The neoliberal policy that I evaluate is the proposed Immigration Inno-vation Act of 2015[1] or "I-Squared," which sought to triple the number of H-1B visas per year. To evaluate this policy proposal, I calibrate the pa-rameters of the model to match key properties of firms and labor market outcomes in the US economy. I project forward how the I-Squared Act affects the stock of skilled workers in the United States. I then compute the transition path of the economy in response to an unanticipated adoption of the I-Squared Act.

This reform generates nontrivial, short-run dynamics in relative wages that differ from their long-run dynamics. In the short run, the wage pre-mium of high-skilled to low-skilled workers contracts *more* than would be predicted by a standard, static constant elasticity of substitution (CES) model. The reason is that immigration induces firm entry and that entrants are likely to be low-skill intensive. Thus, entry bids up the relative price of low-skilled labor and the skill premium decreases by more than a static CES model would predict. This process dissipates as entrants become incumbents and the economy converges to its new stationary equilibrium.

The value added of the model is that I can evaluate the level effects on wages, output, consumption, and welfare — not just the distributional effects. I show that the I-Squared Act generates essentially no negative impact on the level of high-skilled wages. Furthermore, this leads to small increases

1. See https://www.congress.gov/bill/114th-congress/senate-bill/153.

in aggregate gross domestic product (GDP) in year 1, and a 1.5 percentage point increase in GDP fifteen years out.

These gains arise from both a scale and an aggregate productivity effect from adding more skilled labor. These gains are analogous to the gains from trade emphasized in the monopolistic-competition models of Krugman (1980) or Melitz (2003). The surprising result is the *speed* at which these gains are realized—the no-negative wage impact comes from firms entering quickly. The entry of firms is typically thought of as a long-run effect (see, e.g., di Giovanni, Levchenko, and Ortega [2015], who explain this logic well). In my model, however, this benefit is felt in year 2—not in the "long run." The reason is the dynamic, forward-looking nature of the firm. And this detail—the accrual of long-run benefits today—would be overlooked in a steady state to steady state comparison.[2]

The flip side of all these "good" outcomes—higher wages and higher output—is that they come from firm entry, and firm entry must be paid for. There is investment today in the creation of firms to prepare for a larger labor force in the future—and this investment comes at the cost of consumption. Under an assumption about the distribution of profits across workers, the I-Squared Act leads to a drop in consumption of a 0.5 percentage point for both workers (in year 1) and stays depressed relative to previous levels for at least four years. This experiment makes an important conceptual point about who bears the burden of the adjustment to the I-Squared policy—it's the owners of the firm, not the workers.

The nationalistic policy that I evaluate is a complete elimination of the H-1B visa program.[3] Mimicking the results above, this policy delivers the following: the skill premium expands with negative effects on low-skilled workers; firms' exit and entry contracts; output contracts, and yet consumption overshoots, as there is a reduction in investment in new firms.

A unique outcome of the nationalistic policy is its unintended negative effects on the wages of low-skilled workers in the short run. As with the I-Squared policy, these consequences work through a change in the distribution of firms. Due to the elimination of the H-1B program, firms foresee a smaller market that results in less entry and more exit. Since entrants and exiting firms are less productive and low-skill intensive, low-skilled workers' wages contract as the demand for their labor services erodes.

As with the I-Squared policy, the normative implications of the nationalistic policy are subtle. While output declines through the scale and productivity effect, consumption increases in the short run. The issue here is that lower wages and lower output come from less entry and exit of firms. This is

2. Lee (2016) also focuses on the transition of the economy in response to changes in immigration. However, the dynamics of the economy arise from workers' life-cycle motives.
3. One current policy proposal is the High-Skilled Integrity and Fairness Act of 2017 (https://www.congress.gov/bill/115th-congress/house-bill/670/text), which seeks to increase the minimum salary requirement for H-1B visa holders.

because there is less need for investment in new firms, as the economy has too many firms given the shrinkage of the labor force (today and in the future). And the reduction in investment comes at the benefit of higher profits and consumption in the short run. While this effect mitigates the negative consequences of a nationalistic policy, it does highlight the following point: the negative consequences of a nationalistic immigration policy are borne by the workers—not by the owners of the firms.

This chapter provides an answer to some fundamental and unanswered questions: What are the distributional and aggregate effects of immigration? Regarding the distributional effects, there appears to be a wide range of answers within the literature. Estimating the distributional effects relies upon estimates of the elasticity of substitution between workers' types. These estimates seem to give wide-ranging answers depending upon the source of identifying variation, categorization of worker types, the instrument, and so forth (see, e.g., the discussions in Card [2009] or Borjas [2014]). Some estimates suggest near-zero impacts on relative wages, and some are larger.

One explanation for this discrepancy is that there are non-labor-market adjustments taking place in the background (see, e.g., the discussion in Lewis [2013]). I contribute to this line of thought by exploring one margin of non-labor-market adjustment: how immigration affects firms' entry and exit decisions. A key result is that changes in labor supply shift labor demand and lead to different short- and long-run wage responses as firms enter and use different skill mixes relative to incumbents.

Regarding the aggregate effects, the typical approach in the immigration literature is to treat the relative wage response (given an estimated elasticity of substitution) as a sufficient statistic for the outcome from immigration. Under certain restrictions on technologies, this is appropriate. However, in my model, the dynamics of the firm lead to outcomes in which the welfare effects of immigration are not captured by changes in relative wages. As discussed above, the adjustment of firms leads to substantial changes in consumption in the short run, even if the wage effects from immigration are negligible.

This chapter owes a large, intellectual debt to the trade literature and its emphasis on the role of the firm. The work of Bernard and Jensen (1999), Melitz (2003), and Bernard et al. (2003) very much focused the trade literature on the role of firms and their adjustments in understanding the positive and normative implications of trade.

Specifically, this chapter builds on two ideas discussed in the recent trade literature. First, my model shares the "skill-biased productivity mechanism" emphasized in Burstein and Vogel (forthcoming), with the key difference that I study the dynamic effects of a supply shock (immigration) rather than on a demand shock (opening to trade). This chapter also borrows from the idea that firm dynamics lead to horizon-varying trade elasticities, as in the work of Ruhl (2008) and Alessandria, Choi, and Ruhl (2014). In the immigration context, I show when firm heterogeneity matters (and does not) and how the characteristics of entering firms affect the elasticity across worker types over different time horizons.

6.2   Model

I outline the model below by describing the consumers (who are also the workers) and the firms. The interesting economics lie with the firms—specifically, how skill mix varies with firm type and the dynamic choices of the firm.

6.2.1   Time and Consumers

Time is discrete and evolves for the infinite horizon. Consumers have the following preferences:

$$(1) \qquad U = \sum_{t=0}^{\infty} \beta c_t,$$

where U is the present discounted value of the instantaneous utility of consuming the final consumption good, and $\beta \in (0,1)$ is the discount factor. The final consumption good is an aggregate bundle of varieties, aggregated with a CES function:

$$(2) \qquad c_t = \left[\int_{M(t)} c_t(\omega)^{(\sigma-1)/\sigma} \, d\omega \right]^{\sigma/(\sigma-1)},$$

where $c_t(\omega)$ is consumption of individual variety ω. The parameter σ controls the elasticity of substitution across variety. The measure M defines the endogenous set of varieties consumed.

I abstract from any decisions of consumers to hold or accumulate assets. Consumers simply consume given their income in each period. Since consumers are the workers and the owners of the firm, their income available for consumption comes from both labor earnings and profits from firms.

6.2.2   Firms

There is a continuum of firms that are heterogeneous in productivity, that are monopolistic competitors on the product market, and that face competitive labor markets.[4] Dropping the time index for clarity, firms producing individual varieties have technologies

$$(3) \qquad q(\omega) = z\left[\phi_s(z)\ell_s^{(\theta-1)/\theta} + \phi_u \ell_u^{(\theta-1)/\theta} \right]^{\theta/(\theta-1)},$$

where z is a firm's productivity, ℓ_s and ℓ_u are skilled and unskilled labor, the ϕs are the skill weights, and θ is the elasticity of substitution between labor types.

The production technology in equation (3) is similar to the aggregate,

4. Competitive labor markets are easy to work with. However, in the context of the H-1B program, this assumption abstracts from important details of the labor market for H-1B visa holders. In particular, that the H-1B program ties workers to firms for the duration of the visa.

"nested CES" structure of different skill types used in the immigration literature (see, e.g., Card 2009; Borjas 2014). The key difference is that skill intensity—the ϕs—may vary with firm productivity. For example, if $\phi_{s,}(z) > 0$, then skilled workers are relatively more productive in high-productivity firms, leading to a complementarity between skill and productivity across firms. This possibility is discussed in more depth below. This specification is similar to the production function in Burstein and Vogel's (forthcoming) study of the skill premium and international trade.

Consumer preferences in equation (2) imply that a firm producing variety ω faces the following demand curve:

$$(4) \qquad p(\omega)^{-\sigma}\left(\frac{Y}{P^{1-\sigma}}\right),$$

where $p(\omega)$ is the price of the variety, Y is aggregate income (both labor and profits), and P equals the CES price index.

Firms' Choice of Skill Mix. Given the production function in equation (3), a firm's relative demand for skilled and unskilled labor is

$$(5) \qquad \frac{\ell_s(z)}{\ell_u(z)} = \left(\frac{\phi_s(z)}{\phi_u}\right)^{\theta}\left(\frac{w_s}{w_u}\right)^{-\theta},$$

where w_s and w_u are the competitively determined wages for skilled and unskilled workers. With one exception, this demand curve is relatively standard: relative demand for labor is inversely related to the relative wage with elasticity θ. The exception is that if the ϕs vary with skill level, a firm's relative demand for skill varies with productivity. The demand curve in skill (5) implies that the within-firm shares of high- and low-skilled workers are

$$(6) \qquad \pi_s(z) = \frac{\phi_s(z)^{\theta} w_s^{-\theta}}{\phi_s(z)^{\theta} w_s^{-\theta} + \phi_u^{\theta} w_u^{-\theta}} \quad \text{and} \quad \pi_u(z) = \frac{\phi_u^{\theta} w_u^{-\theta}}{\phi_s(z)^{\theta} w_s^{-\theta} + \phi_u^{\theta} w_u^{-\theta}}.$$

These share formulas tell us the following: if skilled wages are relatively higher, then firms will employ relatively fewer high-skilled workers. If $\phi_{s,}(z) > 0$, then more-productive firms will employ relatively more high-skilled workers than less-productive firms will. And if the ϕs do not vary with skill type, then all firms will employ the same shares of high- and low-skilled workers. Finally, it will be useful to define an index of "skill":

$$(7) \qquad \Phi(z) = \left[\phi_s(z)\pi_s(z)^{(\theta-1)/\theta} + \phi_u\pi_u(z)^{(\theta-1)/\theta}\right]^{\theta/(\theta-1)},$$

which is a CES aggregate of the share of different skill types. This is a summary statistic of the skill mix of the workers in a firm with productivity z. If high-productivity firms employ relatively more high-skilled workers, then $\Phi(z)$ will be increasing with the productivity of the firm.

Firms' Choice of Price and Quantity. Given the optimal skill mix, I express a firm's (static) profit-maximization problem as

(8)
$$\max_{p(\omega),\ell} p(\omega)z\Phi(z)\ell - \left(w_u\pi_u(z) + w_s\pi_s(z)\right)\ell.$$

That is, choose an output price and labor units (i.e., number of bodies) to maximize period profits. Period profits are revenues minus the skill-share-weighted costs of employing ℓ labor units. This problem leads to the following optimal price:

(9)
$$p(z) = \frac{\sigma}{\sigma - 1}\frac{\left(w_u\pi_u(z) + w_s\pi_s(z)\right)}{z\Phi(z)},$$

where prices are a constant markup over the marginal cost of employing an efficiency unit of labor.[5] Marginal cost is a share-weighted wage bill relative to the firm's productivity, adjusted by the skill mix of the workers employed. Demand for labor units is

(10)
$$\ell(z) = \frac{1}{z\Phi(z)}\left(\frac{\sigma}{\sigma - 1}\frac{\left(w_u\pi_u(z) + w_s\pi_s(z)\right)}{z\Phi(z)}\right)^{-\sigma}\left(\frac{Y}{P^{1-\sigma}}\right).$$

The firm's static profit function is

(11)
$$\pi(z) = p(z)z\Phi(z)\ell(z) - \left[w_u\pi_u(z) + w_s\pi_s(z)\right]\ell(z),$$

which I use in the discussion of the firm's dynamic problem below.

6.2.3   Firm Dynamics

Firm-level productivity, z, evolves stochastically according to a N-state Markov chain with transition matrix $\mathcal{P}$ and an associated invariant distribution $\tilde{\mathcal{P}}$. This stochastic process is meant to capture the observed changes in firms' size and profitability over time. Apple started out as a two-man operation, hand-building wooden computers in Silicon Valley; only a decade ago, Nokia and BlackBerry were world leaders in the design and production of mobile phones. In an exogenous manner, this stochastic process mimics these changes in firm size and productivity over time that are seen in the data.

This process implies that in any period there is a measure $\mu(z)$ over productivity types. This measure will partially reflect the stochastic process in $\mathcal{P}$. It is also determined endogenously by the exit and entry decisions of firms. Thus, the distribution of firms over productivity is an equilibrium object and an endogenous outcome of the model.

Exit comes about as firms face a per-period, fixed cost of operation κ, which is denominated in units of the final good. The timing is such that if a

---

5. Note that the interaction between productivity and skill will generate dispersion in revenue-based productivity (or TFPR in the language of Hsieh and Klenow [2009]), that is, $p(z)\Phi(z)z$ is not independent of z. Furthermore, consistent with Foster, Haltiwanger, and Syverson (2008), revenue-based productivity in my model is correlated with physical-based productivity.

firm pays the fixed cost, it operates in the next period. If the firm does not pay this fixed cost, then it operates in this period and then exits.

Entry takes place via a large pool of nonactive firms that may enter the economy by paying an entry cost $P\kappa^e$ to gain an initial productivity draw. After receiving their productivity draw, entering firms are exactly like incumbents. Entrants receive their productivity draw from density $\mathcal{P}_e$.

Given this environment, I discuss an incumbent firm's problem and the value of entry.

Incumbents' Dynamic Problem. Given the static profit functions (and focusing on a stationary equilibrium motion where aggregate state variables are not changing), the problem of an incumbent firm is to choose between continuing to operate next period and exiting. Since firms are owned by consumers, firms choose exit policies to maximize the expected present discounted value of real profits, discounting with interest rate $r = (1/\beta) - 1$. The value function of an incumbent firm is

$$(12) \qquad v(z_i) = \max\left[\pi(z_i) - \kappa + \beta\sum_{j=1}^{N}\mathcal{P}(i,j)v(z_j), \ \pi(z_i)\right],$$

where the value of the firm is the maximum over two objects. The first objects are the static profit minus the fixed operating costs plus the expected, discounted continuation value of the firm. The second object is the static profit of the firm if it exits.

Entrants. The entry protocol implies that the value of entry is

$$(13) \qquad v_e = \sum_{j=1}^{N}\mathcal{P}_e(j)v(z_j) - \kappa_e,$$

where $v(z_j)$ is the value of a firm in equation (12), and $\mathcal{P}_e(j)$ is the probability of a firm receiving productivity level z_j. Thus, this says that the value of entry equals the expected value of operating in the market net of entry costs.

6.2.4   Equilibrium

Given the environment described above, I formally define a stationary equilibrium:

DEFINITION 1. *A stationary equilibrium is a collection of allocations for consumers c; allocations, prices, and exit decisions for firms; allocations of workers across firms; wages $\{w\}_{s,u}$, a mass of entrants M_e, and a measure of incumbents μ, such that*

- consumers', firms', and workers' problem is solved;
- labor demand equals labor supply, for each skill type;
- the measure over incumbents is stationary; and
- the free-entry condition is satisfied.

Essentially, firms and consumers optimize, markets clear, and the economy is stationary. The economy being stationary means that aggregate outcomes and the measure of firms over individual states are constant, but that individual firms will dynamically move through the productivity distribution, exit, or enter. In the quantitative section, I will study a nonstationary economy as it transits between two stationary equilibria.

6.3   The Aggregate Skill Premium

In this section, I derive the aggregate skill premium and the aggregate elasticity of relative wages to relative supply of skill. This relationship is important because within the aggregate, nested CES structure, it provides the foundation for evaluating and interpreting the distributional effects from immigration. In particular, I show (a) the importance of the complementarily between firm productivity and skill, and (b) the role of firm heterogeneity and dynamics.

To derive the aggregate skill premium and its relationship to aggregate skill supply, I start from the aggregate resource constraint:

$$(14) \quad \sum_i \mu(z_i)\pi_s(z_i)\ell(z_i) = L_s \text{ and } \sum_i \mu(z_i)\pi_u(z_i)\ell(z_i) = L_u.$$

Here, $\pi_s(z_i)$ and $\pi_u(z_i)$ are the within-firm shares of skilled and unskilled labor in equation (6), $\mu(z_i)$ is the measure of firms with productivity type z_i, and $\ell(z_i)$ is the quantity demanded of labor units by firms with productivity z_i. Finally, L_s and L_u are the aggregate supplies of skilled and unskilled labor. All equation (14) says is that firm demand equals aggregate labor supply.

Substitution of equation (6) into the aggregate resource constraint (14) connects the aggregate skill premium and aggregate skill supply. Proposition 1 summarizes the result.

PROPOSITION 1 (THE AGGREGATE SKILL PREMIUM). *Log relative wages relate to aggregate, log relative skill supplies*

$$(15) \quad \log(w_s) - \log(w_u) = \Theta(w_s, w_u, \mu, \ell) - \frac{1}{\theta}\left[\ \log(L_s) - \log(L_u)\right],$$

where

$$(16) \quad \Theta(w_s, w_u, \mu) = -\frac{1}{\theta}\log\left\{\sum_i \frac{\phi_s(z_i)^\theta\ \mu(z_i)\ell(z_i)}{\phi_s(z_i)^\theta w_s^{-\theta} + \phi_u^\theta w_u^{-\theta}}\right\}$$
$$+ \frac{1}{\theta}\log\left\{\sum_i \frac{\phi_u^\theta\ \mu(z_i)\ell(z_i)}{\phi_s(z_i)^\theta w_s^{-\theta} + \phi_u^\theta w_u^{-\theta}}\right\}.$$

Furthermore, the change in the skill premium with respect to a change in relative skill supply is

$$(17) \quad d\log(w_s) - d\log(w_u) = d\Theta - \frac{1}{\theta}\left[d\log(L_s) - d\log(L_u)\right].$$

Proposition 1 yields three important observations. First, the relationship in equation (15) is very similar to the theoretical relationship used in the immigration literature. Changes in relative labor supply lead to changes in relative wages that connect directly with the elasticity of substitution between labor types. The key difference is that this is not a constant-elasticity relationship. In general, the intercept term $\Theta(w_s, w_u, \mu)$ will vary with the skill supply.[6] A change in the $\Theta(w_s, w_u, \mu)$ term represents a shift in the labor demand curve due to a change in relative skill supply.

Second, Proposition 1 shows why the labor demand curve will shift—it is because of the complementarity between skill and productivity. The easiest way to see this point is to "turn off" the complementarity with ϕ_s independent of z. In this case, the intercept term (16) becomes

$$(18) \quad \Theta = -\frac{1}{\theta}\log\left\{\sum_i \frac{\phi_s^\theta \, \mu(z_i)\ell(z_i)}{\phi_s^\theta w_s^{-\theta} + \phi_u^\theta w_u^{-\theta}}\right\} + \frac{1}{\theta}\log\left\{\sum_i \frac{\phi_u^\theta \, \mu(z_i)\ell(z_i)}{\phi_s^\theta w_s^{-\theta} + \phi_u^\theta w_u^{-\theta}}\right\}.$$

And then, after canceling terms in equation (18), we have

$$(19) \quad \Theta = -\frac{1}{\theta}\log(\phi_s) + \frac{1}{\theta}\log(\phi_u),$$

with all endogenous variables dropping out of the intercept. When there is no complementarity between skill and productivity, the elasticity of relative wages is constant with elasticity $1/\theta$.

The intuition for why complementarity matters is that firms are differentially substituting in to or out of labor types. Thus, the distribution of firms and their labor demands matter. When there is no complementarity, all firms substitute in the exact same way, and, thus, the distribution of firms and their labor demand plays no role.

This latter point is closely related to the "skill-biased productivity mechanism" emphasized in Burstein and Vogel (forthcoming). That is, opening to trade reallocates labor demand from low-productivity, low-skill-intensity firms to high-productivity, high-skill-intensity firms, and this mechanism leads to an increase in the skill premium. Their insight shows up in the intercept term in equation (16): shifts in the *distribution* of labor demand (in their case, caused by trade; in my case, immigration) change the skill premium as long as there is complementarity between productivity and skill.

Third, Proposition 1 says that firm dynamics matter for the dynamics of relative wages only when there is complementarity between skill and productivity. Again, equation (19) shows that the distribution of firms and its evolution "separate" from the change in wages. Thus, to have different short- and long-run wage elasticities, it is necessary to have an interaction between skill and productivity.

---

6. A useful exercise would be to abstract from dynamics and assume a distribution over the zs—that is, Pareto, as done in the trade literature (see, e.g., Chaney 2008). With the right function form for the $\phi_s(z)$, some insight may be possible. In particular, I conjecture that the intercept term and how it would respond would depend on the Pareto-shape parameter; thus, the variation in firm-level productivity dispersion would modulate the wage response.

Finally, these observations have a very close relationship to the work on capital-skill complementarity and immigration in Lewis (2011, 2013) and, more generally, Krusell et al. (2000). Capital-skill complementarity gives rise to a non-constant-elasticity relationship between relative wages and relative skill in a very similar way to equation (17). The difference here—and the empirical content—is that $d\theta$ term in equation (17) relates to firms and their differential adjustment to the change in labor supply.

6.4   Quantification

This section discusses the calibration of the model, which proceeds in three steps. First, I describe functional form assumptions. I then describe how the parameter values are chosen such that the model can replicate key features of firm dynamics in the data. Finally, I discuss how labor supply evolves in the model and how I implement the I-Squared policy.

6.4.1   Specification of Shock Process and Skill Bias

To completely specify the model, I must take a stand on the nature of the shock process, the initial productivity of entrants, and a specification relating productivity to the complementarity between skill and productivity.

I construct a Markov process over the zs so that in logs, z mimics an AR(1) process with normally distributed innovations. I achieve this via Tauchen's (1986) method. This implies that there are two parameters to calibrate: the autocorrelation parameter, ρ, and the standard deviation of the shocks, σ_z.

The entrants' productivity distribution is a mean shift of the invariant distribution associated with the Markov process described above. Specifically, μ_e will be the mean of log productivity for entrants. If μ_e is a negative number, then entering firms will be less productive (on average) than incumbents.

I parameterize the ϕs in the following way. First, I normalize ϕ_u equally to one. I then assume that $\phi_s(z)$ is a log-linear function of z with intercept α and elasticity γ. This functional form has the feature that if $\gamma > 0$, then high-productivity firms employ a larger share of high-skilled workers relative to low-productivity firms. This functional form closely resembles the specification in Burstein and Vogel (forthcoming).

6.4.2   Calibration of Parameters

The parameters of the model are grouped into two categories. One set of parameters consists of those that are chosen outside of the model. I call these "predetermined parameters." The second set consists of those chosen match model moments with data moments, that is, "calibrated parameters." The latter are chosen to mimic key properties of firms in the cross section and over time.

Predetermined Parameters. The time period in the model is a year. Thus, I set the discount factor, β, to 0.98. This corresponds with an annualized risk-free real interest rate of 2 percent, which is consistent with recent experience in the US economy.

The value for the demand elasticity, σ, is set to 4. The trade literature has put much effort into estimating this parameter, and the value 4 lies within the middle of the range of recent estimates. The estimates that I prefer come from Simonovska and Waugh (2014a, 2014b). At the lower end of the range are the estimates from Broda and Weinstein (2006), who find that the median elasticity across product categories is around 3. At the upper end of the range are aggregate estimates from Parro (2013) and Caliendo and Parro (2015); using aggregate tariff and trade-flow data, they find values near 5 (see Simonovska and Waugh [2014b] for a discussion of these estimates).

I set the elasticity of substitution across skill types to 3. This parameter is not uncontroversial. Card (2009) reports that estimates of the θ between college and high school workers range from about 2.5 to 4. Ottaviano and Peri (2012) find estimate values of θ that lie between 1.5 and 3. Borjas (2003) estimates an inverse elasticity of around 1.4. Setting θ to 3 is near the upper-middle part of this range.

There is an important caveat regarding the discussion of the elasticity of substitution across skill types. Proposition 1 makes the point that a structural interpretation of these empirical estimates is not clear, as labor demand will shift with changes in labor supply. Thus, the mapping from these estimates to the θ parameter in my model is not obvious. One rationale for picking a value near the upper-middle part of the range is that these elasticities are biased downward in my model (see, e.g., figure 6.2).

The autocorrelation is chosen to match the autocorrelation of establishment size observed in the Synthetic Longitudinal Business Database (LBD) (US Census Bureau 2011). Predetermining this parameter outside the calibration routine simplifies computational matters, with no loss in the model's ability to correctly mimic the persistence seen in the data.

Finally, the entry cost is normalized to 1. The top panel of table 6.1 summarizes the predetermined parameters.

Calibrated Parameters. There are five remaining parameters to calibrate: the standard deviation of the shocks to productivity, the fixed cost of operation, the shift in the entrant distribution, and the intercept and slope for the skill-bias function.

I calibrate these five parameters to match five moments. The first moment is about the size distribution. The Statistics of US Businesses from the US Census Bureau reports data that include firms binned by size with data on the number of firms, the number of establishments, employment, and the annual payroll for most US business. Half of all employment is in firms with more than 500 employees; I abuse terminology here, but I will call this the median firm. The average firm size is about twenty employees. Thus, I target a ratio of the median to mean size of twenty-five. The parameter that is most directly informative about this moment is the standard deviation of the zs.

Table 6.1   **Calibration summary**

Parameter	Value	Source or target
Predetermined parameters		
Discount rate, β	0.98	—
Demand elasticity σ	4.0	—
Skill elasticity θ	3.0	—
Autocorrelation of log z	0.90	Autocorrelation of size, synthetic LBD
Entry cost, κ_e	1.0	Normalization
Calibrated parameters		
Standard deviation of log z	0.20	Ratio of median size to mean ≈ 25
Fixed cost of operation, κ	0.14	Entry rate of 10 percent
Shift in entry distribution, μ_e	−0.13	Probability of survival of entrants after 5 years, 0.50
Intercept of skill-bias function, α	−0.55	Skill premium, 1.90
Slope of skill-bias function, γ	1.00	Size-wage premium, 1.30

The second and third moments are computed using the Synthetic Longitudinal Business Database (US Census Bureau 2011). The entry rate is computed as the new establishments relative to the total number of establishments. This number is computed to be about 10 percent in the later time periods of the data set. Here, I am just focusing on recent experience in the US economy and abstract from the long-run declines in start-up activity as Decker et al. (2014), Hathaway and Litan (2014), and others document.

The survival rate is computed as establishments staring in a given-year period that remain open (over some time horizon) relative to all establishments starting in that year. This number is about 50 percent at a five-year horizon. The parameters most informative about these moments are fixed operating cost, κ, and the shift in the entrant distribution μ_e.

The fourth and fifth moments are the aggregate skill premium and the firm-size-wage premium. The former is computed as the relative earnings of skilled to unskilled workers using the Current Population Survey. Specifically, I compare the median usual weekly earnings of workers with a bachelor's degree or above with those workers with less than a bachelor's degree. This provides the estimate that skilled workers earn 1.89 times that of unskilled workers.

The size-wage premium is determined as follows. Using the Statistics of US Businesses, I compute the payroll divided by employment for those firms with more than 500 employees—I call this the average wage above the median. Then, I compare this to the average wage or workers in firms below 500 employees. For the period from 2010 to 2013, this value is 1.30. That is, the average wage in firms with more than 500 employees is 30 percent larger than in firms with fewer than 500 employees.

The size-wage premium moment speaks directly to the slope of the skill-bias function, γ. In the model, since size and productivity correspond with each other, there must be some skill bias to match the fact that larger firms pay higher wages. Thus, the calibration finds that high-productivity firms demand and use relatively more high-skilled workers. Consistent with my findings, Burstein and Vogel (forthcoming) find a value of γ near 1 when calibrated to match the skill intensity of Mexican firms.

The bottom panel of table 6.1 summarizes the results.

6.4.3   Labor Supply and Its Dynamics

To compute the initial stationary equilibrium, I use labor endowments from aggregate data. I take L_u to stand for the US labor force with less than a college degree. This value is normalized. I then take L_s to stand for the US labor force with a college degree or higher. This value is set at 57 percent of L_u as seen in recent US data.

I want to use the model to evaluate two different policy proposals. The first policy focuses on the Immigration Innovation Act of 2015 or "I-Squared," which seeks to triple the number of H-1B visas. Current policy in the United States allows for a maximum of 65,000 H-1B visas, with an additional 20,000 visas for foreign graduates of US universities with advanced degrees. Thus, current policy allows up to 85,000 visas per year. The I-Squared Act raises the cap to 195,000 visas per year and eliminates the advanced degree exception. Furthermore, the policy proposal contains "escalators" that restrict the visa increase by 20,000 visas per year until reaching the cap of 195,000.

The second policy proposal is a "nationalistic" policy that restricts the movement of labor into the United States. I model this policy as a complete elimination of the H-1B visa program, allowing existing H-1B visas holders to remain until the expiration of their visa, but preventing H-1B visa holders from transitioning to permanent status.

There are several challenges to evaluating the effects of these policies. First, I need to know about the current stock of H-1B visa holders. Second, I need an estimate of how changes in the flow of immigrants affect the stock over time.[7] Unfortunately, little is known about the current stock of H-1B visa holders and how they transition to permanent status or exit the United States as their visa expires (or before). Thus, to construct an estimate of the current and future stock of H-1B visa holders, I build on the work of Lowell (2000) and make some educated guesses.

I start from the fact that the visa cap has been binding in recent years. The H-1B visa is a three-year visa with an option for an additional three-year extension. Thus, I assume that H-1B visa holders stay the maximum period of six years. At current caps, this implies that the stock of H-1B visa holders

---

7. In a static model or steady state-to-steady state comparison, it may be reasonable to assume that the change in the steady state stock is proportional to the change in the flow. First, one needs to know the original stock to evaluate the level of the effects from this policy. Furthermore, I want to evaluate the transition; thus, I need an estimate of how the stock transitions to the new steady state.

is 510,000. This is consistent with projections of the stock of H-1B visa holders by Lowell (2000) and updated projections by Kerr and Lincoln (2010).

To compute the change in the stock, I need to know how H-1B visa holders may (or may not) transition to permanent status. Lowell (2000) suggests that up to 50 percent of expiring H-1B visa holders transition to permanent status. This may be an exaggeration, as there are numerical caps on those with permanent status. Also, processing time is a nontrivial barrier. This assumption implies that, at current rates, each year 42,500 H-1B visa holders transition to permanent status, while the remaining half exits.

The final issue is to connect the H-1B visa holders that transition to permanent status with the permanent stock of high-skilled workers in the United States. To do so, I assume that the stock of labor evolves according to a simple "perpetual inventory" law of motion, and I infer the rate at which high-skilled workers exit the labor force under the assumption that the stock of high-skilled workers is stationary. Specifically, the stock of high-skilled labor evolves according to

$$(20) \qquad L^p_{s,t+1} = (1 - \delta)L^p_{s,t} + \text{new graduates}_t + \text{H-1B transitions}_t,$$

where $L^p_{s,t}$ is the stock of permanent, high-skilled workers. This law of motion implies that in the steady state,

$$(21) \qquad L^p_{s,ss} = \frac{1}{\delta}(\text{new graduates}_t + \text{H-1B transitions}_t).$$

We know that the current stock of high-skilled workers (net of H-1B visa holders) is about 48.5 million (averaged over 2010–2015). The flow of new graduates entering the workforce is about 1.10 million over the same time period (see, e.g., Spreen 2013). The (guesstimated) flow of H-1B visa holders into the permanent workforce is 42,500. This implies a δ of 2.36 percent.

The total stock of the skilled labor force is

$$(22) \qquad L_{s,t} = L^p_{s,t} + \text{stock of H-1B Visas}_t,$$

or the sum of permanent residents and the stock of H-1B visa holders at that time.

I use these assumptions to project the effects of immigration policy on labor supply. Two final comments on this procedure are warranted. In equations (20) and (22), I assume that native and foreign-born workers are the same. If high-skilled immigrants are positively selected (as the evidence in Grogger and Hanson [2011] suggests), then this implies that I am missing an additional margin. Specifically, that the number of new effective labor units associated with an increase in immigration is larger than I am estimating. Second, I assume that the skill choice is not responding to shifts in labor supply; Bound, Khanna, and Morales (chapter 4, this volume) evaluate this margin of adjustment within the context of the H-1B visa program.

6.5 I-Squared Policy

This section evaluates the economic effects of the I-Squared policy. Below, I first discuss the effects on relative wages and then the aggregate, level effects, and I conclude with a discussion of welfare.

To compute the effects of this policy, I treat the change in policy as unanticipated from the perspective of firms. After the policy is announced, firms understand what the entire projected path of the work force in figure 6.1, panel B, will be. I then compute the transition path of the economy to its new stationary equilibrium.

Figure 6.1, panel A, plots the evolution of the stock of H-1B visa holders from the I-Squared Act.[8] Year 0 is the estimated stock of H-1B visas under the current policy. The new policy is enacted in year 1. From steady state to steady state the stock about doubles from 510 thousand to 1.15 million. The transition does take time to play out, about ten years. This is due partly to the natural addition of new visas at the higher limit. The escalators also play an important role in slowing down the transition.

Figure 6.1, panel B, plots the evolution of the stock of all high-skilled labor. This includes new H-1B visas and the new mass of H-1B visa holders that transition to permanent status. It is normalized to 1 in year 0. When in enacted in year 1, the stock of high-skilled labor increases by a little less than .10 of a percent. Fifteen years out, the I-Squared Act leads to a 2 percent increase in the stock of high-skilled labor. Approximately 1 percentage point of the 2 percent is just from an expansion of the number of visas. The remaining 1 percentage point is from the increases in the flow of transitions to permanent status. Steady state to steady state, this policy leads to a 6 percent increase in the stock of high-skilled labor.

6.5.1 Relative Wages and Wage Elasticities

Measuring Changes in Relative Wages. In discussing the distributional effects of this policy, I focus on the measured elasticity of relative labor supply with respect to wages. I compute this measure by dividing the log change in relative labor supply by the log change in relative wages:

$$(23) \qquad \hat{\theta}_t = \frac{d\log(L_{st}) - d\log(L_{ut})}{d\log(w_{st}) - d\log(w_{ut})}.$$

I call this $\hat{\theta}_t$. Per Proposition 1, this is an interesting statistic because $\hat{\theta}_t$ and how it evolves reveals the extent to which firm dynamics and the complementarity between productivity and skill matter.

To understand this point, note that the estimator in equation (23) will recover the structural parameter θ, if there is no interaction between the skill

---

8. As an additional detail, I evaluate the policy with the proposed escalators described in the Immigration Innovation Act of 2015; that is, the number of H-1B visas increase only by 20,000 per year until the cap of 195,000 is reached.

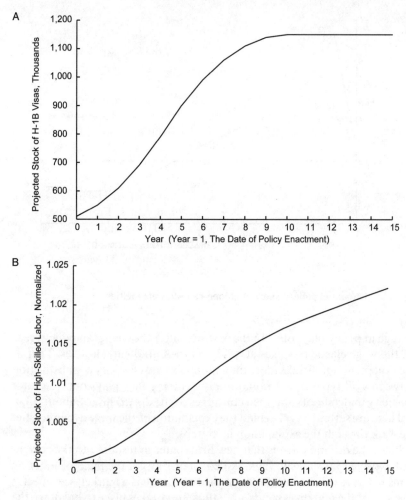

Fig. 6.1   Projected stocks of labor under the I-Squared Act

Notes: A, projected stock of H-1B visas; *B*, projected stock of high-skilled labor (normalized).

of the worker and the productivity of the firm. The calibrated model, however, finds a nontrivial amount of complementarity between high-skilled workers and firm productivity (see the last row of table 6.1). Thus, Proposition 1 tells us that equation (23) will (a) deviate from the structural parameter θ, and (b) vary over time. Thus, plotting $\hat{\theta}_t$ and how it evolves reveals the new insights that the model can deliver about the change in relative wages.

Results: Wage Elasticities. Figure 6.2 plots $\hat{\theta}_t$. Year 1 is the date of policy enactment; I plot this statistic going out only fifteen years. The dotted line plots the elasticity in the long run—that is, the wage response as the economy converges to the new stationary distribution.

Figure 6.2 shows that the wage elasticity is not constant and varies as the

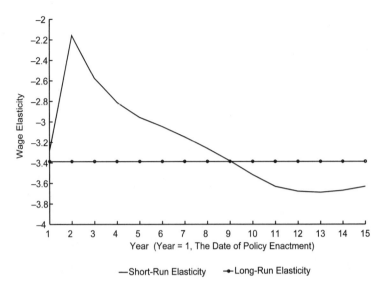

Fig. 6.2   I-Squared policy: Short- and long-run wage elasticities

change in policy plays out.[9] In the first year after the change in policy (year 2), the wage elasticity spikes at −2.2 and then gradually declines. That is, the skill premium shrinks more than the calibrated elasticity of substitution between skill types of −3 would imply. As the policy plays out, the wage elasticity undershoots and then converges to the dotted line of about −3.4.

There are several layers behind the explanation of the wage dynamics. Let me walk through the explanation in in steps.

First, the driving force is that new firms enter in response to the current and expected increases in high-skilled labor.[10] I plot the mass of entering firms in figure 6.3. I conjecture that the key reason is a market-size effect.[11] The size of the market expands, and, thus, entry takes place to bid down the returns of operating in the market and to equalize the free-entry condition in equation (13). This is analogous to variety expansion effects emphasized in monopolistic-competition models in Krugman (1980) or Melitz (2003).

Firm entry, however, is not sufficient to generate the dynamics in figure

9. The slight "bulge" between years 5 and 11 corresponds with when the escalators come off and the growth in stock of high-skilled labor accelerates slightly (see figure 6.1, panel B).

10. An interpretation of firm entry is that this is a form of "product innovation" in the language of Atkeson and Burstein (2010) and, thus, meshes well with the evidence in Kerr and Lincoln (2010).

11. I suspect other mechanisms are also at work. In particular, it raises the option value of entering. This policy makes high-productivity firms relatively more profitable, as the factor that they are using intensively has become more abundant. Firms stay in the market only if they have sufficiently high productivity. Thus, the downside (exit) is the same and the upside is more beneficial, and, hence, the option value of entering increased.

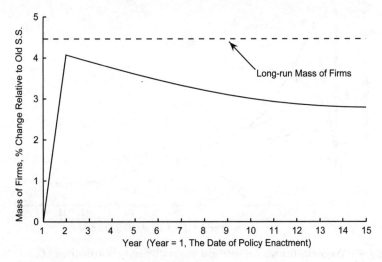

Fig. 6.3   I-Squared policy: Mass of firms (relative to old SS)

6.2. Proposition 1 says that there must be some form of skill bias across firms. Thus, the dynamics in figure 6.2 come from the interaction of firm entry and the skill bias across firms.

The intuition for how this interaction works is the following. First, new firms are likely to be low-productivity firms for two reasons: (a) entrants are not selected, as they come from an unconditional distribution, and (b) that unconditional distribution is also worse (the $\mu_e < 0$). Second, low-productivity firms use low-skilled labor more intensively. Thus, the expansion of low-productivity firms through entry bids up low-skilled wages more than would be expected. Thus, the skill premium decreases more than predicted by a constant-elasticity model.[12]

Changing the properties of the entry distribution and how the wage elasticity varies illustrates this point. For example, if $\mu_e = 0$, then new entrants will not be as unproductive relative to incumbents.[13] Thus, entry should not cause additional wage pressure for low-skilled workers to lead to a less responsive elasticity. This is exactly what figure 6.4 shows. The dashed line reports the wage elasticity when $\mu_e = 0$; the skill premium displays less dramatic dynamics.

12. The intuition here is closely related to the results of Burstein and Vogel (forthcoming) and their skill-biased productivity mechanism in response to trade liberalizations. The key distinction is the focus on the dynamic effects of a supply shock (immigration) rather than on a demand shock (opening to trade). Furthermore, my effects are driven by entry where as the model of Burstein and Vogel (forthcoming) has a fixed mass of firms.

13. This does not imply that entrants look like incumbents. Incumbents will be positively selected, as there is endogenous exit. Thus, even in this case, entrants will be less productive and demand relatively more low-skilled workers.

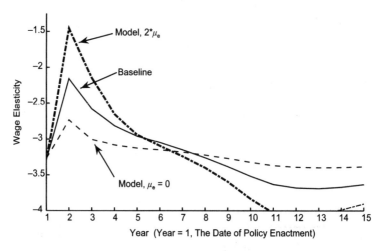

Fig. 6.4   Wage elasticities, baseline and alternative entry distributions

The corollary is that if entrants are even more (relative to the calibrated model) unproductive relative to incumbents, then the wage elasticity should vary more. Why? Entrants will be very unproductive, demand relatively more low-skilled workers, and place even more pressure on wages for low-skilled workers, leading to a more responsive elasticity. Again, this is exactly what figure 6.4 shows. The dash-dot line reports the wage elasticity when the shift in the entry distribution is twice its calibrated value $2^*\mu_e$; the skill premium displays more dramatic dynamics.

To summarize: figure 6.2 shows that the skill premium contracts—and much more than a standard, constant-elasticity model would predict. The reason is that immigration makes the size of the market larger (today and in the future) and, thus, entry occurs. The calibrated models find that entrants are less productive and are low-skill intensive. Thus, entry bids up the relative price of low-skilled labor, and the skill premium decreases by more than a standard model would predict. The strength of this response depends on how different entrants are relative to incumbents.

Evidence Supporting the Mechanism. There are two aspects of the mechanism behind the results in figure 6.2: (a) firm entry responds to a change in labor supply, and (b) new firms are likely to be low productivity and low-skill intensive. There is evidence supporting both aspects of the mechanism.

First, research finds that changes in labor supply affect firm entry. In the context of changes in immigration, Olney (2013) presents compelling evidence in support of this piece of the mechanism; in US data, he finds a strong correlation between immigration and the new entry of establishments at the MSA level. In German data, Dustmann and Glitz (2015) show that firm entry and exit make important contributions to the absorption of labor supply shocks. Karahan, Pugsley, and Şahin (2016) explore how demographic changes effect firm entry; using cross-state and industry data, they find that demographic changes have a large effect on the start-up rate of firms.

Second, there is evidence new firms are likely to be low productivity. To match the high exit rate of new firms, the model finds that new firms are less productive than the average incumbent is. This fact has been well documented (see, e.g., Baily, Hulten, and Campbell (1992); Bartelsman and Doms 2000).

What about how a firm's skill intensity varies with its productivity? Bernard and Jensen (1995) show that exporters (who are larger and more productive) pay higher wages relative to nonexporters. Thus, this suggests that high-productivity firms (exporters) demand more skilled workers and, hence, pay (on average) higher average wages. Schank, Schnabel, and Wagner (2007) discuss a similar finding in German data but establish that observable worker characteristics (e.g., education) account for the wage premium of exporters. This latter fact is very much in line with the calibration result that high-productivity firms employ relatively more high-skilled workers.

Burstein and Vogel (forthcoming) provide multiple pieces of evidence in support of the relationship between skill intensity and productivity. One compelling piece of evidence is that they find using the March CPS that the share of workers with a college degree is larger in larger firms in the United States. Using the correspondence between size and productivity in the model, this implies that high-productivity firms employ relatively more high-skilled workers.[14]

6.5.2   Wage Levels, Output, Consumption

The results in figure 6.2 show that the skill premium is shrinking—and shrinking more than the calibrated elasticity of substitution would imply. The temptation is to jump to the normative conclusion that high-skilled workers are worse off because of the I-Squared policy. The value added of a completely specified model is that I can evaluate the level effects on wages, output, and consumption. And, under certain conditions about the distribution of profits, a welfare evaluation.

Figure 6.5, panel A, plots the level of high- and low-skilled wages after the policy enactment. Again, year 1 is the date of the policy enactment; I plot statistics going out only fifteen years. In year 1, the level of high-skilled wages declines by −0.011 percent—essentially zero. In year 2, high-skilled workers' wages *increase* by 0.02 percent relative to prepolicy

14. Another piece of evidence builds on the observation in footnote 4. This model generates dispersion in TFPR and arises from differences in a firm's wage bill. Fox and Smeets (2011) use matched employer-employee panel data and find that (a) adjusting for labor quality reduces dispersion in TFPR, and (b) a firm's wage bill summarizes well the contribution of labor-quality differences to dispersion in TFPR.

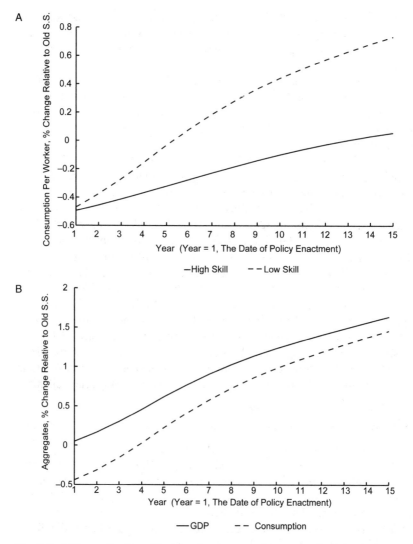

Fig. 6.5 I-Squared policy: Wage levels, output, and consumption

Note: A, I-Squared; *B*, I-Squared policy: output and consumption, percent change relative to old steady state.

levels—small, but not negative. Thus, one year after the policy, high-skilled workers are better off (in terms of labor earnings) than before the enactment of the policy.

Scale and productivity effects are the reasons high-skilled workers earn more. First, a larger labor force leads to more firms (product variety) and higher real wages for all. This expansion in the mass of firms is clearly seen in figure 6.3 with a 4 percent increase in the mass of firms in year 1. Second, there is a productivity effect. More high-skilled labor at a relatively lower price allows firms to substitute into more productive labor, and this is happening for the most productive firms. The analogue to the trade literature is that opening to trade reallocates resources toward the most productive firms, as in Melitz (2003).

The entry of firms is typically thought of as a long-run effect (see, e.g., di Giovanni, Levchenko, and Ortega 2015). However, this benefit is felt in year 2—not in the "long run." The reason is the dynamic, forward-looking nature of the firm. In year 1, the mass of firms increases by 4 percent even though the stock of high-skilled labor expands by only 0.20 percent at that point. Thus, firms respond forcefully to the current and foreseen increases in labor supply.

These effects show up in GDP. Figure 6.5, panel B, plots the path of aggregate output (solid line). In year 1, there is a 0.05 percent increase in GDP. After the complete transition, the I-Squared Act delivers a 4.5 percent increase in GDP, given a 2 percent increase in the total stock of labor.

These benefits are not without costs—and these costs show up as a loss in consumption. The dashed line in figure 6.5, panel B, plots aggregate consumption. In year 1, there is nearly a −0.50 percent loss in consumption. It is not until year 4 that the level of consumption is at its prepolicy level.

The issue is that all the "good" outcomes—higher wages and higher output—come from firm entry. However, firm entry must be paid for. There is investment today in the creation of firms to prepare for a larger labor force in the future—and this investment comes at the cost of consumption. This result makes clear that near-zero wage impacts (e.g., figure 6.5, panel A) do not imply near-zero effects on economic outcomes that are closer a measure of welfare. Thus, the normative implications of immigration policy are more nuanced than just the change in wages.

I made some important modeling choices that might change the consumption result. The first one regards the lack of curvature over period utility in consumers' preferences in equation (1). If consumers have a finite intertemporal elasticity of substitution, then the interest rate firms' profits are discounted would be endogenous and depend on the path of consumption. A growing path of consumption would lead to an increase in the interest rate; firms would discount profits more heavily, and then firm entry would not be as strong. A related issue is the closed economy assumption—international borrowing would allow consumers to smooth consumption while these investments are made.

The second important modeling choice was the denomination of the entry and fixed costs in units of output versus the alternative being the denomination in units of labor. The upside of this choice was that (a) I avoided having to make choices regarding the skill intensity of these activities and then feeding into the distributional effects, and (b) it provides a long-run motive for immigration through the introduction of a scale effect. The downside is that (a) it introduces a scale effect that may be empirically implausible, and (b) the increases in firm entry lead to losses in consumption as more investment in new firms takes place.

6.5.3   I-Squared Policy: Welfare

The I-Squared policy leads to essentially no negative wage effects; yet, aggregate consumption falls on impact and stays depressed for up to four years. This implies that the welfare effects depend critically on the distribution of firms' profits across workers. Below, I illustrate this issue by taking a stand on the distribution of profits and then discuss alternatives.

To compute welfare, I assume that consumers of a skill type receive a wage-bill weighted share of profits net of entry costs. This allocation rule implies that consumption of skilled and unskilled workers is

$$c_s = w_s + \Pi \left(\frac{w_s}{w_u L_u + w_s L_s} \right),$$

$$c_u = w_u + \Pi \left(\frac{w_u}{w_u L_u + w_s L_s} \right),$$

where Π is aggregate profits; and $w_s/(w_u L_u + w_s L_s)$ is the wage-bill share that a skilled worker receives.

Figure 6.6 plots consumption per worker. Consumption for both workers falls on impact and stays depressed, relative to the old steady state, for four and five years for low- and high-skilled workers. Figure 6.5, panel A, shows that labor income is little changed. Thus, consumption falls because the profit that both worker groups receive falls as new entry takes place. Because the workers are also the owners of the firms, they bear the cost of investment today for the creation of firms tomorrow.

As a formal welfare metric, I compute the present discounted gain in consumption for both worker types over the entire transition path into the infinite future. The I-Squared policy amounts to 1.29 and 0.22 percent increases in present discounted consumption for low- and high-skilled workers. This is a substantial—especially for such a seemingly small expansion in the H-1B visa program. With that said, it is also about 50 percent less than a simple, long-run evaluation that compares across steady states would suggest (2.46 percent and 0.65). Thus, the adjustment to this policy is an important consideration.

I do not believe the conjectured profit-sharing rule is accurate or realistic. But this thought experiment makes an important conceptual point: the owners of the firm, not the workers, bear the burden of the adjustment to the I-Squared policy. Mark Zuckerberg and Bill Gates—who are large shareholders of the firms that they operate (or operated) and who advocate policies such as the I-Squared Act—bear the short-run burden.

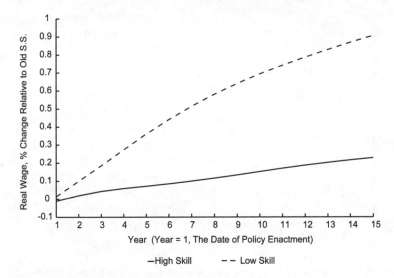

Year (Year = 1, The Date of Policy Enactment)

—High Skill   – – Low Skill

Fig. 6.6   I-Squared policy: Consumption per worker

6.6   Nationalistic Policy

Since I started writing the chapter, the policy environment in the United States has changed. Currently on the table are discussions about policies that are "nationalistic," in the sense that they restrict the movement of labor and goods with the goal of protecting national interests. This section evaluates the economic benefits/costs of one such policy: a complete elimination of the H-1B visa program.

To evaluate this policy, I build on the discussion in section 6.4.3 and change several things. First, no new H-1B visa holders are allowed in the United States. Thus, there is no longer a flow of 85,000 high-skilled workers into the economy each year. However, I do allow existing H-1B visas holders to remain for the maximum duration of six years. Finally, existing H-1B visa holders are prevented from changing their visa status and transitioning into permanent status—that is, H-1B transitions in equation (20) are set to zero. This is probably an extreme assumption, as it implies that nonemployment transitions into permanent status (e.g., marriage) are not possible.

Figure 6.7 plots the projected evolution of the stock of all high-skilled labor. It is normalized to 1 in year 0. The nationalistic policy is enacted in year 1, and the stock of high-skilled labor decreases by a little more than .10 of a percent—essentially, the 85,000 visa holders who exit and are not replaced. Over the next six years, the stock of high-skilled labor falls as H-1B visa holders are not replaced. The stock of high-skilled labor continues to decline as the inflow of domestic college graduates is not sufficient to

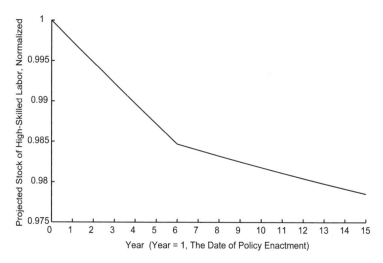

Fig. 6.7   **Nationalistic policy: Projected stock of high-skilled labor (normalized)**

replace the outflow of high-skilled workers. This latter statement is about the δ parameter, which was calibrated such that labor supply was stationary under current policy. Fifteen years out, the nationalistic policy leads to a 2 percent decrease in the the stock of high-skilled labor.

As in the previous analysis, I treat the closing of high-skilled immigration as unanticipated from the perspective of firms. After the policy is announced, firms understand the entire projected path of the workforce. I then compute the transition path of the economy to its new stationary equilibrium.

The next two subsections discuss the impact of this policy on the structure of wages and then on consumption, output, and welfare.

6.6.1   Nationalistic Policy: Wages

Figure 6.8, panel A, plots the level of high- and low-skilled wages after the policy enactment. Again, year 1 is the date of policy enactment; I plot this statistic going out only fifteen years. In year 1, the level of high-skilled wages increase by 0.04 percent—essentially zero. In year 2, high-skilled wages are unchanged, and by year 3 they decrease −0.02 percent relative to prepolicy levels. In the near term, reducing the supply of skilled workers does essentially nothing to increase their wages relative to before the enactment of the policy.

As discussed in the previous section, it is both a scale and productivity effect that leads to high-skilled workers now earning less. In this case, a smaller labor force leads to fewer firms and to lower real wages for all. Figure 6.8, panel B, shows how the mass of firms drops dramatically, with a 6 percent decrease in the mass of firms in year 2. Again, to emphasize this point, this is contrary to the conventional wisdom that the entry of firms is

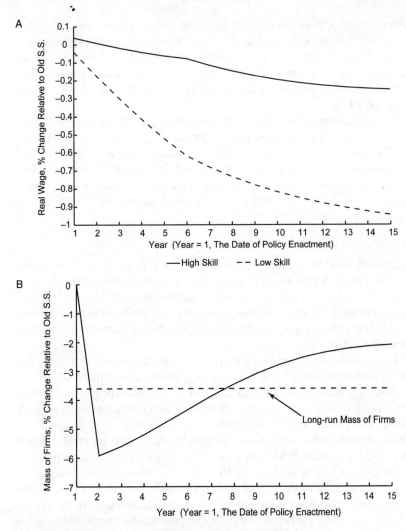

Fig. 6.8   Nationalistic policy: Wages and the mass of firms
Note: A, wage levels; *B*, mass of firms.

a long-run effect. Because of the dynamic, forward-looking nature of the firm, the long-run costs of a more restrictive immigration policy are quickly felt. Furthermore, the productivity effect comes from firms substituting into low-skilled labor as high-skilled labor is now relatively more expensive (discussed below).

Restricting high-skilled immigration has unintended, negative consequences on the wages of low-skilled workers. The dashed line in figure 6.8, panel A, plots the level of low-skilled wages after the policy enactment; these drop relatively sharply in the near term and then more gradually over the transition. The key reason for the drop in low-skilled wages (relative to high-skilled workers) is that the firms who are not entering anymore and the firms that are exiting are low-productivity and, hence, low-skill-intensive firms. In other words, the shrinkage of the market differentially lowers the demand for low-skilled labor because it is the low-skill-intensive firms that leave.

The negative impact on low-skilled wages further illustrates the mechanisms (but in the opposite direction) seen in the I-Squared policy. In this case, firms foresee a smaller market, which results in less entry and more exit, and entrants and exiting firms are less productive *and* low-skill intensive. Thus, the skill premium increases and does so at the expense of those workers at the bottom—not at the top—as the demand for their labor services decreases by relatively more.

6.6.2   Nationalistic Policy: Output, Consumption, Welfare

The reduction in the labor force and the mass of firms shows up as a drop in GDP. Figure 6.9 plots GDP (solid line) relative to its old steady-state value. In year 1, there is a 0.13 percent decrease in GDP. This decline continues as fewer firms enter, existing firms exit, and the labor force contracts. After the complete transition, the nationalistic policy delivers a 3.7 percent decrease in GDP.

These losses in wages and output do come with the benefit of a short-run gain in consumption. Figure 6.9 plots aggregate consumption relative to its old steady-state value. On impact, there is a 0.5 percent increase in consumption, but over time this effect dissipates, and consumption eventually declines in a similar manner as GDP.

In the nationalistic policy, lower wages and lower output come from firm entry, or lack thereof. What this means is that there is no need to invest in the creation of new firms because the economy has too many firms, given the reduction in the labor force (today and in the future). And, the reduction in investment comes at the benefit of higher consumption in the short run.

As in evaluating the I-Squared policy, the normative implications of the nationalistic immigration policy are more nuanced than just the change wages and depend on how profits are redistributed throughout the economy. Using the conjectured profit-sharing rule discussed in section 6.5.3, I compute the present discounted gain in consumption. The nationalistic policy amounts to a 0.20 decrease in present discounted consumption for high-skilled workers. For low-skilled workers—whom this policy is presumably intended not to affect—the welfare decrease is nearly six times as large, at a 1.13 percent decrease in present discounted consumption.

Interestingly, the consequences of the nationalistic policy are borne by the workers, not by the owners of the firms. The firms' owners benefit from this policy as they enjoy higher profits in the short run as a smaller market size reduces the necessity to invest in the creation and maintenance of firms.

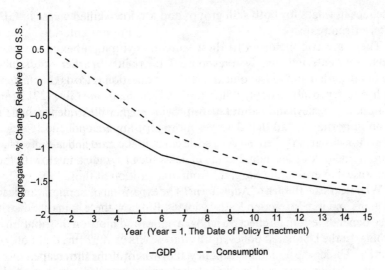

Fig. 6.9   **Nationalistic policy: GDP and consumption**

6.7   Conclusion

This chapter places the firm and its dynamics at the center of economic issues regarding immigration—in particular, the distributional effects, aggregate outcomes, and welfare. This chapter provides a useful place to start, but questions remain.[15] To conclude, let me outline three key lessons and, within each lesson, some open empirical questions.

Firm Dynamics and the Distributional Impacts of Immigration. The dynamics of the firm at the micro level generate nontrivial, short-run dynamics in relative wages that differ from their long-run dynamics. An expansion of skilled labor leads the wage premium of high-skilled to low-skilled workers to shrink more than a standard, static CES model would predict. Similarly, a contraction of skilled labor leads to an increase in the skill premium by more than the standard model would predict. Crucial to delivering this result is entering firms' skill bias relative to incumbent firms. Understanding this last point and what the data say about it is important. This result also raises, perhaps, questions about the structural interpretation of empirical evidence on the wage response to immigration.

The Aggregate Impacts of Immigration. In the chapter's evaluation of the I-Squared Act, wages essentially never declined and there was a 1.5 percent increase in GDP after fifteen years. The nationalistic policy quickly led to

---

15. Kerr, Kerr, and Lincoln (2014) provide a nice summary of the many open questions regarding firms and immigration. Xu (2016) moves in this same direction by focusing on the impact of high-skilled immigration in a growth model with firm dynamics in which firms engage in innovative and growth-enhancing activity.

declines in wages for both skill groups and a 1.5 percent decrease in GDP after fifteen years.

There are two elements to these outcomes. First, these effects came from firms entering quickly in response to the policy. In other words, labor demand shifted and did so quickly. An open question regards the elasticity of firm entry to labor supply. Olney (2013), Dustmann and Glitz (2015), and Karahan, Pugsley, and Şahin (2016) provide suggestive evidence, but this is an important detail that deserves more scrutiny. Second, the aggregate gains/losses partially depend on a scale effect in the model. Scale effects are hard to identify in the data, but (as in fields such as trade and growth) they are critical to evaluating the gains from immigration.

Who Bears the Burden of Adjustment? The expansion of immigration leads to gains and its contraction leads to losses. But how these gains are distributed depends less on its effect on labor earnings and more on distribution of profits. In the I-Squared policy, it was the owners of the firms that bore the burden. Under the nationalistic policy, the owners of the firm reaped short-run gains, while workers (low-skilled workers in particular) lost. Essentially, these observations place the wealth distribution at the center of the analysis. While perhaps obvious to me now, this came as a surprise, and it opens the door to many interesting questions about the winners and losers from changes in immigration and the distribution of wealth.

Appendix A

Data

This section describes the data used to calibrate the model.

1. Autocorrelation of establishment size. These moments were computed using the Synthetic Longitudinal Database (US Census Bureau 2011) by regressing the logarithm of establishment size across consecutive years for those establishments that are present in both years. Only establishments with more than one employee were used. This procedure yields an autocorrelation coefficient of 0.90, which I found to be stable across years and unaffected by incorporating industry fixed effects (at the SIC3 level).

2. Entry and survival rates. These moments were computed using the Synthetic Longitudinal Database (US Census Bureau 2011). The entry rate is computed as the new establishments relative to the total number of establishments. This number is computed to be about 10 percent in the later time periods of the data set. The survival rate is computed as establishments starting in a given-year period that remain open (over some time horizon) relative to all establishments starting in that year. This number is about 50 percent at a five-year horizon.

3. Fraction of skilled to unskilled workforce and earnings. These moments

were computed using the Current Population Survey. Unskilled workers were computed as the sum of the labor force with less than a bachelor's degree (series id: LNS11027659, LNS11027660, LNS11027689). Skilled workers were computed as those with a bachelor's degree or more (series id: LNS11027662). To abstract from long-run trends in the skill composition of the labor force, I focused on the average ratio of skilled to unskilled workers for the time period from 2010 to 2015; this led to an estimate of 0.57.

The relative earnings of skilled to unskilled workers were computed using the Current Population Survey. Using the same definition as above, I compared median usual weekly earnings for skilled and unskilled workers (series id: LEU0252916700, LEU0252917300, LEU0254929400, LEU0252918500). This provides an estimate that skilled workers earn 1.89 times as much as unskilled workers.

4. Firm size and size-wage premium. I used the Statistics of US Businesses from the US Census Bureau. The Statistics of US Businesses reports data that include firms binned by size with data on the number of firms, the number of establishments, employment, and the annual payroll for most US businesses. To compute a measure of the dispersion in firm size, I find that half of all employment is in firms with more than 500 employees; I abuse terminology here, but I will call this the median firm. The average firm size is about twenty employees. Thus, I target a ratio of the median to mean size of twenty-five.

The size-wage premium is determined as follows. I compute the payroll divided by employment for those firms with more than 500 employees— I call this the average wage above the median. Then, I compare this to the average wage or workers in firms below 500 employees. For the period from 2010 to 2013, this value is 1.30. That is, the average wage in firms with more than 500 employees is 30 percent larger than in firms with fewer than 500 employees.

Appendix B
Computing the Transition Path

This section describes how to compute the deterministic transition associated with an unexpected change in a primitive. The basic idea is to guess a sequence of endogenous values and (a) work backward solving for the policy function of the firm, then (b) solve the distribution of firms going forward using the policy function, and (c) check that the guessed endogenous values are consistent with market clearing implied by (b). Finally, update the conjectured about the endogenous variables in a smart way until market-clearing conditions are satisfied.

1. First, hand the computer several things: the value function associated

with the new stationary equilibrium (call it $v_T(z,\mathbf{p}_T)$), and an initial distribution of firms (call it $\mu_0(\mathbf{p}_0)$) that describes the mass of continuing and new firms at the end of the period, just prior to the change in the labor force.

2. Guess a sequence of $\{\mathbf{w}_t, Y_t, M_t\}_{t=1}^T$ where T is the end point that corresponds to the new stationary equilibrium; $\mathbf{w}$ is the vector of wages per efficiency units for each skill type; Y_t is aggregate output; M_t is the mass of entering firms. To economize on notation, denote this sequence as $\{\mathbf{p}_t\}_{t=1}^T$.

3. Given $\{\mathbf{p}_t\}_{t=1}^T$ and $v_T(z,\mathbf{p}_T)$, work backward to compute the value and policy functions where the explicit dependence on $\mathbf{p}$ is made. So, the value of the firm must respect

$$(B.1) \quad v_{T-1}(z_i,\mathbf{p}_{T\text{-}1}) = \max\left[\pi(z_i,\mathbf{p}_{T\text{-}1}) - \kappa + \beta\sum_{j=1}^{m}\mathscr{P}(i,j)v_T\!\left(z_j,\mathbf{p}_T\right), \pi\!\left(z_i,\mathbf{p}_{T\text{-}1}\right)\right].$$

Then, as we walk this backward, this generates a sequence of policy functions—call it $g(\mathbf{p}_t)$ for each date t.

4. Given the policy functions, take the initial distribution of firms $\mu_0(\mathbf{p}_0)$ and solve forward to compute how the mass of firms evolves given the policy functions that solve equation (B.1)

$$(B.2) \qquad\qquad M_t\tilde{\mathscr{P}}_e + \mu_t^*\!\left(P \circ g(\mathbf{p}_t)\right) = \mu_{t+1},$$

which yields a sequence of measures over firms for every date $\{\mu_t(\mathbf{p}_t)\}_{t=1}^T$.

5. Given the sequence of measures over firms, check whether markets clear and the free-entry condition is satisfied at each date t. A second condition is that, at date T, the economy should have converged to the new stationary equilibrium. Thus, check whether $v_{T-1}(z_i,\mathbf{p}_{T-1})$ is close to the value function $v_T(z_j,\mathbf{p}_T)$ associated with the new stationary equilibrium.

6. If these conditions are not satisfied, update the guessed sequence of prices $\{\mathbf{w}_t, Y_t, M_t\}_{t=1}^T$ and work until they are met.

References

Alessandria, George, Horag Choi, and Kim Ruhl. 2014. "Trade Adjustment Dynamics and the Welfare Gains from Trade." NBER Working Paper no. 20663, Cambridge, MA.

Atkeson, Andrew, and Ariel Burstein. 2010. "Innovation, Firm Dynamics, and International Trade." *Journal of Political Economy* 118 (3): 433–84.

Baily, Martin Neil, Charles Hulten, and David Campbell. 1992. "Productivity Dynamics in Manufacturing Plants." *Brookings Papers on Economic Activity: Microeconomics* 1992:187–267.

Bartelsman, Eric J., and Mark Doms. 2000. "Understanding Productivity: Lessons from Longitudinal Microdata." *Journal of Economic Literature* 38 (3): 569–94.

Bernard, Andrew, Jonathan Eaton, J. Bradford Jensen, and Samuel Kortum. 2003. "Plants and Productivity in International Trade." *American Economic Review* 93 (4): 1268–90.

Bernard, Andrew B., and J. Bradford Jensen. 1995. "Exporters, Jobs, and Wages in US Manufacturing: 1976–1987." *Brookings Papers on Economic Activity* 1995:67–119.
———. 1999. "Exceptional Exporter Performance: Cause, Effect, or Both?" *Journal of International Economics* 47 (1): 1–25.
Borjas, George J. 2003. "The Labor Demand Curve Is Downward Sloping: Reexamining the Impact of Immigration on the Labor Market." *Quarterly Journal of Economics* 118 (4): 1335–74.
———. 2014. *Immigration Economics*. Cambridge, MA: Harvard University Press.
Broda, Christian, and David E Weinstein. 2006. "Globalization and the Gains from Variety." *Quarterly Journal of Economics* 121 (2): 541–85.
Burstein, Ariel, and Jonathan Vogel. Forthcoming. "International Trade, Technology, and the Skill Premium." *Journal of Political Economy*.
Caliendo, Lorenzo, and Fernando Parro. 2015. "Estimates of the Trade and Welfare Effects of NAFTA." *Review of Economic Studies* 82 (1): 1–44.
Card, David. 2009. "Immigration and Inequality." *American Economic Review* 99 (2): 1–21.
Chaney, Thomas. 2008. "Distorted Gravity: The Intensive and Extensive Margins of International Trade." *American Economic Review* 98 (4): 1707–21.
Decker, Ryan, John Haltiwanger, Ron Jarmin, and Javier Miranda. 2014. "The Role of Entrepreneurship in US Job Creation and Economic Dynamism." *Journal of Economic Perspectives* 28 (3): 3–24.
di Giovanni, Julian, Andrei A. Levchenko, and Francesc Ortega. 2015. "A Global View of Cross-Border Migration." *Journal of the European Economic Association* 13 (1): 168–202.
Dustmann, Christian, and Albrecht Glitz. 2015. "How Do Industries and Firms Respond to Changes in Local Labor Supply?" *Journal of Labor Economics* 33 (3, part 1): 711–50.
Foster, Lucia, John Haltiwanger, and Chad Syverson. 2008. "Reallocation, Firm Turnover, and Efficiency: Selection on Productivity or Profitability?" *American Economic Review* 98 (1): 394–425.
Fox, Jeremy T., and Valerie Smeets. 2011. "Does Input Quality Drive Measured Differences in Firm Productivity?" *International Economic Review* 52 (4): 961–89.
Grogger, Jeffrey, and Gordon H. Hanson. 2011. "Income Maximization and the Selection and Sorting of International Migrants." *Journal of Development Economics* 95 (1): 42–57.
Hathaway, Ian, and Robert E. Litan. 2014. "Declining Business Dynamism in the United States: A Look at States and Metros." *Brookings*. https://www.brookings.edu/research/declining-business-dynamism-in-the-united-states-a-look-at-states-and-metros/.
Hopenhayn, Hugo A. 1992. "Entry, Exit, and Firm Dynamics in Long Run Equilibrium." *Econometrica: Journal of the Econometric Society* 60 (5): 1127–50.
Hopenhayn, Hugo, and Richard Rogerson. 1993. "Job Turnover and Policy Evaluation: A General Equilibrium Analysis." *Journal of Political Economy* 101 (5): 915–38.
Hsieh, Chang-Tai, and Peter J Klenow. 2009. "Misallocation and Manufacturing TFP in China and India." *Quarterly Journal of Economics* 124 (4): 1403–48.
Karahan, Fatih, Benjamin Pugsley, and Ayşegül Şahin. 2016. "Demographic Origins of the Startup Deficit." Working Paper, Federal Reserve Bank of New York. https://economics.nd.edu/assets/217341/pugsley_demographics_startups_1_.pdf.
Kerr, Sari Pekkala, William R. Kerr, and William F. Lincoln. 2014. "Firms and the Economics of Skilled Immigration." NBER Working Paper no. 20069, Cambridge, MA.

Kerr, William R., and William F. Lincoln. 2010. "The Supply Side of Innovation: H-1B Visa Reforms and US Ethnic Invention." *Journal of Labor Economics* 28 (3): 473–508.

Krugman, Paul. 1980. "Scale Economies, Product Differentiation, and the Pattern of Trade." *American Economic Review* 70 (5): 950–59.

Krusell, Per, Lee E. Ohanian, José-Víctor Ríos-Rull, and Giovanni L. Violante. 2000. "Capital-Skill Complementarity and Inequality: A Macroeconomic Analysis." *Econometrica* 68 (5): 1029–53.

Lee, Hyun. 2016. "Quantitative Impact of Reducing Barriers to Skilled Labor Immigration: The Case of the U.S. H-1B Visa." Working Paper no. 2016-35, Department of Economics, University of Connecticut.

Lewis, Ethan. 2011. "Immigration, Skill Mix, and Capital Skill Complementarity." *Quarterly Journal of Economics* 126 (2): 1029–69.

———. 2013. "Immigration and Production Technology." *Annual Review of Economics* 5 (1): 165–91.

Lowell, B. Lindsay. 2000. "H-1B Temporary Workers: Estimating the Population." CCIS Working Paper, Center for Comparative Immigration Studies.

Melitz, Marc. 2003. "The Impact of Trade on Aggregate Industry Productivity and Intra-Industry Reallocations." *Econometrica* 71 (6): 1695–725.

Olney, William W. 2013. "Immigration and Firm Expansion." *Journal of Regional Science* 53 (1): 142–57.

Ottaviano, Gianmarco I. P., and Giovanni Peri. 2012. "Rethinking the Effect of Immigration on Wages." *Journal of the European Economic Association* 10 (1): 152–97.

Parro, Fernando. 2013. "Capital-Skill Complementarity and the Skill Premium in a Quantitative Model of Trade." *American Economic Journal: Macroeconomics* 5 (2): 72–117.

Ruhl, K. J. 2008. "The International Elasticity Puzzle." Unpublished Manuscript, Penn State University.

Schank, Thorsten, Claus Schnabel, and Joachim Wagner. 2007. "Do Exporters Really Pay Higher Wages? First Evidence from German Linked Employer-Employee Data." *Journal of International Economics* 72 (1): 52–74.

Simonovska, Ina, and Michael E. Waugh. 2014a. "The Elasticity of Trade: Estimates and Evidence." *Journal of International Economics* 92 (1): 34–50.

———. 2014b. "Trade Models, Trade Elasticities, and the Gains from Trade." NBER Working Paper no. 20495, Cambridge, MA.

Spreen, Thomas Luke. 2013. "Recent College Graduates in the US Labor Force: Data from the Current Population Survey." *Monthly Labor Review* 136 (3): 3–12. https://www.bls.gov/opub/mlr/2013/02/art1full.pdf.

Tauchen, G. 1986. "Finite State Markov-Chain Approximations to Univariate and Vector Autoregressions." *Economics Letters* 20 (2): 177–81.

US Census Bureau. 2011. Synthetic LBD Beta version 2.0. [computer file]. Washington, DC and Ithaca, NY: US Census Bureau and Cornell University, Synthetic Data Server [distributor].

Xu, Rui. 2016. "High-skilled Migration and Global Innovation." SIEPR Discussion Paper no. 16-016, Stanford Institute for Economic Policy Research, Stanford University. https://siepr.stanford.edu/sites/default/files/publications/16-016.pdf.

Contributors

John Bound
Department of Economics
University of Michigan
Lorch Hall, 611 Tappan Avenue
Ann Arbor, MI 48109-1220

Gordon H. Hanson
IR/PS 0519
University of California, San Diego
9500 Gilman Drive
La Jolla, CA 92093-0519

John Horton
Leonard N. Stern School of Business
Kaufman Management Center
New York University
44 West Fourth Street, 8-81
New York, NY 10012

Nir Jaimovich
Department of Economics
University of Zurich
Schönberggasse 1
8001 Zurich, Switzerland

William R. Kerr
Harvard Business School
Rock Center 212
Soldiers Field
Boston, MA 02163

Gaurav Khanna
School of Global Policy and Strategy
University of California, San Diego
9500 Gilman Drive
La Jolla, CA 92093

Chen Liu
Department of Economics
University of California, San Diego
9500 Gilman Drive no. 0508
La Jolla, CA 92093-0508

Nicolas Morales
Department of Economics
University of Michigan
Lorch Hall, 611 Tappan Avenue
Ann Arbor, MI 48104

Henry E. Siu
Vancouver School of Economics
University of British Columbia
6000 Iona Drive
Vancouver, BC V6T 1L4 Canada

Christopher Stanton
210 Rock Center
Harvard Business School
Harvard University
Boston, MA 02163

Sarah Turner
Department of Economics
University of Virginia
248 McCormick Road
Charlottesville, VA 22903

Michael E. Waugh
Stern School of Business
New York University
44 West Fourth Street, Suite 7-160
New York, NY 10012

Stephen Ross Yeaple
Department of Economics
The Pennsylvania State University
520 Kern Building
University Park, PA 16802-3306

Author Index

Subject Index